P9-DCC-570

THE
GRAMMAR
HANDBOOK

IRWIN FEIGENBAUM

OXFORD UNIVERSITY PRESS

Oxford University Press

198 Madison Avenue
New York, N.Y. 10016 USA

Great Clarendon Street
Oxford OX2 6DP England

Oxford New York
Athens Auckland Bangkok Bogota Bombay Buenos Aires
Calcutta Cape Town Dar es Salaam Delhi Florence Hong Kong
Istanbul Karachi Kuala Lumpur Madras Madrid Melbourne
Mexico City Nairobi Paris Singapore Taipei Tokyo Toronto Warsaw

and associated companies in
Berlin Ibadan

OXFORD is a trademark of Oxford University Press.

Copyright © 1985 by Oxford University Press

Library of Congress Cataloging in Publication Data

Feigenbaum, Irwin.
    The grammar handbook.

    Includes Index.
    1. English language—Text-books for foreign speakers. 2. English
language—Grammar—1950-Handbooks, manuals, etc. I. Title.
PE1128.F35   1984   428.2'4   84–19063
ISBN 0-19-434107-0

No unauthorized photocopying.

All rights reserved. No part of this publication may be reproduced,
stored in a retrieval system, or transmitted, in any form or by any
means, electronic, mechanical, photocopying, recording, or otherwise,
without the prior written permission of Oxford University Press.

This book is sold subject to the condition that it shall not, by way of
trade or otherwise, be lent, resold, hired out, or otherwise circulated
without the publisher's prior consent in any form of binding or cover
other than that in which it is published and without a similar condition
including this condition being imposed on the subsequent purchaser.

Printing (last digit): 10

Printed in Hong Kong

Contents

Preface

This book was begun in response to a need in upper-level ESL courses: a grammar handbook. Although native speakers of English have had a wide variety of such reference books, the learner of English has not. Native-language handbooks do not serve the nonnative speaker: very often, they rely on a feel for the language that the student does not have; they deal with problems that the student does not have (for example, uneducated or nonstandard usage); and they do not deal with the problems that this student does have (such as, using a present perfect or a past verb form). This handbook is designed to meet this need.

In advanced ESL composition courses

The Grammar Handbook was developed for use in advanced ESL composition courses. Here the pedagogical emphasis is on English structures above the sentence, but students still need help in producing correct words and sentences. One important problem, however, is that students have different requirements: the frequency and the types of mistakes vary widely, even in a relatively homogeneous class. This reference handbook accommodates such variation. The teacher can individualize instruction by referring a student to a helpful section. The teacher can provide class instruction when many students require help with a problem. And students can use the handbook to check and correct their own work without a teacher's direction.

In intermediate and advanced ESL classes

This handbook can be useful in intermediate and advanced ESL classes, where new material is being learned and where there is emphasis on increased accuracy (fewer errors) in the use of previously learned material. It can provide the basis for a review of grammar in which students restudy large portions of English grammar or focus on smaller problem areas (see ORGANIZATION OF THE HANDBOOK below). Intermediate students too can profit from this handbook: the material that they have already studied is presented in a clear step-by-step format; and as the students' level in English rises, more of the book becomes useful.

Editor's Note: The masculine pronoun is generally used throughout the book. It is used for simplicity's sake rather than to indicate a philosophical viewpoint.

Contents of the handbook

The Grammar Handbook is intended to provide a reasonably complete coverage of word, phrase, and sentence grammar. There is also some coverage of intersentential relations; this is seen in sentence (or clause) combining and rearranging. The underlying principle is that language is for communication; therefore, the language student must learn to produce language forms and to use them to convey information.

The style of English covered in the *Handbook* is a relatively formal one appropriate for writing and public speech; however, there is some reference to the style appropriate for informal conversation. Differences between British and American English are also noted where they are important.

Decisions of what to include in this book were based on five principal sources:

1. Other grammar texts that indicate what students should learn.
2. Composition texts that indicate, by statement and by implication, what students require in order to deal with written texts.
3. Professional journals and books that indicate student problems and requirements.
4. Organized meetings and informal discussions in which teachers voiced their needs and their students' needs.
5. The author's experience in teaching ESL for many years in the United States and abroad, and his work with many experienced and new teachers.

Organization of the handbook

The description of English structure does not follow any one linguistic model; instead, the aim has been to present an analysis that is understandable to people with limited background in formal grammar analysis. Even in sections where particular presentations are unique, the teacher and students will be able to find their way without special preparation.

Chapters and sections within chapters are intended to be independent. The material is presented in separate sections, each focusing on one specific point; form and function have been separated to facilitate this focus. Thus, it is not necessary to use this book from the first page. Go directly to the section(s) that deal with the issue in point.

Each section ends with a short exercise. While the exercise provides some practice, its principal purpose is to check mastery of the rules, processes, and/or examples in the section. For this reason, some items in some exercises are unusual. Changing *parry* to the third person singular will indicate whether the student can use the appropriate spelling rule; on the other hand, using a familiar word may indicate that the student has learned a particular form, but not a general means for producing many forms.

Throughout the *Handbook*, common student mistakes are pointed out in sections called "Notes," and incorrect and correct forms are regularly contrasted to help students see their problems clearly.

Conventional terminology is used, to help in locating information in the Table of Contents, the chapters, and the index. The information in the chapters is arranged by language structure:

1. Sentences: structures and purposes
2. Nouns and noun-equivalents
3. Verbs
4. Adjectives and adverbs
5. Combining sentences
6. Rearrangement of sentence patterns
7. Punctuation

This arrangement will facilitate finding material in the book, when specific terms are not known or used.

The structural presentation is also intended to show useful processes and patterns in English. For this reason, such issues as question formation and negation are addressed separately as productive processes. This idea of patterning has also been used in the chapter on punctuation, where the organization is by use and not by a list of the marks. The arrangement provides an overall view of language use and structure. In addition, the processes themselves are laid out so that students can learn how to produce correct forms. Self-instructional step-by-step procedures allow independent learning of material, and they allow students to find and correct their own errors.

Further reading

To those teachers and students whose interest in the structure of English continues beyond this handbook, I would like to suggest the following books for further reading and reference:

Randolph Quirk, Sidney Greenbaum, Geoffrey Leech, and Jan Svartvik, *A Grammar of Contemporary English*
Leech and Svartvik, *A Communicative Grammar of English*
Quirk and Greenbaum, *A Concise Grammar of English*.

Acknowledgments

Many people have influenced the development of this handbook, including students who used parts of it and fellow teachers whose ideas and reactions influenced the content and form. I would like to thank three people whose work has most directly contributed to the present volume, suggesting important improvements as it moved from proposal through editing to final form. Marilyn S. Rosenthal was the Manager of the English Language Teaching Department at Oxford University Press when the proposal was submitted; I would like to thank her for accepting a book unlike others on the market and setting the project on its course. Cheryl Pavlik was hired as the editor for the (very long) manuscript; I would like to thank her for her thoughtful work. Once accepted, this project came under the direction of Debra Sistino, an ESL editor at Oxford University Press; I would like to thank her for the myriad tasks she performed in managing the project over a long period of time.

Irwin Feigenbaum
The University of Texas at Arlington

THE
GRAMMAR
HANDBOOK

Chapter 1
Contents

Chapter 1

1 Sentences: Structures and Purposes

A   SIMPLE SENTENCE PATTERNS

Every sentence has two basic parts, the subject and the predicate. The subject contains a noun or noun-equivalent that names the topic of the sentence. The predicate contains the verb.

In addition to a subject (S) and a verb (V), some sentences have other parts. All the parts of a sentence are related by grammar and meaning; the parts work together to express a thought or idea.

Note: Every simple sentence must have a subject (S) and a verb (V). If not, it is a **sentence fragment**, not a sentence.

   (1) Sentence fragment: no verb
     ✗ A television set next to the stereo in the living room.
   (2) Sentence fragment: no subject
     ✗ Then drove my car to a garage.

Exercise

Some of these sentences are correct; some are not, because they are fragments. In each sentence, underline the subject with one line and put two lines under the verb. If the sentence has a subject and a predicate with a verb, write **OK**. If the sentence does not have a subject, write **S**. If the

3

sentence does not have a complete predicate (if there is no verb), write **V**.

<u>OK</u>   **1.** I have classes from 9:00 a.m. to 1:30 p.m.

_____   **2.** Therefore, had a choice.

_____   **3.** I could go to the post office before my classes.

_____   **4.** Or could go there after my classes.

_____   **5.** The post office open until 5:30 p.m.

_____   **6.** My roommate needed some things at the post office.

_____   **7.** Some stamps for domestic letters and five international air letters.

_____   **8.** I bought them for him.

_____   **9.** And carried them around with me all morning.

_____ **10.** I gave them to him after my last class.

A1 **Sentence Pattern With Intransitive Verbs**

This sentence pattern has two necessary parts: a subject (S) and a verb (V).

	S	V
(3)	John	is singing.
(4)	It	must have snowed.

It is used to describe an action or activity. The S indicates the doer of the action; the V indicates the action.

This pattern is also used to describe the weather. When verbs like *snow* and *rain* are used, they require the **empty it** as the S. (The term "empty *it*" means that the word *it* does not have any meaning; it does not refer to any other word or idea.)

Only certain verbs can be used in this pattern. They are called **intransitive verbs**; this means that there are no nouns or noun-equivalents after the verb to indicate people or things affected by the activity.

Exercise

The following simple sentences have intransitive verbs. Underline the subjects with one line. Underline the verbs with two lines.

1. In the United States, <u>offices</u> <u><u>open</u></u> around 8:00 or 9:00 in the morning.

2. They close at around 5:00 or 6:00 p.m.
3. Some stores close at 9:00 or 10:00 at night.
4. People work for about eight hours a day, with an hour for lunch around noon.
5. However, places of business do not close during lunch-time.

Exercise

This is a list of simple sentences. However, some of the sentences are not correct: they do not have a subject or a verb. Decide if the sentence is complete. If it is, write **OK**. For each incorrect sentence, decide what is missing—the subject or the verb—and write **S** or **V**.

<u>OK</u> 1. Peter works part-time in the school cafeteria.

_____ 2. Sometimes he helps in the kitchen.

_____ 3. Other times serves in the food line.

_____ 4. His boss around a lot.

_____ 5. She can work anywhere in the cafeteria.

A2 **Sentence Patterns With Transitive Verbs**

In addition to the subject (S) and the verb (V), these sentence patterns have a third necessary part called the **direct object** (DO).

The DO is the person or thing directly affected by the verb; it is the direct receiver of the action. The DO is a noun or noun-equivalent.

	S	V	IO	DO	OC
(5)	We	saw		them.	
(6)	Paul	should kill		that rat.	
(7)	Most of the students	know		the answers.	
(8)	Elaine	bought	Alex	a new shirt.	
(9)	She	asked	his mother	his size.	
(10)	She	will give	him	the gift.	
(11)	The people	elected		Truman	President.
(12)	Anne	likes		black coffee.	
(13)	Anne	likes		coffee	black.

S = Subject **IO** = Indirect Object **OC** = Object Complement
V = Verb **DO** = Direct Object

These sentence patterns are used to describe actions or activities. They can be used when there is no observable action. In example 7, the verb *know* does not indicate an action; the direct object *the answers* does not receive any action and is not affected by any action.

A verb that is used with a direct object is called a **transitive verb**. Sentence patterns with transitive verbs are the ones that can be changed to the passive voice (see Chapter 6, page 259).

Exercise

The following sentences have transitive verbs. Underline the subjects with one line. Underline the verbs with two lines. Put parentheses around the direct objects.

1. John writes (all his checks) very carefully.
2. On the line "Pay to the Order of," he puts the person's or the company's name.
3. He always spells names correctly.
4. Next to the dollar sign ($), he uses numbers for the amount of the check.
5. All his checks have periods for decimal points.

Exercise

Some of the following sentences are not complete: one of the necessary parts is missing. If the sentence is complete, write **OK**. If the sentence is not complete, decide which part is missing, and write **S**, **V**, or **DO**.

_OK_ 1. On the third line of his checks, he must write in words, not numbers.

_____ 2. Next to the word "For," writes the reason for the check.

_____ 3. Sometimes he puts "rent."

_____ 4. Last signs his name on the line.

_____ 5. John writes his name very clearly.

A3 **Sentence Patterns With Indirect Objects**

Some of the sentences with a direct object (DO) can also have an indirect object (IO).

The IO is usually a person, although it can be an animal or a thing. It indicates the person who receives the benefits or bad results of the action.

In example 8, *Elaine* is the subject; she did the action. The action was to buy; the verb is *bought*. *A new shirt* was the direct receiver of the action; it is the direct object. *Alex* is the indirect object, the person who received (or will receive) the benefit of the action: he received or is going to receive a gift from Elaine. In example 9, Alex's mother is involved in the action of asking; *his mother* is the indirect object.

The indirect object in examples 8 and 9 is a noun or noun-equivalent. It appears after the verb and before the direct object.

There is another way to indicate the person who is the indirect object. This way is to use a phrase with the prepositions *to, for, from*, or *of*; the phrase appears after the direct object.

       S   V   IO   DO

(14) She bought him a new shirt.

       S   V   DO   Prep phrase

(15) She bought a new shirt for him.

Examples 14 and 15 have the same meaning.

Some transitive verbs can be used both ways to indicate an indirect object: (1) a noun or noun-equivalent before the direct object or (2) a prepositional phrase after the direct object. Other transitive verbs use only a prepositional phrase after the direct object. The verb *tell* is used both ways, but *say* can use only the prepositional phrase.

       S   V   DO

(16) They told a story.

       S   V   IO   DO

(17) They told the children a story.

       S   V   DO   Prep phrase

(18) They told a story to the children.

       S   V   DO

(19) They said hello.

```
        S      V    DO   Prep phrase
```
(20) They said hello to her.

```
        S      V    IO    DO
```
(21) X They said her hello.

The chart in Appendix B shows some transitive verbs and their ways of indicating an indirect object.

Exercise

The following sentences have transitive verbs plus a phrase with *to*, *for*, or *from*. Rewrite the sentences, indicating the indirect objects another way. Underline the subject once. Underline the verb twice. Put parentheses around the indirect object, and write **IO** above it. Put parentheses around the direct object, and write **DO** above it.

Some of Paula Gibson's close friends decided

1. Some of Paula Gibson's close friends decided to throw
(to throw) (her) (a surprise party).

   a surprise birthday party for her.
2. They told their plans to Paula's mother.
3. Mrs. Gibson would bake a birthday cake for Paula.
4. She would lend her stereo to them.
5. She gave the key to Paula's apartment to Paula's friends.

Exercise

Rewrite the sentences, using phrases with *to*, *for*, *from*, or *of*.

On the day of the party, Paula's mother left

1. On the day of the party, Paula's mother left her a
a message for her at the dormitory.

   message at the dormitory.
2. At 7:00 that evening, Paula should bring her father the car.
3. The automobile company had sent him a letter.
4. For a few days, the company would lend Mr. Gibson another car.
5. Paula asked Maria a favor: to drive her back to the dormitory from her home.

A4 Sentence Patterns With Object Complements

Some of the sentences with a direct object (DO) can also have an **object complement** (OC).

An object complement describes or identifies the direct object in the clause. In example 11, the subject did an action, and there was a direct receiver of that action: *Truman* is the direct object (DO). But there is more information. The result of the election was that Mr. Truman was chosen as President.

One way to think about the meaning connection between the DO and the OC is to think of the verb *be*. In example 11, Mr. Truman was elected to *be* President.

Examples 12 and 13 are similar in grammar and meaning, but they are not the same. In both examples, there are the same subject (S), verb (V), and direct object (DO). The difference in meaning is seen in the last unit of grammar and meaning. The sentence pattern with a DO is often used to answer a question about *what* or *who(m)*.

> (22) WHAT does Anne like?
> Black coffee. (short answer)
> She likes black coffee. (complete sentence)

An object complement (OC) is used to answer the question *how?*, *in what form?*, or *to be what?*

> (23) How/In what form does Anne take her coffee?
> Black. (short answer)
> She takes it black. (complete sentence)
> (24) What did they elect Mr. Truman to be?
> President. (short answer)
> They elected him (complete
> President. sentence)

The object complement is a noun or noun-equivalent (example 24) or an adjective (example 23). It appears after the DO (if it appears before the DO, it is part of the DO, as in example 22).

Exercise

The following sentences have object complements. Underline the verb with two lines. Put parentheses around

9

the direct object and write **DO** above it. Put parentheses around the object complement and write **OC** above it. Label each OC **N** or **Adj**.

1. In the United States, voters elect(a person) (President).
2. On election day, they make him happy.
3. This leaves other candidates very unhappy.
4. The President names someone Secretary of State.
5. The Secretary of State must keep the President informed.

Exercise

Answer each question, using a complete sentence. Use the sentence pattern with S V DO or the pattern with S V DO OC.

1. What do people in your country drink in the morning?

   They drink coffee.

2. How do they take it?
3. In 1978, what did the College of Cardinals in Rome elect Pope John Paul II to be?
4. What do Americans usually drink in the morning?
5. How do you take your tea?

Exercise

All of the sentences have transitive verbs (they have direct objects). Underline the verb with two lines. Put parentheses around each direct object, indirect object, and object complement, and label them **IO**, **DO**, and **OC**.

_____ 1. They made (Mary) (the class president.)
_____ 2. They made Mary a cake.
_____ 3. In spite of the large number of students in that class, no one could tell the professor the answer.
_____ 4. Some Americans eat their big meal of the day in the early afternoon.
_____ 5. However, most have theirs in the evening.
_____ 6. They call the big meal of the day "dinner."
_____ 7. Few Americans drink wine with their meals.
_____ 8. They have hot coffee or a soft drink.
_____ 9. In hot weather, many people prefer iced tea.
_____ 10. Still others drink a lot of cold beer.

A5 Sentence Patterns With Linking Verbs

	S Subject	V Linking Verb	SC Subject Complement	Adv Adverbial
(25)	It	was		in 1860.
(26)	Abraham Lincoln	became	President of the United States.	
(27)	He	had been	a legislator.	
(28)	That	was		in Illinois.
(29)	He	might be	the most famous American President.	
(30)	The Gettysburg Address and the Emancipation Proclamation	have remained	very important.	

These sentence patterns have **connecting** or **linking verbs**. These verbs connect the subject (S) and the subject complement (SC) in the pattern.

The subject complement is an adjective, noun, or noun-equivalent that (1) appears after the verb and (2) describes or identifies the subject. (Remember that an object complement describes or identifies the direct object.)

The connection between the subject (S) and the subject complement (SC) is indicated by a connecting verb. Connecting verbs are not meant to indicate actions, even though some activity may be involved. For instance, in example 26, becoming President involves actions.

In addition to the verb *be*, connecting verbs or linking verbs include: *appear, become, feel, get* (= *become*), *grow* (= *become*), *look, occur, remain, seem, smell, sound, taste,* and *turn* (= *become*).

This sentence pattern is used for a condition. The subject is described (with an adjective) or identified (with a noun or noun-equivalent) by the subject complement.

The pattern is often used with the "empty *it*" subject, to discuss weather (example 31); to specify days, dates, and times (example 25); and to identify people and things (examples 32 and 33).

$$\text{S} \quad \text{V} \qquad \text{SC}$$

(31) It was very cloudy.

11

(32) (What is that?)

<pre>
 S V   SC
</pre>
It is a hot dog.

(33) (Who was in the car?)

<pre>
 S   V   SC
</pre>
It was my friend Alice.

In these examples, the "empty *it*" does not refer to a particular person or thing; it is used to fill the subject part of the sentence pattern.

Exercise

The following sentences have linking verbs. Underline the subject once. Underline the verb twice. Underline the subject complement once and write **SC** above it. Label each SC as a noun (**N**) or an adjective (**Adj**).

1. Telephone calls are relatively inexpensive. *SC Adj*
2. They are also a very fast method of communication.
3. However, a phone call in a foreign language can be a hard job.
4. It can be hard even for a talkative person.
5. Even some native speakers are uncomfortable on the phone.

Exercise

Some of the following sentences are not complete: one of the necessary parts is missing. If the sentence is complete, write **OK**. If the sentence is not complete, decide which part is missing, and write **S**, **V**, or **SC**.

_OK_ 1. My friend Catherine is happy with her bank.
_____ 2. Her money is safe.
_____ 3. But is always available in her checking account.
_____ 4. The people in the bank helpful with any problems.
_____ 5. For almost two years, she has remained.

Linking Verbs With Adverbials

A linking verb can appear in a sentence pattern with an adverbial (Adv). The verb connects the subject and the adverbial, as in examples 25 and 28.

The adverbial is an adverbial of place or time. The pattern is used to tell the location of the subject: it tells where or when the subject is.

Exercise

These sentences have linking verbs and adverbials. Underline the verb twice. Underline once the adverbial of place or time. Then complete the sentences with a subject, a linking verb, or an adverbial of place or time.

1. In my country, the main meal of the day is _dinner_.
2. Washington, D.C._____about 220 miles south of New York City.
3. New Year's Day is_____.
4. _____are every four years.
5. _____is south of India.

B FOUR TYPES OF SENTENCES

Another way to look at sentences is to consider their use in communication. In this section, we consider the purpose of a sentence:

1. What does the speaker or writer intend to communicate?
2. What kind of response or reaction is expected?

B1 Statements (Declarative Sentences)

One type of sentence is called a **statement** or a **declarative sentence**. Statements are the most common type of sentence. Statements are used in all types of situations: in spoken and written English, and in formal and informal styles.

Form of statements

There are three signals that a sentence is a statement:

1. The word order has the subject before the verb.

$$\underset{\text{S}}{\underline{\quad}} \quad \underset{\text{V}}{\underline{\quad}}$$

(34) The door closed slowly.

13

2. A statement is spoken with falling intonation at the end.
   (35) The door closed slowly.
3. The end punctuation for a written statement is a period.
   (36) The door closed slowly.

Statements are affirmative or negative. Negative statements are signaled by *not* (*n't*), by a negative like *never* or *at no time*, or by a near-negative like *seldom* or *hardly ever*.

Sometimes, it is necessary to adjust the form of the verb.

(37) affirmative
   The door *closed* slowly.
(38) negative
   The door *did not close* slowly.

These negative signals often appear next to the verb in the sentence.

(39) She is seldom at work on Saturdays.

At the beginning of a sentence, a negative signal requires a rearranged sentence.

(40) *At no time* has he told us why he needs to leave early. (See Chapter 6, page 254 for the grammar and the meanings of negative sentences.)

Form of responses to statements

The hearer or reader—the receiver—of a statement is expected to respond with an understanding of what has been presented. In a conversation, the hearer may indicate this understanding by nodding his head or by using short oral responses like "I see," "Yes," or "OK." After receiving the statement, the hearer or reader may indicate his understanding by using the information or idea in his own sentences at a later time.

Exercise

The following sentences are statements. Underline the subject once and the verb twice. If the verb has more than one word, underline the entire verb twice.

1. Albert and his two roommates were going to register early.
2. They wanted to get the same physics course and lab.

3. Unfortunately, Albert had to work on the first morning of registration.
4. He told them to register without him.
5. Registration started at 8:00 a.m.
6. Late registrants always seemed to get the worst choices.
7. The two of them stood in line for almost two hours.
8. They got the preferred course and lab.
9. Albert did not register until the second day.
10. He was not happy about his course schedule.

Exercise

Each of the following sentences has a subject and a predicate with a verb plus a direct object or a subject complement. Make a statement, arranging the 3 parts of each sentence in correct order. Then match each of the responses with one of the statements: write the letter of the response.

1. choose / most of their own courses / university students
   University students choose most of their own courses.
   Response: *b*
2. different requirements / each major / has

   _____

   Response: _____
3. all their classes in the morning / like / some students

   _____

   Response: _____
4. easy to get a good schedule / is not / it

   _____

   Response: _____
5. best to register early / is / it

   _____

   Response: _____

   a. But I can't. I haven't picked my courses yet.
   b. I like the idea of having some choices.
   c. I know it. Pat spent several hours trying to work out a good one.
   d. We found them printed in the university catalog.
   e. My roommates want theirs in the afternoon so that they can sleep late.

15

B2 **Questions (Interrogative Sentences)**

The second type of sentence is called a **question** or an **interrogative sentence**.

There are two kinds of interrogative sentences. We ask questions to learn something new or to confirm information that we already have.

Questions to learn
1. Information or wh-questions
2. Affirmative yes/no questions

Questions to confirm
3. Negative yes/no questions
4. Tag questions
5. Restatements

Two very common signals show that a sentence is a question, not a statement:

1. The question mark at the end of a written question

   (41) What is the difference between a college and a university?

In writing, a question mark is a sure signal of a question: every question has one, and it is used only with a question.

2. Question word order

A question has an auxiliary or the verb *be* in front of the subject. When the hearer or reader finds a verb form in front of the subject, he has a clear signal that the sentence is not just a statement. In question word order, the verb form in front of the subject is one of the following: *is, am, are, was, were, have, has, had, do, does, did, will, would, shall, should, can, could, may, might, dare* (very rare), and *need* (very rare).

Step 1. If the verb has 2 or more words, MOVE the first word of the verb in front of the subject.

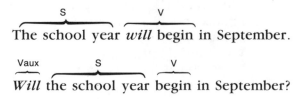

The school year *will* begin in September.

Will the school year begin in September?

Step 2. If the verb has only one word and if that word is a form of *be,* MOVE it in front of the subject.

S   V

Albert *is* in my calculus class.

V   S

Is Albert in my calculus class?

Step 3. If the verb has only one word and if that word is not *be,* then look at the tense of the verb.

   a. If the verb is in the past tense, ADD the auxiliary *did* in front of the subject and change the verb to the simple form.

S   V

Albert registered for calculus this semester.

Vaux   S   V

Did Albert register for calculus this semester?

   b. If the subject is *he, she, it,* or an equivalent and the verb is in the present tense, ADD *does* in front of the subject and CHANGE the verb to the simple form.

S   V

Henry likes his mathematics class.

Vaux   S   V

Does Henry like his mathematics class?

   c. In all other cases, ADD the auxiliary *do* in front of the subject, but DO NOT CHANGE the form of the verb.

S   V

Albert and Henry study together.

Vaux   S   V

Do Albert and Henry study together?

The verb *have* is the only verb in English that has two possible word orders for questions. It can be treated like the verb *be* in Step 2, or it can be treated like all other verbs in Step 3.

(42a) statement
　　　Albert has two physics classes.
(42b) Question word order, Step 2

　　　　V　　S
　　　　‾‾‾　‾‾‾
　　　Has Albert two physics classes?
(42c) Question word order, Step 3b

　　　　Vaux　　S　　V
　　　　‾‾‾‾　‾‾　‾‾
　　　Does Albert have two physics classes?

Both arrangements are correct. Step 2 is more common in British English; Step 3 is more common in American English.

Question word order is a very common signal of a question, but it is not a completely sure signal. Some questions do not have this order, (see Chapter 5, pages 214-215), and some statements have it (see Chapter 6, page 254).

Exercise

Change the following statements into questions. Use both of the signals discussed previously.

1. A college is similar to a university.
   Is a college similar to a university?

2. They both provide advanced education for their students.
3. They are also different from one another.
4. A college has only one course of study.
5. It could be a college of engineering.
6. Marie has decided to go to a liberal arts college.
7. A university is a collection of colleges.
8. Universities often have medical and law schools.
9. Clara and her brother had been trying to choose between a small college and a big university.
10. They were willing to work hard to get a good education.

Exercise

Change the following questions into statements. Eliminate the two question signals.

The first year at a college or university is called the "freshman" year.

1. Is the first year at a college or university called the "freshman" year?
2. Are the second and third years called the "sophomore" year and the "junior" year?
3. Has William decided to transfer to a university?
4. Will he get credit for his two years of study at the state college?
5. Does Marsha work part-time?
6. Do her parents help her with her college expenses?
7. Did they buy her that car?
8. Are many students working their way through college?
9. Can they expect to work hard?
10. Is it worth the effort?

Information or Wh-questions

An information question usually has a question word. Because most information questions have these question words and because most of these question words begin with the letters *w* and *h,* information questions are often called **wh-questions** in grammar texts.

Form of information questions

Four signals show that the sentence is an information question:

1. An information question begins with a question word or a phrase with a question word.

   (43) *When* will you be registering for classes?
   (44) *At what time* will you be registering for classes?

Question word	Asks for this information
who subject	the identification of a person, people
whom { *direct object indirect object object of preposition	
whose	the identification of the possessor
what	the identification of the place(s), thing(s), idea(s)

19

Question word	Asks for this information
which	the indication of a choice
how	manner
how (*often, far,* etc.)	degree
how much/many	quantity
when	time
where	place
why	reason

***Note:** In informal conversation, many people use *who* for both subjects and objects.

The question word *which* is used when the possible choices are known. If the possible choices are not known, use another question word, such as *what* or *who*.

(45) Alan told me that you were considering three typewriters.
Which did you buy?

(46) I saw your sister at the store yesterday buying clothes.
What did she buy?

2. An information question usually has question word order: there is a verb auxiliary or a form of the verb *be* in front of the subject (see Chapter 5, page 215).

Vaux   S

(47) Why have you chosen that college?

There is one situation when an information question does not have the question word order: when the question word refers to the subject of the clause.

S   V

(48) Who likes American food?

In this case, the verb looks like the verb in a statement; it doesn't take an auxiliary.

(49) X Who does like American food?
(50) X Does who like American food?

3. An information question is spoken with falling intonation.

(51) Why have you chosen that college?

Note: It is important to signal information questions with falling intonation. Falling intonation signals that the answer should be information. Rising intonation signals a different kind of answer. (See Chapter 1, pages 22 and 31.)

4. The end punctuation mark for a wh-question is a question mark.

(52) How did you come to this country?

Exercise

Look at the answer that follows each question. Then add the appropriate question word.

1. *When* did you find out about the accident?
At about 4:30.

2. _____told you about it?
Mr. and Mrs. Applewhite.

3. From_____did they hear about it?
From their cousin in Detroit.

4. _____did they tell you about it?
Because they know that we are concerned about drunk driving.

5. _____are you going to do with the information?
We are going to add it to the report we are sending to our congressman.

Exercise

Make wh-questions from the statements. The underlined words indicate where to use question words.

1. The last year of college is called the "senior" year .

What is the last year of college called?

2. Most students attend college for four years .

3. Working students often need five years to complete their education.

4. They are studying hard because they have a test tomorrow .

21

5. A student can get a good education <u>at a state college or university</u> .

6. Bill lost <u>his brother's calculator</u> .

7. Bill lost <u>his sister's</u> book.

8. It was <u>her expensive chemistry</u> book.

9. He found the book <u>after class</u> .

10. He bought his brother a new calculator <u>by paying for it in installments</u> .

Yes/No Questions (Affirmative)

The second type of question is called a **yes/no question**. The asker of this question wants to find out if something is true or not; he expects the answer to be *yes* or *no*.

Form of affirmative yes/no questions

Three signals show that a sentence is a yes/no question:

1. A yes/no question has question word order: there is a verb auxiliary or a form of the verb *be* in front of the subject (see Chapter 5, page 214).

      Vaux   S

(53) Did the door close slowly?

2. The end punctuation for a yes/no question is a question mark.

(54) Did the door close slowly?

3. A yes/no question is spoken with rising intonation at the end. The rise tells the hearer to answer *yes* or *no*.

(55) Did the door close slowly?

In speaking, many people ask yes/no questions without changing word order. They merely use rising intonation.

(56) The door closed slowly?

Form of responses to affirmative yes/no questions

In informal conversation, a one-word answer is all right. However, in more formal English, two other answers often occur. One of these answers has the word *yes* or *no* plus a complete sentence.

> (57) Is today Tuesday?
> Yes, today is Tuesday.
> (or)
> No, it is not Tuesday.

A complete sentence is always appropriate as an answer.

The other common way to answer a *yes/no* question is with the word *yes* or *no* plus a short answer; it is used when we do not wish to repeat a lot of information that is already clear in the conversation. To many people, this type of answer is more polite than a one-word answer.

> (58) Is today Tuesday?
> Yes, it is.
> No, it is not.

Note: In examples 57 and 58, there is a comma between the *yes* or *no* and the rest of the answer.

Note: When the tag statement is affirmative, the subject pronoun and the form of the verb can not be contracted. When the tag statement is negative, they can be contracted.

> (59) Yes, we are.
> (60) X Yes, we're.
> (61) No, we are not.
> (62) No, we're not.

(See Chapter 6, page 251 for more information about contractions.)

A short answer is part of a sentence pattern: it has a subject plus an auxiliary verb or a form of the verb *be;* if it is negative, it also has *not* or *n't.*

$$(\text{Yes,}) + \text{Subject} + \left\{ \begin{array}{l} \text{Vaux} \\ be \end{array} \right.$$
(pronoun)

> (63) Were the guests satisfied?
> Yes, they were.

$$(\text{No,}) + \text{Subject} + \left\{ \begin{array}{l} \text{Vaux} \\ be \end{array} \right\} + \left\{ \begin{array}{l} not \\ \text{n't} \end{array} \right.$$
(pronoun)

> (64) Were Tom and Sara there?
> No, they weren't.

The subject (pronoun)

The subject in a tag statement is usually a pronoun. Because a short answer is a response to another sentence, the subject has already been stated. Therefore, we can use a pronoun as the subject.

(65) Did he like the chili?
Yes, he did.
(66) Will all the students register for classes at the same time?
No, they will not.

Sometimes a short answer is a short form of a statement with the word *there* (see Chapter 6, page 267). In this case, the word *there* is used in the subject position.

(67) Is there enough time to eat lunch before we leave?
Yes, *there* is.

The verb form in short answers

1. If the verb has 2 or more words, divide the sentence after the first word in the verb phrase (and include *not* or *n't* if the statement is negative).

(68) *Have* they ever *eaten* southern fried chicken?
Yes, they have.

2. If the verb has only one word and if the word is a form of the verb *be,* divide the sentence after the verb (and include *not* or *n't* if the statement is negative).

(69) *Was* the chicken very spicy?
No, it wasn't.

3. If the verb has only one word and if the word is not a form of the verb *be,* divide the sentence after the subject and look at the tense of the verb and the subject.
   a. If the verb is in the past tense, add the auxiliary *did* after the subject.

(70) Did we *like* it?
Yes, we did.

   b. If the subject is *he, she, it,* or an equivalent, add the auxiliary *does* after the subject.

(71) Does your mother make it?
No, she doesn't.

c. In all other cases, add the auxiliary *do* after the subject.

(72) Do you want to learn how to make it?
     Yes, I do.

The verb form in a short answer is one of the following: *is, am, are, was, were, have, has, had, do, does, did, will, would, shall, should, can, could, may,* or *might*. Notice that these are the same verb forms that are used to form question word order.

Exercise

Make yes/no questions from the following statements.

1. Americans eat chicken with their hands.
   Do Americans eat chicken with their hands?
2. A hot dog is also eaten with the hands.
3. Many types of food are found in the United States.
4. Mexican food has become very popular recently.
5. During the visit, Pierre's wife ate Chinese food for the first time.
6. She was crazy about cheeseburgers.
7. You can find Italian food in almost every city.
8. You find all kinds of food in the big cities.
9. Pierre and his wife found good regional food in small towns.
10. Visitors to the United States should try all the different types of food.

Exercise

Answer the following questions, using **yes** or **no** plus a tag statement.

1. Are there over 100 countries in the United Nations?
2. Was the U.N. founded in 1955?
3. Did the U.N. set up its headquarters in New York?
4. Has the International Court been meeting in the United States?
5. Have all the Secretaries-General been from Third World countries?
6. Is there a part of the U.N. concerned with health problems?
7. Can the General Assembly discuss any subject?

8. Does the General Assembly have the power to enforce its decisions?
9. Does the Security Council have the power to enforce its decisions?
10. Do all the members of the Security Council have a "veto"?

Negative Questions

One type of confirmation question is the **negative question**. The user of this question wants to confirm that something is correct.

Form of negative questions

There are three signals that a sentence is a negative yes/no question:

1. The word order in a negative question has a verb auxiliary plus not before the subject. (See Chapter 5, page 215.)

     Vaux   S   V

(73) *Wasn*'t this book written in the United States?

The negative word *not* is almost always contracted. Using the full form is very formal.

(74) Was this book not written in the United States?

2. A negative question is spoken with rising intonation at the end.

(75) Wasn't this book written in the United States?

3. The end punctuation is a question mark.

(76) Wasn't this book written in the United States?

Form of answers to negative questions

Naturally, the expected answer to a negative question includes the word *yes* or *no*. However, the answer—the *yes* or *no*—does not refer to the question; the *yes* or *no* refers to the facts of the situation.

For example, the situation is the following: (1) this handbook was written in the United States, and (2) it was written in 1983.

(77) Wasn't this handbook written in the United States?
       Yes, it was (written in the United States).

(78) Was this handbook written in the United States?
Yes, it was (written in the United States).

The difference between examples 77 and 78 is that the asker of 77 expected the answer to be *yes;* he would have been surprised to find out that the book had been written in another country. Therefore, when the answer to a negative question is *no,* it is a good idea to provide the correct information.

(79) Wasn't this book written in 1980?
No, it wasn't (written in 1980). It was written just last year.

(80) Was this book written in 1980?
No, it wasn't. It was written in 1983.

The asker of 79 thought that he knew when the book was written; he asked for a confirmation that he was correct. The asker of 80 did not expect a confirmation; he asked for information that he did not know.

A negative question should be answered in exactly the same way you answer any affirmative question—according to the facts of the situation.

(81) Didn't they arrive earlier than you did?
Yes, they *did.*
(or)
No, they *didn't.* We got here first.

The following two examples are not correct responses in English.

(82) X *Yes,* they *did not arrive* earlier than we did.
(83) X *No,* they *arrived* earlier than we did.

Exercise

A friend of yours has heard some things about the English system of measurement; but he is not sure about them, so he asks you some questions to get confirmation. If your friend's conclusion or knowledge is accurate, answer with **yes** plus a short answer. If it is not correct, answer with **no** plus a short answer, and add another sentence with the correct information.

1. Isn't the English system easier to learn and use than the metric system?

No, it isn't. They're both pretty easy.

27

2. Isn't some of the opposition to change due to people's habits?
3. Isn't a quart larger than a liter?
4. Haven't most countries in the world adopted the English system?
5. Doesn't water boil at 200 °F?
6. Isn't -40 °C the same as -40 °F?
7. Isn't a kilometer longer than a mile?
8. Don't children find it hard to remember that (1) 12 inches = 1 foot, (2) 3 feet = 1 yard, and (3) 5280 feet = 1 mile?
9. Can't scientists communicate more easily when they all use the same system?
10. Don't pints and quarts measure weight?

Exercise

Change the statements into negative questions. You want confirmation.

1. The metric system is used in the United States.

    Isn't the metric system used in the United States?

2. Temperature is commonly measured according to the Fahrenheit scale.
3. Goods are weighed in pounds and ounces.
4. Quantities are sometimes measured in pints, quarts, and bushels.
5. Some people have wanted to change to the metric system.
6. They stress the ease of using it.
7. There has been a lot of opposition to the change.
8. Scientists are using metric measurements.
9. Some manufacturers have changed to metric.
10. Some goods are labeled in both the metric and English systems.

Tag Questions

Another type of confirmation question is called a **tag question**. The person asking this type of question wants the answer to confirm (or not) information that he already has. This information is included in the sentence, for the answerer's response. Tag questions are most often found in conversation; they are not common in writing, except sometimes in informal writing.

Form of tag questions

Four signals show that a sentence is a tag question:

1. The first part of the sentence is a statement that includes the information to be confirmed.

    (84) statement

$$\overbrace{\text{Elena}}^{\text{S}} \quad \overbrace{\text{will open}}^{\text{V}} \quad \overbrace{\text{a checking account,}}^{\text{DO}}$$
$$\text{won't she?}$$

2. The second part of the sentence is the tag question. It has question word order.

    (85) Elena will open a checking account, $\overbrace{\text{won't she?}}^{\text{tag question}}$

We look at the complete question in order to decide how to form the correct tag question. Tag questions are formed like this:

$$\left.\begin{array}{l}\text{Vaux}\\[4pt]\textit{be}\end{array}\right\} \ + \ \text{Subject (pronoun or \textit{there})}$$

$$\left.\begin{array}{l}\text{Vaux}\\[4pt]\textit{be}\end{array}\right\} \ + \ \textbf{\textit{n't}} \ + \ \text{Subject (pronoun or \textit{there})}$$

The verb auxiliary is one of the following: *is, am, are, was, were, have, has, had, do, does, did, will, would, shall, should, can, could, may,* or *might.*

If the statement in the first part of the sentence is affirmative, the tag question is negative, as in example 86. If the statement is negative, the tag question is affirmative, as in example 87.

(86) Elena $\underset{\uparrow}{\text{AFFIRMATIVE}}$ *will open* a checking account, $\underset{\downarrow}{\text{NEGATIVE}}$ *won't* she?

(87) Elena $\underset{\uparrow}{\text{NEGATIVE}}$ *won't open* a savings account, $\underset{\downarrow}{\text{AFFIRMATIVE}}$ *will* she?

The subject in a tag question is usually a pronoun.

(88) *Elena* will open a checking account, won't *she?*

29

Sometimes a tag question is a short form of a question with *there*. In this case, *there* is used in the subject position.

> (89) There are different types of bank accounts, aren't *there*?

3. The tag question has falling or rising intonation. It has falling intonation if the asker is sure that the answerer will agree with him.

> (90) Today is August 19, isn't it?

In example 90, the user is sure of the date. In example 91, the tag question has rising intonation because the user is not so sure that the answerer will agree with him.

> (91) Today is August 19, isn't it?

4. The end punctuation for a tag question is a question mark.

> (92) Today is August 19, isn't it?

Form of answers to tag questions

Tag questions call for agreement or disagreement from the hearer. A person answers a tag question with *yes* or *no* according to the correct information, that is, the information in the statement part. (See Chapter 1, page 23.)

Exercise

Rewrite the following sentences, adding tag questions.

1. Checking accounts are very useful.

   Checking accounts are very useful, aren't they?

2. There is no danger of losing money.
3. Your money is always available when you need it.
4. Canceled checks can be good records of money that you spend.
5. A savings account is also a useful account.
6. The bank pays interest on the money in a savings account.
7. However, the money is not always immediately available.
8. People should talk to their banker to decide on the best type of account.
9. You and I do not need a savings account to pay for our school expenses.

10. Sandra, on the other hand, will be better off with both a checking account and a savings account.

Exercise

Answer the following tag questions, using **yes** or **no** plus a short answer.

1. A savings account will increase in value, won't it?

    Yes, it will.

2. The money in a savings account is safe, isn't it?
3. A checking account is best for everyone, isn't it?
4. Banks can change foreign currency, can't they?
5. Grocery stores in the United States will accept travelers checks in dollars, won't they?
6. Grocery stores in the United States will not accept travelers checks in foreign currency, will they?
7. Money in a checking account is not always available, is it?
8. There is a good reason to have a bank account, isn't there?

Restatement Questions

The third type of confirmation question is a **restatement**. The person who asks this type of question wants confirmation (or not) that he heard or read something accurately. What he observed or concluded is included in the question. He is asking, "Did I hear that correctly or come to the correct conclusion?"

Restatement questions usually occur in conversation. They do not occur often in written English. A more formal way to ask for this type of confirmation is to use a sentence like: *Is it true that . . . ?* or *Am I correct in assuming that . . . ?* These sentences occur in formal speech and in writing.

Three signals show that a question is a restatement question:

1. A restatement question usually has the structure of a statement.

    (93) She dialed Abu Dhabi from her own apartment?

2. A restatement question has rising intonation. The rise tells the hearer to answer with *yes* or *no*.

31

(94) She dialed Abu Dhabi from her own apartment?

3. The end punctuation for a restatement is a question mark.

(95) She dialed Abu Dhabi from her own apartment?

Exercise

You have heard some things about American food, but they surprise you. Change these groups of words into restatement questions to show that you are surprised and that you want someone to confirm what you have heard.

1. Americans / corn-on-the-cob / eat

Americans eat corn-on-the-cob?

2. eat it / they / with their hands
3. a very popular food / is / it
4. do not get sick / from it / they
5. are expected to try it / too / visitors
6. I / might have to eat some / myself
7. can politely refuse / I / if I want to
8. mind / they / won't

B3 Imperatives

The third type of sentence is called an **imperative sentence**. In an imperative, the speaker or writer indicates that he wants some action or situation to result from his words. An imperative may be affirmative or negative.

Form of imperative sentences

Five signals show that a sentence is an imperative:

1. Many imperatives do not have grammatical subjects. Unlike all other sentences, there is nothing in the subject (S) part of the clause.

        S   V   DO

(96) _____ Write your name at the top of the page.

2. The verb form is the simple form (sometimes called the **base form** or the **infinitive without to**); this is also known as the **imperative mood**.

(97) *Be* on time for the test.

(98) *Answer* all the questions on the test.

The negative is formed by adding *do not* or *don't*.

(99) *Don't* begin to work before 8:30.

3. Polite words or phrases are often used in imperative sentences, especially if they are requests or suggestions.

(100) *Please* bring me your test paper when you have finished.

(101) *Would you please* answer the telephone.
(Note that here the subject *you* is used.) *Would you please* answer the telephone.

4. The usual end punctuation for a written imperative sentence is a period.

(102) Be on time for the test.

(103) Would you please answer the telephone.

However, when the imperative is very strong, the end punctuation is an exclamation mark.

(104) Don't touch that poison ivy!

5. The usual intonation for an imperative is falling intonation at the end.

(105) Be on time for the test.

However, when the imperative has the grammar structure of a yes/no question, the intonation may be rising or falling (see Chapter 5, page 233).

(106) Would you please answer the telephone.

(107) Would you please answer the telephone.

Form of responses to imperative sentences

The receiver of an imperative is expected to help the user. He helps by understanding the new action or situation. He may indicate this understanding by responding orally with an utterance like "Yes" or "OK" or by nodding his head. Also the receiver often helps by doing something. If the imperative does not call for him to act, he responds only by showing that he understands the imperative and agrees that it is possible and/or good to do.

Commands and Instructions

A common use of imperatives is to command or instruct people to do something.

(108) Do not come back until you have finished the job.
(109) Read the examples before beginning the test.

The term **you-understood** is often used to describe the doer of an imperative sentence: we understand that the subject is *you*, that is, the person spoken to. Sometimes, but not often, the doer of the action is expressed in an imperative sentence, for emphasis or clarity.

(110) You lift up that end of the table.
(111) Robert and Mary, lift up this end.
(112) Theodore, open the door for them.

The conversational situation and the verb in the simple form indicate that these sentences are imperatives.

Requests

Request imperatives are grammatically similar to commands and instructions, but requests usually have polite words or phrases. The most common polite addition is the word *please.*

(113) Please open the door for me.

There are other ways to make requests.

(114) Could you tell me the time.
(115) Would you return this book to the library for me.
(116) I wonder if you could lend me a pen.

Examples 114 and 115 look like questions, but they do not have that purpose; therefore, they do not have question marks. Example 116 is not a statement. These three sentences are requests; they have the same meanings as 117, 118, and 119, respectively.

(117) Please tell me the time.
(118) Please return this book to the library for me.
(119) Please lend me a pen.

Examples 114, 115, and 116 are imperatives; their purpose is to get some action from the hearer or reader. One appropriate response to 114 is "Yes. It's 2:35."

Suggestions

Suggestion imperatives are like other imperatives: (1) they call for acknowledgement and/or approval of the new action or situation, and (2) an expected response is the action. But suggestions are also different from other imperatives: the doer of the action may be another person besides the "you" of **you-understood**.

(120) Let's have lunch before the test.

When Mary says sentence 122 to John, she is suggesting that both John and she should have lunch. John could respond by (1) saying "OK" and (2) putting on his jacket and walking to the cafeteria with Mary.

The negative form of a suggestion imperative with *Let's* uses *not.*

(121) Let's *not* have lunch before the test.

There is a second suggestion imperative.

(122) Shall we have lunch before the test.

It is similar to a yes/no question: it has the question word order. But it does not have the purpose of a question; it is a suggestion. In writing, it is clearly a suggestion; the end punctuation is a period, not a question mark. In conversation, the situation will often indicate the purpose of the sentence.

The third type of suggestion imperative is shown in examples 123 and 124.

(123) Why don't you come to my house at 7:00.
(124) Why don't they finish their work after lunch.

Examples 123 and 124 are similar to information questions: they begin with a question word, and they have the question word order. And sometimes a sentence like 123 or 124 is used to ask a question (then it has a question mark at the end). On the other hand, a sentence like 123 or 124 is often used to make a suggestion or invitation. When it is written, there is no question mark at the end; when it is spoken, the conversational situation is the clue to the expected response. These invitations are very informal.

Examples 125, 126, and 127 show two suggestions and one question, with appropriate responses.

(125) Why don't you come to my house at 7:00.
OK. I'll be there then.

(126) Why don't they finish their work after lunch.
All right. I'll tell them to stop for lunch now and to finish work after they eat.

(127) Why don't they finish their work after lunch?
Because they are going on their vacation this afternoon.

This type of informal suggestion has the following structure:

$$\text{Why} + \left\{ \begin{array}{ll} \text{don't} & \text{they} \\ & \text{we} \\ & \text{you} \\ & \text{I} \\ \text{doesn't} & \text{he} \\ & \text{she} \\ & \text{it} \end{array} \right\} + \begin{array}{l} \text{V (imperative} + \text{other words in the} \\ \quad\text{mood)} \qquad \text{imperative sentence} \end{array}$$

Exercise

Write imperative sentences for the following.

Tell your friend what to do when he arrives in the United States.

1. Tell him that he should open a checking account in a bank.

   Open a checking account in a bank.

2. Tell him to change some of his travelers checks into cash.

3. Tell him not to change all of them into cash.

4. Tell him to use his passport for identification until he has some local form of identification such as a driver's license or school I.D.

Request something.

5. Ask someone for the correct time.

   Could you tell me the time.

6. Ask someone to tell you how to get to the nearest post office.

7. Ask the teller at the bank to cash your 50-dollar check.

Make some suggestions.

8. Suggest that you and a friend go to the bookstore together this afternoon.

Let's go to the bookstore this afternoon.

9. Invite a friend to come to a party at your apartment
tomorrow evening.

10. Suggest to your friend that she should bring her two
roommates to the party.

Exercise

Match the responses to the imperative sentences. The
responses are words and/or actions.

1. Write your name on the first line of this form.
Response: Action__*e*__

2. Would you two mail this letter for me.
Response: Words_____

3. Answer all 50 questions in half an hour.
Response: Action_____

4. Can you tell me where the library is.
Response: Words_____ Action_____

5. Please open the door for me.
Response: Action_____

6. Don't use a pen. You may want to change an answer.
Response: Action_____

Responses

Words
a. Yes, we'd be happy to.
b. Yes. It's right behind that tall building.

Actions
c. You start immediately.
d. You open it.
e. You write your full name very carefully.
f. Point it out to her.
g. You take out a pencil.

B4 Exclamations

The fourth type of sentence is called an **exclamation** or
exclamatory sentence. In an exclamation, the speaker or
writer indicates that he feels very strongly about a situation: he is very happy, very angry, very surprised, etc.

Exclamations do not occur often in written English, except when speech is written down. Exclamations should not be used often because too many at one time decreases their individual effect.

Form of exclamations

Two signals show that a sentence is an exclamation:

1. Many exclamations begin with the words *what* + a noun or *how* + an adjective or adverbial.

    (128) What an interesting meal that was!
    (129) How sweet American food is!
    (130) How quickly Americans eat!

The word *what* or *how* indicates that the next unit of meaning (the noun, adjective, or adverbial) is the cause of the strong emotion in the situation. This is a rearrangement of the usual word order in a sentence, so that the cause of the strong emotion follows the introductory word. Exclamations that begin with *what* or *how* can only be affirmative.

2. The end punctuation for a written exclamatory sentence is called an exclamation mark or exclamation point.

    (131) How quickly Americans eat!

There is a second type of exclamation. The grammar of the sentence is like the grammar of a statement. The written end punctuation or the spoken loudness and emotion are the only indications of an exclamation.

    (132) That was an interesting meal!
    (133) American food is sweet!
    (134) Americans eat quickly!

Form of responses to exclamations

There is no clear way to respond to an exclamation. The hearer or reader is expected to understand that there are strong feelings about the situation. Often, the receiver will agree or disagree with the sentence or say something else to let the speaker or writer know that the message has been understood. Example 135 shows several likely responses to an exclamatory sentence.

    (135) How sweet American food is!
          Do you really think so?
          Yes, I certainly agree.
          Do you think so?
          I haven't found it especially sweet.

Exercise

Change the following statements into exclamations, using **what** or **how** and an exclamation point. The underlined words show the causes of the strong emotion.

1. The summers in the South are hot .

   How hot the summers in the South are!

2. The sun rises early .

3. It sets late in the evening .

4. There is a pleasant change in temperature when the sun goes down.

5. The summers in the North are pleasant .

6. The days usually are warm .

7. We have cool nights after sundown.

8. They had a severe winter in Milwaukee last year.

9. It was lucky that they could take a vacation in Florida.

10. They quickly forgot the cold weather.

Chapter 2
Contents

2 Nouns and Noun-Equivalents

A COMMON AND PROPER NOUNS

Most nouns are **common nouns**; they are not names, for example, *book* and *friend*. **Proper nouns** are the names given to particular people, places, things, and ideas, for example, *California* and my friend *Howard*. Both *friend* and *Howard* are nouns; but *friend* is a common noun, a noun that is used in many different situations; *Howard* is a proper noun, the name of a particular person.

Proper nouns begin with capital letters, for example, *California*. The following are some frequently used types of proper nouns.

1. Names of people: Thomas Jefferson
2. Titles of people when used with their names: President Jefferson
3. Days of the week: Sunday, Monday, etc.
4. Months of the year: January, February, etc., but not seasons: spring, summer, fall/autumn, winter
5. Geographical features: the Atlantic Ocean, Mt. Everest
6. Countries, states, cities: England, Los Angeles
7. Nationalities: American, Polish
8. Languages: English, Thai

9. Specific course/class names: History 104, Design Graphics, but not the field of study: history
10. Heavenly bodies: Mercury, Alpha Centauri; as a special case, earth, sun, moon are generally not capitalized except when used in connection with other heavenly bodies or for clarity of reference, for example, *The space capsule drifted back toward Earth.*

Exercise

Indicate whether the noun is common (**c**) or proper (**p**).

_____ c **1.** a red pencil
_____ **2.** Mrs. Alice Gennaro
_____ **3.** fear
_____ **4.** an island
_____ **5.** Uncle Sam (a symbol of the U.S.)
_____ **6.** white paper
_____ **7.** my cousin
_____ **8.** first place (in a race)
_____ **9.** boxes of candy
_____ **10.** the Prime Minister

Exercise

Capitalize the proper nouns in the following sentences.

He began working on this book in the fall of 1979;

1. He began working on this book in the fall of 1979; it was august or september, I think.
it was August or September, I think.

2. The earth rotates on its axis once every 23 hours and 56 minutes.

3. They could not tell me if president kennedy had been elected in 1960.

4. Did you study english and chemistry?

5. The tour includes a two-day visit to cairo after a trip through the suez canal.

B **COUNTABILITY**

English nouns can be divided into two groups: those that we can count and those that we can not count.

The nouns that we can count are called **countable nouns** or **count nouns** (*one chair, two chairs, three chairs*). (Uncountable nouns are discussed in Chapter 2, pages

48-49.) Sometimes we understand why a noun is countable or not; other times we do not. For example, *information* may seem to be countable (*one information, two informations*), but it is not a countable noun in English.

B1 Singular and Plural Form

Countable nouns have two forms: **singular** (one *book,* an *idea,* the *word*) and **plural** (two *books, ideas,* the *words*).

The plural form of regular nouns is written by adding the letter *s* to the end of the singular form.

Singular	+ s =	Plural
book	+ s =	books
horse	+ s =	horses
calendar	+ s =	calendars

Sometimes adding the letter *s* also requires a change in the spelling. Turn to Appendix A for the correct rule.

Exercise

The word *one* is used with singular nouns; words for other numbers are used with plural nouns. Read the following sentences. Add **one**, **two**, or **four** in each blank and correct any mistakes in the form of singular and plural nouns.

1. It takes *two* hand to drive a car carefully.
2. Each person has_____parent and_____grandfather.
3. But we have only_____father.
4. Yesterday I had_____cup of coffee:_____at breakfast and_____at lunch.
5. When I replaced all the tires on my car, I found out how expensive_____tires are.
6. The word *noun* has_____letters.
7. We have_____choice: to leave now or to wait until tomorrow morning.
8. Mrs. Jackson has_____daughter:_____daughter who is 7 years old,_____daughter who is 4 years old, and_____twins who were born last week.

Irregular Singular and Plural Forms

There are a number of common irregular plural forms:

Singular	Plural
child	children
foot	feet
man	men
tooth	teeth
woman	women

Some English nouns have the same form for the singular and the plural. Some have a form which looks like a singular: that is, there is no final *s: Chinese, sheep, fish*. Others of these nouns look like plurals: that is, there is a final *s: series, means*.

Some specialized or technical words have kept their Latin or Greek forms in English:

	Singular	Plural
-us/-i	stimulus	stimuli
-a/-ae	alumna	alumnae
-um/-a	stratum	strata
-is/-es	thesis	theses
-on/-a	criterion	criteria
-ex/-ices	index	indices

Some Latin and Greek nouns are being made into regular English nouns. Therefore, we find two plural forms—one foreign, the other English:

Singular	Plural
medium	media (foreign)
	mediums (English)
formula	formulae (foreign)
	formulas (English)

Latin and Greek forms present special problems. It is best to check a dictionary for the correct singular and plural forms.

Exercise

Complete the chart of singular and plural noun forms.

	Singular	Plural
1.	*man*	men
2.	apex	_____
3.	_____	media
4.	sheep	_____

5. child	_____
6. _____	teeth
7. base	_____
8. basis	_____
9. _____	means
10. foot	_____
11. _____	data
12. series	_____
13. boot	_____
14. alumnus	_____
15. _____	fish
16. criterion	_____
17. _____	cases
18. _____	appendixes
19. _____	appendices
20. _____	women

Singular and Plural Nouns: Special Problems

Some English nouns are always plural. They have no singular forms:

1. Pairs: two equal parts joined together

binoculars	pliers	eyeglasses
scissors	shears	pajamas, pyjamas
pants	shorts	jeans
trousers		glasses ("eyeglasses")

2. Plurals in *s*

fireworks	earnings
manners	grounds
oats	wages
quarters	savings
surroundings	stairs
tropics	looks ("good looks")
ashes	minutes (of a meeting)
clothes	odds (in betting)

3. Plurals not in *s*

cattle	people	police
(singular - cow)	(singular - person)	(singular - police officer)

Another problem in countable nouns is the **collective nouns**. The collective nouns refer to groups of people (for example, *family, team,* and *committee*), but most of the time they are considered singular nouns. The plural usage is much more common in British English than it is in American English.

Although most of the time a collective noun refers to a group, it may refer to the members of a group.

    (1)   Our team is playing well this season.

    (2)   The team are doing their exercises.

The singular meaning of *team* in example 1 requires the verb form *is.* The plural meaning in 2 requires the verb form *are.* (See Chapter 2, page 55 and Chapter 3, page 86 for subject-verb agreement and Chapter 2, page 66 for pronoun forms.)

There is no problem with the singular and plural forms. The collective nouns are regular in their formation:

Singular	Plural
family	families
team	teams
committee	committees

Some English nouns are **complex**: they are a combination of noun and adjective or prepositional phrase. The plural is formed by putting the *s* after the noun, not after the adjective or prepositional phrase.

one son-in-law   two sons-in-law
                      X two son-in-laws

a postmaster general   several postmasters general
                      X several postmaster generals

Other examples of complex nouns are the following:

mother-in-law	attorney general
father-in-law	body politic
daughter-in-law	court-martial
sister-in-law	notary public (American English)
brother-in-law	Secretary-General (of the United Nations)

Exercise

Choose **is** for singular nouns and **are** for plural nouns.

1. The police_____investigating the crime.
2. Our team_____playing for the championship tonight.
3. The rich_____getting richer.
4. Nowadays some diseases_____less serious than in past centuries.
5. The people_____waiting for a bus.
6. His sisters-in-law_____cooking Thanksgiving dinner.

B2 Uncountable Nouns

In addition to nouns that can be counted (*one book, two books, three books,* etc.), there are nouns that can not be counted. For example, we can not count ink in the same way we count books, as ✗ *one ink,* ✗ *two inks,* ✗ *three inks.*

The nouns that we can not count in this way are called **uncountable nouns**, **non-count nouns**, or **mass nouns**. Sometimes it is not possible to figure out if a noun is countable or uncountable. For example, *news* may look like a countable noun (*one new, two news, three news,* etc.), and *vocabulary* may seem like something that you can count; but they are uncountable nouns in English. Therefore, when you are uncertain whether the word is countable or not, you should consult your dictionary.

An uncountable noun has only one form; it does not have singular and plural forms like countable nouns. The uncountable nouns *information* and *news,* for example, never change to ✗ *informations* and ✗ *new.*

Since an uncountable noun does not have singular and plural forms, it can not appear with other words that indicate the meaning of singular or plural. For example, we can not have ✗ *several news* or ✗ *an information.* (Turn to Chapter 4, pages 133, 143, and 145 for more information about uncountable nouns and quantifiers.)

Commonly, uncountable nouns are used for materials or substances: for example, *ink, chalk, soap, air,* and *milk.* They are also commonly used for abstract qualities: for example, *honesty, beauty,* and *danger.* There are always exceptions to this rule. For example, the abstract nouns *difficulty* and *worry* have both plural and singular forms.

Here are some common uncountable nouns that look like countable nouns:

1. Diseases: mumps, laryngitis, measles
2. *-cs* subjects: statistics, physics, politics
3. Some games: checkers, billiards, darts, dominoes

Some common uncountable nouns are:

advice	garbage	money
baggage	homework	music
china	information	news
clothing (clothes is	knowledge	punctuation
countable plural)	luggage	spelling
education	machinery (machine	traffic
equipment	is countable)	vocabulary
food	mail	writing
furniture		

Note: *Clothes* is a countable plural which can be used with quantifiers such as *few,* 'She has few clothes.' but never with numbers. ✗ She has five clothes.

Exercise

Identify each noun as uncountable (**u**), countable-singular (**sing.**), or countable-plural (**pl.**).

___u___ **1.** equipment   _____ **6.** water
_____ **2.** oxygen   _____ **7.** happiness
_____ **3.** television   _____ **8.** people
_____ **4.** politics   _____ **9.** car
_____ **5.** clothes   _____ **10.** scissors

Exercise

Choose **much** for uncountable nouns and **many** for countable-plural nouns.

1. I did not find very_____information in that report.
2. Did you see_____cattle when you visited Texas?
3. Road construction requires_____heavy machinery.
4. _____machines used in road construction can be very expensive.
5. Don't use the freeways during rush hours: you will find too_____traffic then.

Counters

Since we can not count uncountable nouns, we have to use another way if we want to discuss amounts. We use **counters**. Counters allow us to count uncountable nouns. For example, we can not count *soap*, but we can count *bars of soap*; we can not count *milk*, but we can count *bottles of milk*.

A counter is a countable noun that specifies an amount, either specifically (a *gram*) or generally (a *box*). Common counters indicate quantities, units, and containers.

1. quantities

a *pound* of butter	a *cup* (8 fluid
a *kilo* of flour	ounces) of oil
two *feet* of rope	an *ounce* of gold
several *quarts* of	ten *grams* of silver
orange juice	one *meter* of ribbon

2. units

a *cake* of soap	a *piece* of advice
a *bar* of soap	two *items* of news
several *pieces* of	a *bit* of information
equipment	

3. containers

a *bottle* of milk	a *bag* of salt
some *jars* of jam	many *cups* of coffee
a *box* of sugar	a *glass* of water

A number can be a counter in a few situations where the quantity is clear and conventional. For example, in a restaurant, we might order *two coffees*; it is clear that we mean *two cups of coffee.* If a person asks for *one sugar* in his coffee, he wants one teaspoon of sugar or one lump of sugar in it.

Exercise

Complete this shopping list. Put in an appropriate counter. Use **pound** (0.45 kilo), **quart** (0.946 liter), **box**, **head**, or **can**.

5 *pounds* of apples

1 _____ of orange juice

1 big _____ of laundry detergent

1 _____ of bleach

2 _____ of veal chops
1 _____ of milk
1 big _____ of cabbage
2 small _____ of baked beans
1 _____ of hot dogs
10 _____ of cat food

Exercise

Put in an appropriate counter or an appropriate noun.

1. In December 1981, one _ounce_ of gold cost about $400.
2. I keep a _____ of black ink in my desk.
3. I like one teaspoon of _____ in my black coffee.
4. My car holds 10 gallons of _____ .
5. Every time I fill up my car, I have to add a _____ of oil.
6. When she read the letter, she got two _____ of bad advice.
7. Do you think he drinks too many _____ of coffee each day?
8. We used almost two feet of _____ to tie up the package.
9. For her birthday, he bought a large _____ of perfume.
10. When I bought the toothbrushes, I remembered to buy a tube of _____ .

B3 Uncountable Nouns and Countable Nouns: Two Meanings

Many English nouns have two meanings: an uncountable noun meaning and a countable noun meaning. A few of these nouns are presented in the following chart.

Countable Meaning	Noun	Uncountable Meaning
a company _He owns many businesses._	business	commerce; trade _Business is good this year._

51

Countable Meaning	Noun	Uncountable Meaning
a dessert made of flour and sugar *She made three cakes.*	cake	food made of flour and sugar *Do you want any cake?*
a difference *There have been many technological changes in the past ten years.*	change	money returned after a purchase *You didn't give me the correct change.*
an activity to practice a skill *I didn't finish the grammar exercises.*	exercise	effort used doing something *We don't get much exercise.*
a container *Give me a glass, please.*	glass	material used in making windows *The statue was made of glass.*
a written report; a newspaper *I bought three papers.*	paper	material on which we write *We need some paper.*
a machine for receiving pictures *They just bought a new television.*	television	technology of visual communication *Some people say that television is bad for children.*
a moment when an event takes place *She always talks about the good times.*	time	what is measured by hours, days, etc. *Time passes slowly when you are bored.*

An uncountable noun can be made into a countable noun in order to signal the meaning *different kind(s) of*.

(3) Many people drink wine with their meals.

(4) The wines of California are not as famous as the wines of France or Germany.

In example 3, we are discussing the drink—wine (which is uncountable). In example 4, we are discussing several different types of wine, for example, white wine and red wine.

Note: A countable noun can not be made into an uncountable noun. For instance, example 5 is incorrect.

(5)　X Computer had not been invented then.

The subject of the sentence—*computer*—refers to any computer or to all computers in general. Nevertheless, the *computer* is a countable noun: it must have a determiner when it appears in the singular form. (See Chapter 4, page 133 for general reference.)

(6)　The computer had not been invented then.

Exercise

Identify whether each underlined noun has an uncountable meaning (**u**) or a countable meaning (**c**).

___u___ **1.** Radio has allowed us to communicate quickly over very large distances.

_____ **2.** My radio can pick up signals from half-way around the world.

_____ **3.** Marie Antoinette said, "Let them eat cake!"

_____ **4.** They had left the papers on the couch in the living room.

_____ **5.** The glass was broken, and we had to get a new rear window for the car.

_____ **6.** The glass was broken, and the wine spilled all over the table.

_____ **7.** The wines of Australia are not as famous as the wines of Germany.

_____ **8.** There are exercises throughout this handbook.

_____ **9.** Exercise is important in maintaining good health.

C　NOUNS AND NOUN PHRASES

A noun can appear alone in a clause, for instance, *answers* in example 7.

(7)　*Answers* are sometimes not reliable.

However, nouns also appear with other words in noun phrases. A **noun phrase** includes a noun and other words, phrases, or clauses. In a clause, a noun phrase fills the same place as a noun. Adjectives come before nouns in noun phrases.

noun phrase

(8)   Simple *answers* are sometimes not reliable.
Prepositional phrases come after nouns in noun phrases.

noun   prepositional phrase

(9)   *Answers* to complex questions are sometimes not
      reliable.
Articles come before nouns, and clauses come after them
in a noun phrase.

article   noun   clause

(10) The *answers* which we receive are sometimes not
      reliable.
A noun is sometimes used as an adjective.

noun   noun

(11) Computer *answers* are sometimes not reliable.
(See Chapter 4, page 157.)

In a noun phrase, it is important to know which noun
is the principal one. For instance, in example 9, the subject of the sentence is *Answers*; it is not *questions* because
answers is the principal noun.

Exercise

For each underlined noun phrase, identify the principal
noun (pn) and the other parts of the phrase. Enter the information in the chart.

1. This is the common method of making change.

2. It is used in various parts of the United States and
    Canada .

3. Of course, it is nice to have a good system that works
    well .

4. The principal benefit of the method is fewer mistakes.

5. The addition method may seem very odd to you.

	Article	Adjective	PRINCIPAL NOUN	Prepositional phrase	Clause
1.	the	common	method		
2.					
3.					
4.					
5.					

D **SUBJECT-VERB AGREEMENT**

The singular or plural form of a noun may affect the form of the verb.

                           S   V

(12) The different *procedure* was not useful in dangerous conditions.

                           S   V

(13) The different *procedures* were not useful in dangerous conditions.

The singular noun *procedure* is the subject (S) of the sentence; it requires the singular verb form *was*. The plural subject (S) *procedures* requires the plural verb form *were*. (See Chapter 3, page 86 for more information about subject-verb agreement.)

An uncountable noun may affect the form of the verb in a clause.

(14) The *information* was not welcome at that time.

(15) *News* comes quickly via television.

The uncountable nouns usually require the singular form of the verb: *was* and *comes*.

Exercise

Find the principal noun in the subject noun phrase and

underline it. Supply the correct verb form: **is**, **are**, **was**, or **were**.

1. Very little business _was_ conducted today because of the holiday.
2. The first holiday which we celebrate each year _____ New Year's Day, January 1.
3. Other holidays _____ celebrated during the year.
4. But January 1 _____ just the first day of the year.
5. New Year's parties _____ usually very noisy.
6. The noise from the parties _____ very loud.
7. People _____ singing from 10:00 p.m. until dawn today.
8. The reason for all those noisy songs _____ New Year's Eve.
9. The neighbors who just moved in across the hall _____ not noisy.
10. The news tonight _____ full of stories of war.

E   ### NOUN-PRONOUN AGREEMENT

The singular or plural form of a noun affects the pronouns that can refer to it.

singular

(16) An artificial heart is not practical for

plural

all of the patients.

singular   plural

(17) It is not practical for all of them.

An uncountable noun also affects the pronouns that can refer to it: only *it* can be used.

uncountable

(18) News comes quickly via television.

uncountable

(19) It comes quickly via television.

The pronouns *they*, *their*, and *theirs* can not be used for an uncountable noun, even if the amount is very large.

uncountable

(20) We used such a large volume of information that we needed a computer.

uncountable

We used such a large volume of it that we needed a computer.

Exercise

Fill in the blanks with **it** or **they**.

1. Information is important because _it_ helps us make decisions.
2. Newspapers provide information with lots of details, but _____ can be read only by literate people.
3. Radio is more useful than newspapers because _____ is available to people who can not read.
4. Television has an advantage over radio: _____ is seen as well as heard.
5. But not everyone has a television set because _____ are expensive.
6. A family needs money for rent and food before _____ can invest in a television set.
7. A radio is more practical because _____ is not as expensive as a television.
8. Through radio and television, the countries of the world are in close contact. Will _____ understand each other better?
9. Does news from around the world help? Will _____ improve our understanding?
10. People have access to information. Will _____ use _____ properly?

F **NOUN-EQUIVALENTS**

A **noun-equivalent** is any word, phrase, or clause that (1) refers to a person, place, thing, or idea and (2) appears in one of the usual noun places in a clause.

One common noun-equivalent is a pronoun. (See Chapter 2, page 59.)

Another common noun-equivalent is a verb form. There are two of these: (1) an infinitive (*to* + the simple form of the verb) and (2) a gerund (the simple form of the verb + *-ing*).

(22) noun direct object (DO): *sports*
    Howard likes sports.
(23) infinitive direct object (DO): *to run*
    Howard likes to run.

57

(24) gerund direct object (DO): *hiking*
Howard likes hiking.

There are several uses of infinitives. Example 23 shows only one: its use as a noun-equivalent in a clause. A gerund has only one use: it is a verb form that has the function of a noun in a sentence. (See Chapter 5 for more about gerunds and infinitives as noun-equivalents.)

An entire clause can function like a noun.

(25) noun phrase direct object (DO): *the answer*
Mary knows the answer.

(26) clause pattern as direct object (DO):
that a meter is longer than a yard
Mary knows that a meter is longer than a yard.

Clause patterns used like nouns are called **noun clauses.** (See Chapter 5 for more about noun clauses.)

Exercise

Identify the underlined nouns or noun-equivalents:

    a. Noun
    b. Pronoun
    c. Verb form: infinitive
    d. Verb form: gerund
    e. Clause

_____ 1. In English, we say "ten pounds" and "ten dollars."

_____ 2. It would be more logical to write 10£ and 10$, but we do not write them that way.

_____ 3. On the other hand, we do follow logic by writing 25¢, with the ¢ after the number.

_____ 4. And we say "twenty-five cents," with cents after the number.

_____ 5. Students of English must forget logic .

_____ 6. They must imitate how we do it in English.

F1 **Pronouns**

Pronouns: Use

Pronouns can appear in clauses wherever nouns can appear: the word **pronoun** means *in place of a noun*. Pronouns are often used to replace a noun or noun-equivalent in a clause pattern.

> (27) *Anita* is working part-time.

> (28) *She* wants to pay her own school expenses.

> (29) With this job, she is able to pay almost all of *them*.

It would be possible to repeat the name *Anita* in example 28, but we avoid repetition by using *she*. And the pronoun *them* is used in order to avoid repeating *her own school expenses*. The pronouns *she* and *them* refer to the nouns *Anita* and *expenses*; the nouns are the **antecedents** of the pronouns.

Pronouns can shorten a sentence by reducing the number of words in it; for instance, in example 29, *them = her own school expenses*.

Pronouns also show that several sentences are part of the same message; for instance, examples 27, 28, and 29.

A pronoun can be used to point to persons, places, things, or ideas that are clear in the message.

> (30) X Anita and Martha have jobs. *She* works in the evening.

The message in example 30 is not clear, because the pronoun *she* does not have a clear antecedent, that is, it can refer either to *Anita* or to *Martha*. Example 31 may also be unclear: Who is referred to by the pronoun *we—you and I?, someone else and I?,* or *you, someone else, and I?*

> (31) We are reading about the pronouns in English.

Note: A noun and a pronoun are not used together if they refer to the same person, place, thing, or idea.

> (32) X All students in this school they must come to class.

The verb *must* has a subject: *all students*. The pronoun *they* refers to this same subject; therefore, example 32 is incorrect. The correct sentence is Example 33.

> (33) All students in this school must come to class.

Exercise

Underline each pronoun and draw an arrow from the pronoun to its antecedent.

Many international students have studied English for many years before they go to study in an English-speaking country. After many years, they feel that they can read and write it well. And, of course, most of them can. However, frequently their experience in speaking it has been limited.

Last month, Li came to ask a question after class. He felt that it was very important. Several of his friends came along to hear the answer. The problem was that an American student had walked up to Li in the Student Union and had asked him where the nearest bathroom was. Li told him that there were no bathing facilities in the whole building. The American student laughed at the answer.

Li's English teacher told him and his friends that in American English, *bathroom, washroom, restroom,* and *men's room* or *ladies' room* mean *toilet.* They laughed, too, when they understood what had happened.

Exercise

Correct any mistakes in pronoun use.

1. Lack of practice speaking a new language it can cause problems.

2. Li's teacher thought of Li and the American student. She understood his reaction.

3. Li's friends had learned some new words. They were very funny.

4. Each student he or she must expect some embarrassing moments.

5. The important thing is that the student should be ready to learn from any mistakes that they might make.

Form of Pronouns: First, Second and Third Person

A pronoun points to a person, a place, a thing, or an idea in the conversation or composition. A pronoun can be used only when it is clear what is pointed to or referred to.

Pronouns can be first, second, or third person.

First person (the speaker or writer): *I, me, we, us*

Second person (the receiver of the message): *you*
Third person (someone or something else): *he, him, she, her, it, they, them*

Note: Whenever a pronoun occurs in a grouping with nouns or other pronouns, the best order is (a) second person, (b) third person, and then (c) first person. Example 34 is not polite in English.

(34) X I and John went to eat after the movie.

3rd person   1st person

(35) John and I went to eat after the movie.

2nd person   3rd person

(36) You and John can finish the work later.

2nd person 3rd person   1st person

(37) The police wanted to talk to you, Elaine, and me.

Exercise

Rearrange the pronouns if necessary.

1. I and you know English.

   You and I know English.

2. You may teach me and them to speak it better.
3. They and I are students.
4. We and they are studying two foreign languages.
5. It is hard for you, us, and them to remember all the vocabulary.

Form of Pronouns: Subjects and Objects

Pronouns in English have many different forms. Before you can decide on a form, you must know how it is used. For example, you must know what position it occupies. If a pronoun fills the position of a subject or a subject complement, it should be a subject pronoun. If it fills the position of a direct object, an indirect object, object of a preposition, or an object complement, it should be an object pronoun.

61

Subject Pronouns	Object Pronouns
I	me
you	you
he	him
she	her
it	it
we	us
they	them

Note: The pronouns *it* and *you* are used for subjects and objects.

S   IO

(38) I told her the news.

S   DO

(39) He bought them in the morning.

S   DO   Object of preposition

(40) We gave it to them.

However, when identifying yourself there are two ways which are considered correct.

S   V   SC

(41) It 's I.

S   V   SC

(42) It 's me.

Example 41 is correct according to formal English usage: the subject pronoun for the first person singular is *I*. However, sentences like 42 occur very often in conversational English. Although example 42 does not follow the rules of formal usage, it is accepted informal English.

When the subject or object is complex, people often make pronoun usage mistakes such as the following:

(43) ✕ Me and John went to eat after the movie.

(44) ✕ They saw John and I.

(45) ✕ To you and I, it really sounds like a bad idea.

Errors like these can be avoided by using this simple test:

separate the two parts of the subject or object and use each part with the verb *went*. The sentence *John went to eat after the movie* sounds all right, but the sentence *Me went to eat after the movie* is clearly wrong.

In sentence 44, we need the object pronoun for the direct object: *me*. The sentence *They saw I* is obviously wrong.

Exercise

Choose the correct pronoun form. Circle your answer.

1. Is the package for you or for I/me?
2. When did the postman give she/her the notice about the package?
3. It could not have been after 8:30, because she/her leaves for work then.
4. Perhaps he/him left the notice with the next-door neighbors.
5. But if he saw the neighbors, why didn't he give they/them the package?
6. I think that either you or I/me must sign for it in person.
7. We/us can go to the post office tomorrow morning.
8. Maybe you can, but I/me can not.
9. My boss asked I/me to work tomorrow.
10. Then I/me will go alone. Do you think they/them will give I/me the package if only I/me sign?

Exercise

Correct any mistakes in pronoun form.

1. You and him are learning about English.
   You and he are learning about English.
2. Between you and I, this is very good advice.
3. To them, it may seem odd.
4. However, she and I have looked into the matter.
5. And you and me can benefit.

Form of Pronouns: Masculine, Feminine, and Neuter

The masculine forms *he/him* and the feminine forms *she/her* are used only for human beings and animals whose sex is known. The neuter form *it* is used for animals whose sex is not known, things, ideas, and uncountable nouns. The masculine and feminine forms are also used to refer to objects or ideas that the speaker feels very close to. For example, a captain might use sentence 46 in discussing a ship.

(46) She is a fine ship.

(This use of the masculine and feminine forms for inanimate objects is not common.)

The plural forms *they/them* are used for countable nouns. They are used for masculine, feminine, or neuter nouns, or for any combination of them.

There is often a problem in deciding whether to use a masculine pronoun (*he, him*, or *his*) or a feminine pronoun (*she, her*, or *hers*). This problem exists when the pronoun substitutes for an indefinite, such as *everyone,* or for a noun that can be either masculine or feminine (such as *parent).*

Very conservative formal usage says that the pronoun *he, him*, or *his* should be used if the person is clearly a man (example 47) or if it is not possible to determine *he* or *she* (example 48).

(47) Every father decides how *he* wants to raise *his* children.

(48) Every parent decides how *he* wants to raise *his* children.

If the person is clearly a woman, the pronoun *she, her*, or *hers* should be used.

(49) Every mother decides how *she* wants to raise *her* children.

Modern usage presents another possibility: the combinations *he/she* (read as "he or she"), *him/her, his/her*, and *his/hers*. They are used if it is not possible to determine *he* or *she*.

(50) Every parent decides how *he/she* wants to raise *his/her* children.

It is not possible to use a neuter pronoun—*it* or *its*—in this case. While it is true that a neuter pronoun would avoid the problem of deciding on a masculine or feminine pronoun, *it* and *its* can not be used for human beings. (The use of plural pronouns to solve this problem is shown in Chapter 2, page 66.)

Exercise

Fill in the blanks with appropriate pronouns.

1. Police Officer Franklin is not a man, but *she* has not had any problems on the job.
2. The other police say that _____ are satisfied that _____ does the job very well.
3. People in the community are happy that _____ is on the police force.
4. Mr. Franklin is happy that _____ is not the only "breadwinner" in the house.

Exercise

Cross out the noun or noun-phrase subject in the second sentence and substitute the correct pronoun.

1. Most people in this country work 40 hours a week. ~~Many people in this country~~ *They* work five days a week, 8 hours a day.
2. However, Mr. and Mrs. Stone do not. Mr. and Mrs. Stone do not work full-time.
3. Mr. Stone is a writer. Mr. Stone works only 25 hours a week.
4. Mrs. Stone is even luckier. Mrs. Stone only works on weekends.
5. Mr. and Mrs. Stone have two children. Mr. and Mrs. Stone do not need outside care for their children.
6. They are very glad that they don't need such care. Such care is expensive and can be impersonal.
7. Their daughter's name is Mary. Mary is four years old.
8. Robert is their son. Robert is one year old.

Form of Pronouns: Singular and Plural

The pronouns, like the nouns, are singular, plural, and un-countable.

Singular	Plural	Uncountable
I/me	we/us	
you	you	
he/him	they/them	
she/her	they/them	
it	they/them	it

65

There is sometimes a problem in deciding whether to use a singular or plural noun to refer to indefinites (such as *everybody*) or to nouns that can be either masculine or feminine (such as *parent*). Although the indefinites are singular in formal usage (and the verb forms are also singular), informally the pronoun *they* is often used.

>   (51) Everybody decides how *they* want to raise *their* children.

(Notice that the indefinite *everybody* goes with the singular verb *decides*, but that *they* goes with the plural verb *want*.)

The use of *they*, *them*, *their*, and *theirs* to refer to indefinites or singular nouns should be limited to informal, conversational English.

Collective nouns present another problem for choosing singular or plural pronoun substitutes. Collectives refer to groups, for example, *family*, *team*, or *class*. Collectives are countable, and the pronouns (and the verb forms) for the plural form are clear.

>   (52) The four teams were ready for their matches.

The problem is with the singular of a collective noun: it is grammatically singular, but sometimes it is logically plural because the members of the group are considered individually.

>   (53) His family is strong. It has been built on a strong foundation of love and trust.

In example 53, *family* is considered as a unit; therefore, the singular pronoun *it* is used (and the verbs are *is* and *has been built*).

>   (54) His family have not been well. They have had colds and the flu all winter.

In example 54, *family* is made of individual people. The individual people have been ill; the family unit itself has not been ill. The pronoun *they* is used (and the verbs are *have been* and *have had*).

In American usage, a singular collective noun usually requires a singular pronoun to refer to it. British usage more often uses a singular or a plural pronoun for a collective noun, according to the logic of the situation. If the learner of English is not sure which pronoun forms to use, it is possible to avoid the problem and at the same time make the idea clearer.

> (55) *The members of his family* have not been well. They have had colds and the flu all winter.

Exercise

Fill in the correct pronoun.

1. Our team will not arrive at the same time because _they_ are traveling by plane and by car.
2. Every fan at the game will wave a flag to show that _____ supports the team.
3. Each student must determine the best way for _____ to study.
4. The class had been scheduled to meet early in the morning. The registrar had been able to find a room for _____ then.
5. Many people were not happy about this. It seemed that each of the students had _____ own reason to ask for a change.

Pronouns for General Reference: You, One, They

We use the pronoun *you*, *one*, or *they* to make a general statement about people. In this case, the pronoun does not refer to any particular person or people; that is, there is no antecedent for it.

In examples 56 and 57, the pronouns *you* and *one* mean *people in general* or *anyone*.

> (56) You should be especially careful driving on a mid-city freeway.

> (57) One should be especially careful driving on a mid-city freeway.

The use of *you* for *people in general* is informal: it appears in conversation and informal writing. Sometimes, it can be confusing, because the pronoun *you* has two common meanings: *the person(s) spoken to* (the second person) and *anyone* (the third person). For instance, does example 56 include all people or just the receiver of the message?

In American English, the use of *one* for *people in general* is formal: it appears more often in writing. However, in British English, *one* is consistently used in both speaking and writing. Therefore, both are correct: 58 is more common in American English; 59 is more common in British English.

(58) You can easily lose your way in a new city.

(59) One can easily lose one's way in a new city.

Informally, *they* is often used to avoid naming specific people.

(60) They say that Siberia is very cold.

The meaning of *they* is unclear, because there is no antecedent for it. This informal use should be avoided in writing and in careful speech. Instead of the general *they*, use a clearer indication of who is referred to.

(61) Travelers in Asia say that Siberia is very cold.

If the identity of the people referred to by *they* is unimportant or unknown, you simply rephrase the statement.

(62) I have heard that Siberia is very cold.

(63) Siberia is very cold.

Exercise

Indicate whether the pronouns *you*, *one*, and *they* are used for general reference (**gen.**) or for specific reference (**spec.**) to particular people in these sentences.

spec. **1.** I heard that *you* intend to major in computer science.

_____ **2.** It is hard to tell if a book is good until *you* read it.

_____ **3.** *They* say that television will be in every home.

_____ **4.** Yesterday, *they* reported the results of the college survey.

_____ **5.** Several persons together as a group might be able to change Melinda's mind; *one* can not.

F2 **Reflexive Pronouns**

Reflexive Pronouns: Form

The reflexive pronouns are formed from a pronoun plus *self* (singular or uncountable) or *selves* (plural).

	Singular	**Plural**	**Uncountable**
First person	myself	ourselves	
Second person	yourself	yourselves	

	Singular	Plural	Uncountable
Third person, masculine	himself	themselves	
Third person, feminine	herself	themselves	
Third person, neuter	itself	themselves	itself

We often find reflexive forms like 64 and 65.

(64) X hisself

(65) X theirselves

These forms are logical: a possessive pronoun plus *self* or *selves*, similar to *myself*. However, they are not correct. Note the difference in form between the second person singular and the second person plural, *yourself* and *yourselves*.

Exercise

Fill in the blanks with correct forms of reflexive pronouns.

1. Cathy went to buy a new winter coat with the money she had earned _herself_.
2. Her parents were helping her with college expenses, but their income_____was not big enough to pay for everything.
3. Her father had said, "Because college is so expensive, you and your brother will have to help_____."
4. David was already paying for all his school expenses by_____.
5. Their mother thought to_____that independent children will do well.

Reflexive Pronouns: Use

A reflexive pronoun is used in a sentence when the subject and object refer to the same person or thing.

(66a) X Jack hit Jack with the hammer.

(66b) Jack hit himself with the hammer.

(66c) He hit himself with the hammer.

Example 66a is incorrect because both the subject and the object are the same. Compare the examples above with the following ones.

(67a) Jack hit Rick with the hammer.

(67b) Jack hit him with the hammer.

(68) I bought myself a birthday present.

In example 68, the subject and the indirect object are the same person: the speaker/writer.

S   V   Object of preposition

(69) She said to herself that tomorrow was another day.

In example 69, the speaker and the object of the preposition *to* are the same woman.

A reflexive pronoun can be used for emphasis.

(70) Those people did the whole thing themselves.

In example 70, the speaker/writer wants to emphasize that the people acted *alone, with no help* from anyone else.

A reflexive pronoun in a prepositional phrase with *by* means *alone*.

(71) We stood there by ourselves waiting for the bus.

Exercise

Identify the use of the reflexive pronoun in each sentence.

    a. to show that the subject or object are the same person(s) or thing(s)

    b. to emphasize

    c. to mean *alone, without help*

_c_ **1.** My brother traveled all the way around the world by himself.

_____ **2.** He made all the plane reservations himself.

_____ **3.** He bought himself the cheapest ticket he could find.

_____ **4.** He took a picture of himself for his passport.

_____ **5.** And he could only blame himself if anything went wrong.

F3 **Impersonal *It*; Empty *It***

The pronoun *it* has several uses where it does not have an

antecedent: it is used to take the place of the subject of a sentence.

One of these uses is to discuss time (example 72), days and/or dates (example 73), and weather (example 74).

(72) It was 7:45 in the evening.

(73) It is Tuesday, April 2.

(74) It will be sunny and hot tomorrow.

Another use is to identify.

(75) (Who is on the telephone?)
     It is Robert Johnson.

The **empty** *it* is used sometimes for emphasis.

(76) It is very important that we finish before tomorrow.

(77) It was at a sports shop when Phyllis first realized that she missed playing tennis.

(See Chapter 6, page 269.)

F4 Pronoun Uses of *There* and *Then*

The adverbs *there* and *then* are sometimes used as pronouns in order to point to an earlier unit of meaning in the sentence, composition, or conversation.

(78) We arrived at the airport at 3:00 in the morning.
     We had to wait *there* until 5:00 a.m.

In example 78, *there* means *at the airport*.

(79) They could wait only until 7:00 p.m.
     They would have to leave *then*.

In example 79, *then* refers to 7:00 p.m.; it means *at 7:00 p.m.*

The word *there* is often used to fill a noun position in a clause pattern.

(80) Question word order
     Were *there* many people near the ticket counter?

(81) Tag statement
     Yes, *there* were.

(See Chapter 6, page 267.)

Exercise

Fill in each blank with **it**, **there**, or **then**.

1. How many people were *there* at the bank this morning?

2. Do you think that_____is as hot today as yesterday?

3. You should go to the bank at 9:00._____will not be many people_____.

4. Tell me when_____is 2:00 so I can get to the bank before it closes.

5. _____certainly is helpful to have a checking account.

F5 Possessive Form of Nouns and Pronouns

Another form and use of nouns and pronouns is the **possessive**. Although there are several uses of the possessive form, its principal use is to show ownership or possession.

Possessive Nouns: Form

The possessive of nouns is formed in two ways. One of these ways is a prepositional phrase with the preposition *of*.

(82) The agenda *of the meeting* was long.

The second way to form the possessive of nouns is to add an ending. This ending is written with an apostrophe and an *s* (example 83) or with an apostrophe alone (example 84).

(83) The *President's* press conference was on Wednesday.

(84) The *Senators'* press conference was on Thursday.

The noun with the ending appears *before* the noun indicating what or who(m) is possessed; example 85 is not correct.

(85) X The press conference President's was on Wednesday.

It is possible for the possessive to appear without a following noun, if the meaning of the sentence is clear.

(86) The President's press conference was on Wednesday, and the Senators' was on Thursday.

The correct written form—either *'s* or *'*—is determined by following three steps:

1. Write the correct form of the singular, plural, or uncountable noun.
2. Add an apostrophe after the last letter of the noun.
3a. If the last letter is *s*, STOP: do not add anything after the apostrophe.
3b. If the last letter is NOT *s*, ADD an *s* after the apostrophe. For example:

> (87) Step 1 (the) Senators (press conference)
> Step 2 (the) Senators' (press conference)
> Step 3a the Senators' press conference

> (88) Step 1 (the) President (press conference)
> Step 2 (the) President' (press conference)
> Step 3b the President's press conference

> (89) Step 1 (that) man (score)
> Step 2 (that) man' (score)
> Step 3b (that) man's score

> (90) Step 1 (those) men (score)
> Step 2 (those) men' (score)
> Step 3b those men's score

The same three steps can be used when the possessor or possessors are named in a phrase. We look at the last word in the phrase.

> (91) Step 1 John and Mary (house)
> Step 2 John and Mary' (house)
> Step 3b John and Mary's house

Note: With some nouns ending in *s*, there are two possible written forms: *Mr. Jones' car* and *Mr. Jones's car*. The first one follows the three steps. The second is used to show that some people say the possessive form with an extra syllable, like "Joneses." Both forms are correct.

Exercise

Fill in each blank with the correct possessive form of the noun or noun phrase. Use a possessive form with an apostrophe.

1. The United Nations had scheduled a meeting. The _United Nations'_ meeting was held on Monday.

2. The Security Council had a long debate. The_____ debate was very heated.

3. A permanent member called a press conference. The _____press conference did not attract a lot of attention.

4. Two temporary members held a secret meeting. The _____meeting did not produce any noticeable results.

5. The Secretary-General tried for a compromise. Many people were unaware of the_____efforts.

6. On Wednesday, two representatives from UNESCO addressed the Security Council. We all heard the _____address.

Exercise

Fill in each blank with the correct noun or pronoun form.

1. The union's strike was suspended. The management was happy that the _union_ had done this.

2. On the other hand, one corporation chairman's actions did not please the union. The union said that the _____had promised to negotiate.

3. The union mentioned other corporation chairmen's promises to negotiate. The_____promised to negotiate if the strike were suspended.

4. The head of the union's position was clear. Management considered what_____proposed.

5. Management's position was clear, too. Negotiators discussed what_____proposed.

Possessive Nouns: An Apostrophe or *Of*
An ending with an apostrophe

1. Use this ending when the possessor is:

   a) human
   (92) Maurice's first purchase in an American store surprised him.
   (93) He was surprised by the shopkeeper's way of counting change.
   b) an animal that is familiar, such as a pet
   (94) My dog's leg was broken.

c) an animal which is high on the evolutionary scale
(95) An ape's brain is smaller than a human's brain.

2. Use this ending with certain expressions of time and place.

(96) A month's vacation will give you a good rest.
(97) Much of Mexico's border with the United States is the Rio Grande River.

A prepositional phrase with of

Use this phrase when the possessor is:

a) not an animal
(98) The leg of the table was broken.
(99) X The table's leg was broken.

b) an animal which is low on the evolutionary scale
(100) The life of the amoeba is very limited.

c) stated in a long or complicated phrase
(101) It depends on the attitude of *the user of the sentence*.
(102) X It depends on *the user of the sentence's attitude*.

Exercise

Write a correct possessive phrase for each sentence, with an apostrophe (') or with the preposition **of**.

1. My older sister got a driver's license.
   My older sister's driver's license
2. The picture has a frame.
3. It was a vacation that lasted two months.
4. Her husband Alvin wrote the letter.
5. Mr. Jones developed a new rose.
6. His pet cat has a green food bowl.
7. Two of the more outspoken members presented the solution.
8. All snakes have fangs.
9. The problem has unusual aspects.
10. Our aunt found the picture.

Possessive Pronouns with Following Nouns (Possessive Adjectives)

There are two sets of possessive pronouns. One set replaces the possessive noun phrases.

(103) The agenda of the meeting was long.

Its agenda was long.

(104) The Senators' press conference was on Thursday.

Their press conference was on Thursday.

These pronouns are sometimes called **possessive adjectives** because they appear in front of nouns, as adjectives do. The pronouns in this set are:

Singular	Plural	Uncountable
my	our	
your	your	
his	their	
her	their	
its	their	its

Note: Possessive pronouns do not have apostrophes. The word *it's* is not a possessive term: *it's* is the short form of *it is*.

These pronouns do not change form. The noun after them can be singular, plural, uncountable, masculine, feminine, etc.; the noun does not affect the form of the pronoun. The form of the pronoun is affected only by the possessor. For instance, in examples 105 through 108, the form is always *her*, because the possessor is one woman.

(105) Mrs. Thompson has *a son* and a daughter.
(masculine singular)
Her son is in Canada.

(106) Mrs. James has *two sons* and a daughter.
(masculine plural)
Her sons are in Detroit.

(107) Mrs. James has two sons and *a daughter*.
(feminine singular)
Her daughter is at home.

(108) Mrs. James has *a day job* and a night job.
(neuter singular)
Her day job is in television.

Note: These forms are used in discussing the parts of a person's body. Example 109 is not correct English.

(109) ✗ Mary Ann washed *the* hands before lunch.

(110) Mary Ann washed *her* hands before lunch.

Exercise

Fill in the blank with an appropriate possessive pronoun.

1. Mr. and Mrs. Arlington visited _their_ daughters in Dallas.
2. The older daughter is married and lives with _____ husband in a small house.
3. The younger daughter lives with _____ roommate in an apartment.
4. Then, the Arlingtons went to Chicago to visit _____ son.
5. He lives there with one of _____ grandparents.
6. He met _____ parents at the airport.
7. He asked, "How was _____ flight?"
8. _____ mother answered, "We almost missed _____ flight."
9. _____ father said that they were stuck in a traffic jam on the way to the airport.
10. He said, "And that's not all. I forgot _____ pipe in the hotel, too."

Possessive Pronouns with No Following Nouns

The second set of possessive pronouns is used when there is no following noun.

> (111) We saw Bill's new car, but not Ann's.
> We saw his new car, but not *hers*.
> X We didn't see *hers car*.

The pronouns in this set are:

Singular	Plural	Uncountable
mine	ours	
yours	yours	
his	theirs	
hers	theirs	
its	theirs	its

These pronouns do not change form. They do not have apostrophes. The form is determined by the possessor.

77

Exercise

Fill in the blanks with possessive pronoun forms.

1. Those checks belong to Francis.
   They are *his* .
2. Francis and Alice bought a new car.
   It is_____.
3. I paid for the television set myself.
   It is_____.
4. My sister and I own a car. It is_____.
5. Since she bought the book, she insists that it is_____.
6. If you prefer the seat on the aisle, you can have it. It's
   _____.
7. I will drive my car, and you and your wife will drive
   _____.
8. You have your opinions, and they have_____.

Possessive Nouns and Pronouns: Meaning

The possessive can be used to signal several different types of relationships. These are:

1. ownership
   (112) *Carlo's* English book was found yesterday.
2. close relationship
   (113) The cover *of the book* was missing.
   (114) *Carlo's* class in pronunciation meets three times a week.
   (115) This is *his* first day in the school.
   (116) The cost *of the classes* is high.
3. doer of an action
   (117) The President is coming tomorrow. We must finish all the work before *his* arrival.
4. receiver of an action
   (118) The police were unsure about the time of *Alice's* murder. (= the time when someone murdered Alice)
   (119) The renovation *of the school* was overdue.
5. period of time
   (120) Each week the students have *three hours'* practice in the language lab.

(121) There is a break *of 30 minutes* after the weekly test.

Exercise

Identify the meaning of the underlined possessive.
   a. ownership or possession
   b. close relationship
   c. doer of action
   d. receiver of action
   e. period of time

_a_ **1.** My sandwich was stale.

_____ **2.** Actually, Mary's salad did not look good, either.

_____ **3.** In the middle of the movie there will be an intermission of a quarter of an hour .

_____ **4.** Our missing the test was serious, but not a disaster.

_____ **5.** It was her roommate's turn to clean the apartment.

_____ **6.** We were not surprised by their dismissal from their jobs.

_____ **7.** They were lucky not to lose their jobs.

_____ **8.** Where did you leave David's car?

_____ **9.** If you left it in our garage, where is ours ?

Double Possessive Forms

There is a construction that is made of two possessive forms.

   (122) John is a friend of mine.

This sentence has two possessive forms:
1. a prepositional phrase with *of* (*of mine*)
2. a possessive pronoun (*mine*)
Sometimes more than one possessive form is needed. Therefore, example 123 is not correct.

   (123) X John is a friend of me.

Instead of the objective-case form of the pronoun (*me*), example 122 has the form of the possessive pronoun that appears when there is no following noun: *mine*. Example 124

79

is incorrect because it has the wrong possessive pronoun form.

(124) x John is a friend of my.

This **double possessive** is used to mean part of a larger group. For instance, example 122 means that I have several friends and that John is one of them.

Example 125 is correct English, but it does not have the same meaning as 122.

(125) John is my friend.

This sentence discusses only John; there is no indication of other people besides John. Example 126 indicates that all of my friends helped me, while example 127 indicates that some—but not all—helped me.

(126) My friends helped me move into my apartment.
(127) Friends of mine helped me move into my apartment.

Example 128 indicates that I own the pictures (but we do not know who is in the pictures). Example 129 indicates that I am in the pictures (but we do not know who owns them).

(128) Did you see those pictures of mine?
(129) Did you see those pictures of me?

Exercise

Correct any errors in the possessives.

1. Where do they get those ideas of their?
2. Did you see those pictures of hers?
3. Some cousins of him had come for a short visit.
4. Two uncles of ours had come, too.
5. You may bring a friend your if you wish.

Chapter 3
Contents

Chapter 3

3 Verbs

A VERBS: MEANING

The verb is one of the necessary parts in a sentence pattern. Every sentence has a subject (S) and a predicate (Pred.); and every predicate has a verb (V).

$$\overbrace{\underbrace{\text{They}}_{\text{S}} \underbrace{\text{live}}_{\text{V}} \underbrace{\text{in New York}}_{\text{Adv.}}}^{\text{Pred.}}$$

(1) They live in New York.

The verb in a sentence pattern can have one word (as in example 1), or it can have several words.

(2) They *are studying* English.
(3) She *must have finished* the test.

When the verb is a phrase of two or more words, one word is the **main verb** or **principal verb**; for instance, example 3 has the main verb *finish*. Any other part of the phrase is an **auxiliary verb** or **helping verb.** Example 2 has one auxiliary (*are*), while example 3 has two (*must* and *have*).

A1 Two-Word and Three-Word Verbs

Meanings

When we use a dictionary to look up the meaning of a verb, we are used to thinking of one-word verbs like *go, happen*, and *operate*. But in English, there are also two-word verbs and three-word verbs, such as *call up, take after, pass away*, and *put up with*.

83

Two-word and three-word verbs are like idioms; they must be defined as a unit. The meaning of *take* plus the meaning of *after* will not equal the meaning of *take after*; the two-word verb means *resemble*.

> (4) Mary *takes after* her mother. They both have blond hair and blue eyes.

Grammar

In a sentence pattern, the direct object (DO) sometimes affects the order of the parts of a two-word verb.

1. Separable transitive: The verb *call up* is transitive; it has a direct object. (See Chapter 1, page 6.)

> (5) He *called up* his friend.
> (6) He *called* his friend *up*.
> (7) He *called* her *up*.
> (8) ✕ He *called up* her.

The verb *call up* is separable. This means that the two parts may be separated, with the direct object (DO) between them.

a) If the DO is a pronoun, the verb must be separated, as in example 7. Example 8 is incorrect because the verb is not separated.

b) In other cases, there is a choice: the verb can be separated (example 6) or not (example 5).

A very long or complicated DO will not separate a separable two-word verb.

> (9) He *called up* someone who would know the answer.
> (10) ✕ He *called* someone who would know the answer *up*.

Example 10 is too difficult to understand because the two parts of the verb are far from each other.

2. Inseparable transitive: The verb *take after* is transitive; it has a direct object.

> (11) She *takes after* her father.
> (12) ✕ She *takes* her father *after*.
> (13) She *takes after* him.
> (14) ✕ She *takes* him *after*.

The verb *take after* is inseparable: the direct object (DO) never separates the two parts of the verb.

3. **Inseparable intransitive:** The verb *passed away* is intransitive: it does not have a direct object. Therefore, there is no direct object (DO) to separate the parts of the verb. (See Chapter 1, page 4.) All intransitive two-word verbs are inseparable.

(15) He *passed away* after a long illness.

4. **Three-word verbs:** All three-word verbs are inseparable.

(16) She would not *put up with* that kind of behavior.
(17) She would not *put up with* it.

There is a list of common two-word verbs in Appendix B. The list shows if the verb is separable or inseparable.

Exercise

Complete each sentence. Choose a verb and use it with a pronoun (if one is given).

break __ in	=	to break something in order to enter
break in(to) __	=	to enter a place illegally
break in __	=	to enter illegally
break in on __	=	to interrupt someone or something

1. The television program was stopped when the announcer _broke in on it_____. (it)
2. The guard told the police that the thieves _____
   _____.
3. When did they_____the bank?
4. They_____at midnight. (it)
5. The front door of the bank was very heavy, so the thieves were unable to_____. (it)

count __ in	=	to include
count on __	=	to depend
count __ out	=	to exclude

6. He is such a coward that when we mentioned the dangers, he immediately said that we should _____
   _____. (him)
7. When we mentioned the benefits, he said that we should
   _____. (him)

8. Since he changes his mind so often, it is not wise to
_____. (him)

B **VERBS: SUBJECT-VERB AGREEMENT**

Subject-verb agreement means that the subject (S) in a sentence pattern affects the choice of the verb form. For instance, in example 18, the subject *I* requires the verb form *am*.

        am
(18) I i̶s̶   studying English.
       a̶r̶e̶

1. Singular and uncountable nouns appear with the same singular verb form. This is often called the **third person singular, present tense** form.

         singular S
       ⎴   a̶m̶
(19) A good *teacher* is important to him.
                  a̶r̶e̶

        uncountable S
      ⎴   a̶m̶
(20) *Time* is important to him.
           a̶r̶e̶

Plural nouns appear with another verb form.

        plural S
      ⎴   a̶m̶
(21) Easy *tests* i̶s̶ not helpful at all.
              are

2. Compound subjects joined with *and* appear with a plural verb form.

           S   l̶i̶v̶e̶s̶
     ⎴
(22) *Phillip and Charles* live in a dormitory.

Other compound subjects show subject-verb agreement between the last noun and the verb form.

(23) Either her mother or her *brothers* ~~was~~ / were
using the car.

(24) Either her brothers or her *mother* ~~was~~ / were
using the car.

3. Gerunds, infinitives, phrases, and clauses appear with
a singular verb form.

noun clause S

(25) *What I want to know* ~~am~~ / is / ~~are~~ when they will

repay my money.

infinitive S

(26) *To err* ~~am~~ / is / ~~are~~ human.

4. Indefinites (*each, every, any*, etc.) appear with singular
verb forms.

(27) Everyone enjoys a holiday celebration.
~~enjoy~~

The verb form is singular even though the subject (S)
everyone has the meaning of *all people*, that is, a plural
meaning.

5. Sometimes a collective noun refers to a group;
sometimes it refers to the members of a group. The
singular or plural meaning may determine the verb form
to use.

(28) singular meaning: the group

Our family has just gotten a new car.
~~have~~

(29) plural meaning: the individuals in the group

Our family ~~am~~ / ~~is~~ / are well after many colds and

other illnesses this past winter.

A sentence like example 29 is not common in American English, but is very common in British English.

6. If the subject is long or complicated, it is necessary to determine which word(s) will influence the subject-verb agreement.

(30) One of Alice's friends   has   arrived.
                              have

In example 30, the verb form *has* agrees with the word *one*: Alice has many friends, but only one is here.

                                    has
(31) A number of Bill's friends   have   arrived.

In example 31, who arrived? a number? some of Bill's friends?

Of course, subject-verb agreement is a concern only when there are two or three forms to choose from. For example, subject-verb agreement is not a concern in the past tense (except for the verb *be* or with some verb auxiliaries).

(32) Our family *had* just bought a new car.
(33) Studying *should* not occupy one's entire life.

Exercise

Choose the correct words; cross out the wrong ones. Be sure that the subject-verb agreement is correct.

1. One
   Two } dead fish were lying on the shore.

2. Good news { am / is / are } what I want to hear.

3. What I want to hear { am / is / are } good news.

4. Both
   One } of the television programs was very boring.

5. People { has / have } been arriving all afternoon.

6. Either Carla or her roommates { am / is / are } going to help.

7. Carla and her roommates $\begin{Bmatrix} \text{am} \\ \text{is} \\ \text{are} \end{Bmatrix}$ going to be there early.

8. Phyllis and I $\begin{Bmatrix} \text{am} \\ \text{is} \\ \text{are} \end{Bmatrix}$ bringing a baseball and a bat.

9. Each team $\begin{Bmatrix} \text{plays} \\ \text{play} \end{Bmatrix}$ two games.

10. To forgive $\begin{Bmatrix} \text{am} \\ \text{is} \\ \text{are} \end{Bmatrix}$ divine.

C **VERBS: TIME, STATUS, RELEVANCE**

English verbs appear in several forms in order to provide certain information about the situation that they describe.

One type of information is **time**: this tells *when*. We can discuss a situation in the present, the past, or the future.

The second is the **status** of the situation. Is it an action which continues over a period of time, or one which occurs from time to time?

The third type of information is **relevance**. Is an earlier event important at a later time, or does it have no particular relevance later?

Time	Status	Relevance
Present	Progressive or Continuous	Perfect
Past	Simple	Non-perfect
Future		

D **SIMPLE PRESENT TENSE: FORM**

The **simple present tense** form of a verb is the form in a dictionary. It is sometimes called the **infinitive**, **base**, or **simple** form. It is also the first form in a chart of irregular forms. The form is used with most subjects.

(34) My sister and her husband *live* in Chicago.
(35) I *visit* them twice each year.

There is a special form to use when the subject of the verb is *he, she, it,* or any subject that has the same meaning as *he, she,* or *it.* This form is called the **third person singular, present tense** form.

> (36) My sister *works* for a large corporation in downtown Chicago.

Add the letter *s* to the simple form of the verb:

work + *s* = *works*
drive + *s* = *drives*
get + *s* = *gets*

Sometimes adding the letter *s* also requires a change in spelling. Turn to Appendix A for the correct rule.

Changing final *y* to *i* and adding *es*
>   infinitive + *s* = third person singular
>   *carry* + *s* = *carries*

Adding *es*

>   infinitive + *s* = third person singular
> *push* (one syllable) + *s* = *pushes* (two syllables)

Adding *es* or *s* after *o*

>   infinitive + *s* = third person singular
>   *echo* + *s* = *echoes*

Note: Irregular form: *have* + *s* = *has.*

Note: The verb *be* has two possible forms in the present tense. In writing, the full form is usually used. The contracted forms are used in conversation and in very informal writing.

Full Forms: (more formal)	Contractions: (less formal, to use in conversation)
I am	I'm
he is	he's
she is	she's
it is	it's
you are	you're
we are	we're
they are	they're

Exercise

Fill in the correct simple present tense form of the verb in parentheses.

1. My friend Mary Ann (run)___*runs*___ her own business.
2. Some of her customers (travel)_____on business.
3. A tourist (think)_____about expenses when he (travel)_____.
4. He (want)_____to see as much as possible.
5. She (hope)_____that they (like)_____their trips.

E SIMPLE PRESENT TENSE: MEANING

The **simple present tense** is used to describe actions or situations that exist at the present time.

> (37) My sister *works* in one of the skyscrapers downtown.

The present time is a period of time that includes the moment of speaking or writing. However, it does not indicate only the exact moment of speaking or writing. At the moment of writing example 37, my sister may be at work or at home or in a store buying a coat—we cannot tell this from the information given in the example. But we do know what she usually or generally does.

1. The simple present tense is used to describe actions or situations that do not change; these statements are eternal truths.

   > (38) The earth *revolves* around the sun.
   > (39) The square root of 196 *is* 14.

2. The simple present tense is used for repeated or habitual actions.

   > (40) She *meets* many different people each week.

3. The simple present tense is used to describe states, situations which we do not think of as continuous activities. (See Chapter 3, page 103.)

   > (41) She *likes* big-city life.
   > (42) They *have* a new house.

4. With a clear indication of future time, i.e., *tomorrow, tonight,* etc., the simple present tense can be used to describe actions that are scheduled to take place in the future.

91

(43) They *leave* for Los Angeles tomorrow morning.

Note: The future time indicator does not have to be in the same sentence; it can be understood from the context of the conversation or writing.

Do not use the simple present tense:
1) to describe actions that are true or that exist only at the exact moment of speaking or writing. The progressive form is used for this purpose.

(44) Right now my sister *is buying* a new winter coat; she usually *buys* a new one every two or three years.

2) to show that an action began in the past and continues through the present. In this situation, the present perfect form of the verb is necessary.

(45) X Phillip *works* for that company since 1975.
(46) Phillip *has worked* for that company since 1975.

Exercise

Identify the meaning of the following sentences.

        a. an eternal truth
        b. a repeated action

___*b*___ **1.** Only a small percentage of the people vote in local elections every two years.

_____ **2.** A leap year has 366 days.

_____ **3.** The Robinsons move to a new city approximately every five years.

_____ **4.** The sun sets late in the summer and early in the winter.

_____ **5.** After class we study in the library for two or three hours.

        c. an action scheduled for the future
        d. a continuing state or situation

_____ **6.** It is important to vote in all elections.

_____ **7.** My cousins live in California because of the warm weather.

_____ **8.** Next week they travel to another city.

_____ **9.** Some students live in dormitories on campus.

_____ **10.** Both my sister and my brother-in-law enjoy living in a big city.

F **SIMPLE PAST TENSE: FORM**

The **simple past tense** of a regular verb is formed by adding the ending *ed* to the simple form.

(47) Yesterday James *worked* on his term paper all morning.

This form is used with all the subjects (S): *I, he, she, it, you, we,* and *they.* There is no special form for *he, she,* and *it.*

(48) He *wanted* to play first base.
(49) His teammates *wanted* him to play center field.

Sometimes adding *ed* to a verb requires a spelling change. Turn to Appendix A for the correct rule.

Doubling the final consonant
  infinitive + *ed* = past
    prefer + *ed* = *preferred*

Cancelling the final *e*
  infinitive + *ed* = past
    use + *ed* = *used*

Changing final *y* to *i*
  infinitive + *ed* = past
    try + *ed* = *tried*

Irregular Forms

1. The verb *be* is the only verb that has more than one form in the simple past tense:

I he she it	} was	we you they	} were

2. There are many irregular verbs in English. The most common ones are listed in Appendix D.

Exercise

Change the verbs in these sentences. Change simple present tense verbs to the simple past, and change simple past tense verbs to the simple present.

1. Emily knows that the answers are reasonable even though they seem strange. *Emily knew that the answers were reasonable even though they seemed strange.*

2. Our next door neighbors sometimes take us shopping with them.

3. Our favorite professor taught only afternoon and evening classes.

4. The city manager drew up all plans for street improvements.

5. Sometimes the line of students went all the way around the gymnasium.

6. They need to finish the plans before the legislature adjourns.

7. I was seldom in my office in the evenings.

G **SIMPLE PAST TENSE: MEANING—"TIME"**

The simple past tense is used to tell a story, to tell about past events, to tell what happened. It describes single past actions, past states, and repeated actions in the past.

(50) single past action
They *moved* to a new neighborhood.
(51) past state
They *had* a new car.
(52) repeated past actions
She *made* two trips.

This tense is sometimes described as **not current**: the action or state is not currently relevant. In fact, the past tense is often used to indicate that a past action or situation does not exist in the present time; there has been a change from the past time to the present time.

(53) My sister and brother-in-law *had* two children in 1978, when you met them, but now they have three.

The simple past tense is sometimes called the **definite past tense**. It is used when we tell specifically when something happened. It is used with expressions of time that tell *when,* such as *last May, yesterday,* and *after Mary finished the work.*

(54) They *left* Buffalo last May.

(55) We *went* to the movies yesterday.
(56) After Mary *finished* the work, she had lunch.

Exercise

Identify each of the uses of the past tense.

        a. single past action
        b. a past condition or state
        c. several repeated past actions

_*b*_ **1.** Robert Atkins liked the challenge of something new.

_____ **2.** He changed jobs five times in 14 years.

_____ **3.** His wife left him after his last change.

_____ **4.** She was very unhappy about moving from city to city.

_____ **5.** She often complained to him.

_____ **6.** Then she decided to divorce him.

_____ **7.** Every day for two weeks, he tried to change her mind.

_____ **8.** He moved to his new job the day before yesterday.

_____ **9.** They sold their house when he left.

H OTHER PAST FORMS

1. One other indicator of past time is the phrase *used to* + an infinitive. *Used to* emphasizes a change in situation.

    (57) I *used to* swim a mile a day.
       (Indicates that there has been a change.)
    (58) negative
       When she was young, she *did not use to* eat a lot of ice cream.
       (Indicates that now she does.)
    (59) interrogative
       When you were young, *did* you *use to* eat a lot of ice cream?

Note: In the past tense and with the negative, *used to* becomes *use to* with the use of the auxiliary *do*.

Note: The past time indicator *used to* is different from the adjective phrase *be used to*. *Used to* means a habitual activity in the past. *Be used to* means *be accustomed to* or *be familiar with*. *Be used to* is followed by a noun or noun-equivalent.

> (60) I'm *used to getting up* early.

Used to is followed by the base form of a verb.

> (61) She *used to call* me every day.

2. Another indicator of past time is the modal auxiliary verb *would*.

> (62) My grandfather *would* always tell me stories about his boyhood.

3. It is possible to combine the past and future with *be going to*.

> (63) Last month, Maria told me that she *was going to* travel to Brazil.

Example 63 reports a past situation: at that past time (*last month*) Maria had future plans (*travel to Brazil*).

Exercise

If the sentence is correct, write **OK**. If the sentence is not correct, write **X** and correct it.

___X___ **1.** Now, I am used to eat American food.
Now, I am used to eating American food.

_____ **2.** Five years ago, I use to run everyday.

_____ **3.** Did you used to study hard?

_____ **4.** When we lived abroad, we would experiment with different types of food.

_____ **5.** Whenever she visited a foreign country, she used to would not miss a chance to try the native food.

FUTURE TIME

There are several ways to discuss events and states in the **future**.

1. The first way to discuss the future is with the verb *be* and the phrase *going to*.

> (64) She *is going to* consider your proposal.
> (65) They *are going to* leave for Los Angeles tomorrow morning.

There is subject-verb agreement: *she* + *is* and *they* + *are*.

The phrase with *go* does not indicate any motion or going. In example 64, she will make her consideration while she is seated; in example 65, there is motion but it is indicated by the verb *leave,* not by *going.*

2. The second way to discuss the future is with *will* or *shall* in the verb phrase.

(66) I *shall leave* before noon tomorrow.
(67) They *will pick up* their package later.

The verb phrase has the simple form of the main verb: for example, *leave,* not *left* or *leaving.* There is only one form of the main verb when it is used with *will* or *shall:* there is no special form for the third person singular.

In American English, *will* is commonly used with all subjects:

I will leave	we will deny
you will arrive	you will know
he will stay	they will pick up
she will consider	
it will break	

In British English, *shall* is often used with the first person pronouns; *will* is used with all other subjects.

I shall leave	we shall deny
you will arrive	you will know
he will stay	they will pick up
she will consider	
it will break	

(The auxiliaries *will* and *shall* often have uses besides indicating future time. These are discussed in Chapter 3, pages 119 and 121–123.)

Note: Neither *will* nor *shall* nor *be going to* occur in future time clauses with the words *if, when, before, after.*

(68) X She will consider your proposal when you *will present* it to her.
(69) She will consider your proposal when you *present* it to her.
(70) You and I will discuss the proposal before you *type* it.
(71) She will read it after you and I *discuss* it.
(72) I'll tell her if I *see* her tonight.

3. The third way to discuss the future is with the present tense (simple or progressive). With a clear indication of future time, the present tense indicates that something is planned for the future.

   (73) They *leave* for Los Angeles tomorrow morning.
   (74) They *are leaving* for Los Angeles tomorrow morning.

4. The fourth way to discuss the future is with the verb *be* and an infinitive-with-*to*.

   (75) The General Assembly *is to meet* tomorrow afternoon.

There is subject-verb agreement: *General Assembly* (= *it*) + *is*. This indicates that an action has been planned or formally scheduled. It is more formal than the other ways.

Exercise

If the sentence is correct, write **OK**. If the sentence is not correct, write **X** and correct it.

___X___ **1.** Alicia and James going to go around the world when they have enough money. *Alicia and James are going to go around the world when they have enough money.*

_____ **2.** They will save 10% of their salaries each month.

_____ **3.** They estimate that they shall have enough money in three years.

_____ **4.** I am going travel around the world too.

_____ **5.** I leave in six months.

J PROGRESSIVE: FORM

Every **progressive** verb form has two parts: an auxiliary verb and a main verb. The first part is the auxiliary verb *be*. This part tells whether the verb is present, past, future, infinitive, etc.

   (76) present progressive
        He *is* living in Chicago.
   (77) past progressive
        She *was* traveling in Asia at that time.
   (78) future progressive
        They *will be* finishing at the time of our arrival.

(79) infinitive

It is important *to be* working hard when they arrive.

In addition to the auxiliary verb *be* and the main verb, a progressive verb phrase may have other auxiliary verbs.

(80) modal progressive

They *must be* living in an apartment.

(81) present perfect progressive

I *have been* looking for them for an hour.

Note: In the present and past progressives, there must be subject-verb agreement.

(82) X They was looking for you.

(83) They were looking for you.

(84) He was looking for you.

Note: In the present progressive, the form of *be* may be a full form or a contraction.

Full Forms: (more formal)	Contractions: (less formal, to use in conversation)
I am working	I'm working
he is working	he's working
she is working	she's working
it is working	it's working
you are working	you're working
we are working	we're working
they are working	they're working

Note: The contracted form of *is* and the contracted form of *has* are the same: *it* + *is* = *it's; it* + *has* = *it's*. The verb tense becomes clear if you consider the entire verb form.

(85) She*'s doing* it now. = She *is doing* it now.

(86) She*'s done* it now. = She *has done* it now.

Note: There must be a form of *be*.

(87) X He living in Chicago.

(88) He *is* living in Chicago.

The second part of a progressive verb form is sometimes called the **present participle** of the main verb. It is always the simple or base form + *ing*: there are no irregular present participles in English. Sometimes, however, adding *ing* requires a spelling change. Turn to Appendix A for the correct rule.

> Doubling the final consonant
> infinitive + *ing* = present participle
> *prefer* + *ing* = *preferring*

> Canceling the final *e*
> infinitive + *ing* = present participle
> *use* + *ing* = *using*

Exercise

If the sentence has a correct progressive verb phrase, write **OK**. If the verb phrase is incorrect, write **X** and make the verb a correct progressive. Then identify the progressive verb phrase: put the letter in the parentheses.

> a. present progressive
> b. past progressive
> c. modal progressive (modals = *will, can, could, may, must*, etc.)
> d. present perfect progressive
> e. future progressive

<u>OK</u>   **1.** Mr. and Mrs. Miller are packing for their vacation trip. (*a*)

_____   **2.** When Kate walked in, they finishing dinner. ( )

_____   **3.** Actually they were reviewing their proposal. ( )

_____   **4.** They should be visit their cousins in Montreal. ( )

_____   **5.** The police was chasing the robbers down Columbus Street. ( )

_____   **6.** They voting in the next election. ( )

_____   **7.** You are doing that too late to help. ( )

_____   **8.** He has been working for the police department since 1978. ( )

_____   **9.** They will be wait inside if it is cold. ( )

_____ **10.** I am asking everyone to donate some money to this charity. ( )

K   *PROGRESSIVE: MEANING—"STATUS"*

The progressive verb form is used to indicate that an activity is incomplete at a certain time. It is progressing or continuing; therefore, it is not finished. The time should be clear: the form of the verb *be* gives this information, and often there is another indication of when.

> (89) John *was correcting* his history term paper when he saw Mary enter the library.

Example 89 tells us that (1) the action (*correcting the term paper*) was going on at a particular moment (when John noticed Mary's arrival in the library) and that (2) the action was not begun or ended at that moment (John was in the middle of doing the job when Mary walked in). Sentences like 89 and 90 describe an interruption: one action interrupts or breaks into another, continuing action.

> (90) She *is* usually *sleeping* when I *leave* for work.

However, it is not necessary to have an interruption: two activities could be going on at the same time.

> (91) John *was correcting* his history term paper, while Alice *was doing* some research.

1. The progressive verb form is often called **temporary**. The action or situation is happening at a particular time, but there has been a change or there is going to be a change.

> (92) Alfred changed his major last semester; now he *is studying* computer science.

A progressive verb form can describe a continuing situation, a single continuing action, or a series of repeated actions.

> (93) continuing situation
>   The newspaper *was lying* on the couch.
> (94) single continuing action
>   Rob and Marie *are eating* dinner.
> (95) series of repeated actions
>   Claudine *has been making* her own clothes for the past five years.

2. The present progressive can be used to describe an action in the future. The idea is that the action will take place in the future; the plans and preparations are in progress.

(96) The Jeffersons *are leaving* for their vacation in Australia tomorrow.

The adverb *tomorrow* gives a clear indication that this sentence describes a future action.

Note: The present progressive form is not used for situations that began in the past and continue to the present time. To show a connection between a past situation and a present situation, it is necessary to use the present perfect (simple or progressive).

(97) X Mr. and Mrs. Fitzgerald *are living* in Boston since 1973.

(98) Mr. and Mrs. Fitzgerald *have lived* (or *have been living*) in Boston since 1973.

Exercise

Identify each of the meanings of the progressive.

    a. a continuing situation
    b. one single activity
    c. a series of repeated activities

___*a*___ **1.** They are enjoying a two-week vacation in Bermuda.

_____ **2.** At 10:00 last night, I was watching my favorite television program.

_____ **3.** Mary is refereeing all the games in the basketball tournament.

_____ **4.** The Robinsons are planning their son's birthday party.

_____ **5.** For the past six months he has been rebuilding an old car.

_____ **6.** At that time in his life, he was writing one novel every two years.

_____ **7.** His parents will be arriving on the 9:30 flight this evening.

_____ **8.** We are playing tennis tomorrow afternoon around 4:00.

_____ **9.** Right now, they are playing a round of golf.

_____**10.** Martha could still be living near Dallas.

K1 Progressive and State Verbs

The progressive is not usually used for **states**, that is, for situations without activity. To describe states, it is necessary to use the simple form of the verb, even when discussing a situation that is true at a particular moment.

(99) X At that moment, she *was needing* an eraser.

(100) At that moment, she *needed* an eraser.

(101) X Carol *is owning* a blue sportscar.

(102) Carol *owns* a blue sportscar.

(103) X Ted and Mark *have been knowing* the Jensens a long time.

(104) Ted and Mark *have known* the Jensens a long time.

These verbs are commonly used to describe states and therefore do not usually take the progressive form.

appear	hate	resemble
be	hear	satisfy
believe	know	see
belong (to)	like	seem
consist (of)	love	smell
contain	mean	sound
cost	need	suffice
desire	owe	suit
despise	own	surprise
deserve	please	taste
detest	possess	think (about, of)
dislike	prefer	understand
feel	recognize	want
forget	remember	wish
have	require	

Under certain conditions, state verbs can appear in the progressive:

1. When they are used to describe an action.

(105) When I saw Ellen, she *was smelling* the melons to decide which one to buy. (describes an action)

(106) All the melons *smelled* bad, so she did not buy any. (describes a state, since a melon cannot smell in the active sense)

(107) *Are* you *having* a good time on your vacation? (describes an action)

103

(108) They *have* a room with a view of the ocean. (possession, no action)

2. When the emphasis is on a temporary situation that is a change from the usual situation.

(109) He *is being* especially polite this afternoon.
(110) The sharp increase in the price of oil *was costing* some countries more than they could afford.

Exercise

Provide a correct form of the verb in parentheses. Use the simple present, the present progressive, the simple past, or the past progressive.

1. A progressive verb form (consist of)___*consists of*___ two parts, while a simple verb form (have)___*has*___ only one.

2. Why is Peter so quiet?
   He (think about)_____his trip abroad.

3. Why didn't he buy the watch?
   Because it (cost)_____more than he could afford.

4. When we walked in, they (listen to)_____ the latest news.

5. They (hear, negative)_____it very well because there was a lot of noise outside.

6. What's all that noise next door?
   They (have)_____a party, I think.

7. What (mean)_____the word *actual*
   _____?

8. I (understand)_____what the President (mean)_____yesterday.

L **PERFECT: FORM**

1. **Simple perfect**

Every simple perfect verb form has at least two parts: the auxiliary verb *have* and a main verb. The first part, the auxiliary verb *have*, tells whether the perfect is present, past, future, etc.

(111) present perfect
He *has* lived here since 1979.
(112) past perfect
He *had* lived in many countries before coming here.
(113) future perfect
You *will have* finished long before we arrive.
(114) modal perfect
I *would have* told you if you had asked me.

Note: In the present perfect, there must be subject-verb agreement.

(115) X He *have* lived here since 1979.
(116) He *has* lived here since 1979.
(117) We *have* lived here since 1975.

Note: In the present perfect, the verb *have* may be a full form or a contraction.

Full forms: (more formal)	Contractions: (less formal, to use in conversation)
I have worked	I've worked
you have worked	you've worked
we have worked	we've worked
they have worked	they've worked
he has worked	he's worked
she has worked	she's worked
it has worked	it's worked

Note: The contracted form of *has* and the contracted form of *is* are the same: *he* + *has* = *he's; he* + *is* = *he's*. The verb tense becomes clear if you consider the entire verb.

(118) What's *happened* here? = What *has happened* here?
(119) What's *happening* here? = What *is happening* here?

Note: In the past perfect, the verb *had* may be a full form or a contraction.

Full Forms: (more formal)	Contractions: (less formal, to use in conversation)
I had worked	I'd worked
you had worked	you'd worked
we had worked	we'd worked
they had worked	they'd worked
he had worked	he'd worked
she had worked	she'd worked
it had worked	it'd worked

Note: The contracted form of *had* and the contracted form of *would* are the same: *he* + *had* = *he'd; he* + *would* = *he'd.* The verb tense is clearer if you look at the entire verb form.

(120) I*'d gone.* = I *had gone.*
(121) I*'d go.* = I *would go.*

Note: It is important to remember to include a form of *have*; for example, do not say or write example 122.

(122) X He been in Chicago since 1978.

The second part of a perfect verb form is the past participle of the main verb. It is the simple form of the verb + *ed.* For regular verbs, the past tense and the past participle forms are the same.

(123) past tense
He *walked* to the library in the rain.
(124) present perfect
He *has walked* there every day this week.

Sometimes adding *ed* requires a spelling change. Turn to Appendix A for the correct rule.

Doubling the final consonant
infinitive + *ed* = past participle
infer + *ed* = *inferred*

Canceling the final *e*
infinitive + *ed* = past participle
use + *ed* = *used*

Changing final *y* to *i*
    infinitive + *ed* = past participle
        try + *ed* = *tried*

There are many irregular verbs in English. The most common ones are listed in Appendix D.

Note: In American English, the past participle of *get* is *gotten;* in British English, the past participle is *got.*

(125) I have gotten the report. (American English)
(126) I have got the report. (British English)

In conversational American English, *have got* = *have* and *has got* = *has.*

(127) I've got the book = I have the book.

Note: We use *have* as both the auxiliary marker of the perfect and also the verb meaning *to possess.*

(128) present perfect
        She *has had* our book for almost a month.
(129) past perfect
        Before that, Bob *had had* it.

Note: The perfect often occurs with adverbs such as *since, yet,* and *already.*

(130) She has had my book *since* last month.
(131) She started reading it last week, but she hasn't finished it yet.
(132) I have *already* promised to lend it to Jack next.

2. *Perfect progressive or continuous*

The perfect progressive, or continuous, has the past participle of *be* and a verb + *ing.*

(133) present perfect progressive
        She has *been studying* English for several years.
(134) past perfect progressive
        We had *been waiting* for an hour when John finally showed up.

Exercise

If the sentence has a correct perfect verb form, write **OK**. If the verb is not a correct perfect form, write **X** and correct the verb. Then identify the perfect verb phrase in each sentence:

> a. present perfect
> b. past perfect
> c. modal perfect (modals = *may, might, can, could, will, must*)
> d. present perfect progressive

___X___ **1.** The Richmonds aren't home. They *have* already gone on their vacation. (*a*)

_____ **2.** They had talked about it for more than three months. ( )

_____ **3.** There had be several family arguments before they made the final decision. ( )

_____ **4.** They could have visited relatives in Japan, but Mrs. Richmond wanted to go on a safari. ( )

_____ **5.** She said they had been plan to go to Africa for a long time, so they went there. ( )

_____ **6.** As a travel agent, I could have cutted their expenses. ( )

_____ **7.** They would have been able to go for longer than two weeks. ( )

_____ **8.** I have be helping with their travel plans for a long time, but for some reason this time they decided to do it themselves. ( )

M PERFECT: MEANING—"RELEVANCE"

1. Past-through-present continuation

The present perfect is used to describe a single activity, a repeated action, or a state (condition) that began in the past and continues until the present time.

(135) a single activity
> Mark *has worked* in the chemistry lab since 1978.

Example 135 describes a single activity (working in the lab) that began in the past (in this sentence, we know exactly when it began) and continues up to the present time (that is, Mark is working in the lab now).

(136) a repeated action
> They *have visited* us several times.

(137) a state

The car *has been* in the garage for a few days.

All present perfect progressive verb forms indicate actions which began in the past and continue to the present. Some situations can be described with either a simple or a progressive verb form.

(138) Mark *has lived/has been living* in Washington for ten years.

Other situations will take only one of the forms.

Note: Examples 139 and 140 are not correct ways to describe continuation; they require the present perfect.

(139) X Mark *works* in the chemistry lab since 8 o'clock this morning.

(140) X Mark *is working* in the chemistry lab since 8 o'clock this morning.

2. *Completion*

The present perfect is used to describe a single activity, a repeated action, or a state (condition) that took place in the past and ended before the present time, but is still relevant in the present. It may be relevant because the action was recently completed.

(141) The radio can't be broken; it *has* just *been repaired.*

It may be relevant because it describes a single activity that the speaker feels is likely to occur again.

(142) We *have won* the Junior Championship three times.

Compare examples 142 and 143.

(143) When he was young, he won the Junior Championship three times. (He will never win it again.)

The present perfect is sometimes called the **indefinite past tense**. It can be used with general expressions of past time, such as *just* (meaning *immediately before now*) and *since.*

(144) They *have just moved* into a new apartment.
(145) She *has lived* in many places *since* she left Canada.

However, the present perfect cannot be used with definite indications of past time, that is, expressions that tell when.

> (146) X They *have moved* into a new apartment *last May*.

Example 146 is not correct. With an indication of exactly when, it is necessary to use the simple past tense.

> (147) They *moved* into a new apartment *last May*.

However, the present perfect may also include the idea that the situation or action can occur again or can continue.

> (148) He has been President.
> (149) He was President.

Example 148 can describe a situation which began in the past, continues up to the present, and may continue into the future. On the other hand, example 149 is about a situation that existed in the past. Therefore, example 149 may be used to discuss Abraham Lincoln; but example 148 may not, since it describes a person who is still living.

3. *Past-in-the-past*

The past perfect is used to describe one of two past events when one occurred before the other.

> (150) Mrs. Allen *had left* before the telegram arrived.

Mrs. Allen left her apartment at noon; the telegram arrived at 12:30 p.m. Therefore, the verb *had left* is used to make clear that one event (Mrs. Allen's leaving) took place before another event (the arrival of the telegram).

In less formal usage, it is possible to use two past-tense verbs if there is another indication in the sentence of which event took place first.

> (151) Mrs. Allen *left* before the telegram *arrived*.

The word *before* indicates clearly which event came before the other. Example 150 is clearer, however, because the reader or hearer has two indications of the order of events: the verb phrase and the word *before*.

The past perfect also has a progressive form.

> (152) I *had been studying* for 3 hours when Alice arrived.

The progressive form shows that the action continued up to the point of Alice's arrival.

Past-in-the-past is also used in reported or indirect speech, when we are concerned with the sequence of tenses in a complex sentence. (See Chapter 5, page 228.)

Exercise

Identify the type of situation in each sentence.

a. continuation up to the time indicated by the verb
b. completion before the time indicated by the verb

_b_ **1.** She has finished two books of short stories.
_____ **2.** Robert and Phil should have been finishing their homework at that time.
_____ **3.** The flowers have smelled better since the rain.
_____ **4.** The Robinsons have moved into a new house.
_____ **5.** The Robinsons moved into a new house yesterday.
_____ **6.** They had been drinking right before the accident.
_____ **7.** They had been seen only once by the police.

Identify the type of situation in each sentence. If the situation is **d**, underline the part of the sentence that describes the FIRST event.

c. two events at the same time
d. one event before another

_____ **8.** The telegram arrived at 12:30; Mrs. Smith had left.
_____ **9.** The telegram arrived after Mrs. Smith left.
_____ **10.** Mrs. Smith left when the telegram arrived.
_____ **11.** Mrs. Smith left when she had read the telegram.
_____ **12.** The telegram had arrived when Mrs. Smith left.

Exercise

Respond to the sentences. Use the present perfect or the past, whichever is appropriate.

a. He has burned it.
b. He burned it.

1. Why can't she prove that she wrote him a letter?

   _b_

2. What did he do with the letter before he left the house?

   _____

3. He did a strange thing then:_____
4. I can not give you any written evidence._____
5. I saw him destroy the letter;_____.

   c. She studied English.
   d. She has studied English.

6. What did Anne do in New York?_____
7. Why is Betty finding French vocabulary easy to learn?

   _____

8. She prepared for her trip to England._____
9. She can get along in India:_____
10. David: Did she take your advice?
    Leon: Yes._____

N   **VERB + VERB: INFINITIVES AND GERUNDS**

Sometimes a predicate includes a verb + infinitive or verb + gerund. Infinitives and gerunds are sometimes called **verbals.** Appendix C lists which verbs take infinitives and which take gerunds.

V   + infinitive

(153) They decided to produce inefficient cars.

V   + gerund

(154) They delayed producing more efficient ones.

to + V

Some verbs are followed by an infinitive-with-*to; decide* is one of these verbs. There is one actor (*they*) for both actions (*decide* and *produce*) in example 153.

V-ing

Other verbs are followed by a gerund (V-*ing*); *delay* is one of these verbs. There is one actor (*they*) for both actions (*delay* and *produce*) in example 154.

Some verbs can be followed by either an infinitive or a gerund, with no change of meaning; *continue* is one of these verbs.

(155) They continued *to produce* those models.
(156) They continued *producing* those models.

With a few verbs like *forget, remember,* and *stop,* there is a change of meaning.

(157) I *remembered* paying my tuition.
(158) I *remembered* to pay my tuition.

Example 157 indicates that I paid my tuition and I remembered that I had at a later time. On the other hand, example 158 indicates that I paid my tuition; I didn't forget to pay it.

O + to V

Some verbs allow a second actor in the sentence.

First   Second

(159) We advised them to change their production plans.

These verbs are followed by (1) a noun or pronoun in the objective case and (2) an infinitive-with-*to*.

The V-*ing* verbals can also be used to express a second actor.

(160) She anticipated buying a new car.
(161) She anticipated their buying a new car.

Example 160 has one actor (*she*) and two actions (*anticipate* and *buy*), but example 161 has a second actor. The subject (S) of a V-*ing* is expressed with a possessive form; example 161 has *their.*

O + V

A few verbs have a second actor which appears with an infinitive-without-*to*. These verbs fall into two groups. The first group can be called **verbs of sense**. Some of these are: *see, hear, watch, smell.*

(162) I *heard* him leave.
(163) We *will watch* him perform.

The sense verbs may also be followed by the V-*ing* form.

The V-*ing* form of the verb emphasizes that the second action took place over a period of time.

> (164) We *smelled* a fire burning. Then we *heard* the building explode.

The second group is called **causative verbs**. These are: *make, have,* and *let.*

> (165) The teacher *had* all the students write a composition.
> (166) No one did a good job, so she *made* them write it again.
> (167) Tom didn't hand in the second composition, so she *wouldn't let* him leave when class was over.

In these verb + verb sentences, either verb can be negative, depending on the speaker's idea. The way to make a main verb negative is shown in Chapter 6, page 249. Gerunds and infinitives are made negative by putting *not* directly in front of the verbal.

> (168) They decided *not* to produce inefficient cars.
> (169) We advised them *not* to change their production plans.
> (170) She anticipated their *not* buying a new car.

Verb + verb combinations are shown in Appendix C.

Exercise

The verb + verb constructions are incorrect. Correct them by changing the second part of each sentence.

1. We should let them to do it.
   We should let them do it.
2. When did they finish to do it?
3. They encouraged he and I to do it.
4. Despite their lack of success, they kept on to try.
5. He cannot stand you to have the right answers.

Provide a correct form of the verb in parentheses in each sentence. Add the correct form of each pronoun in parentheses.

6. One country threatened (invade)_____
   in order to regain the territory; the other pledged
   (defend)_____its territory.

7. The Secretary-General advised (they, negotiate) _____instead of fighting.
8. He felt that they should begin (talk) _____ as soon as possible.
9. A neutral country endeavored (act)_____ as an intermediary.
10. It was hard to imagine (they, fight)_____ for such a small piece of land.

O VERBS: ATTITUDE

Time, status, and relevance are used to report what happened, what is going to happen, etc. In addition to these three types of information, it is possible to express an **attitude** or evaluation of a situation. For example, we can indicate that an action is probable or that it is contrary-to-fact; we can indicate that there is permission or an obligation to do something. Modal auxiliaries and phrases are used in order to give the speaker's or writer's point of view about a situation.

P MODALS

Modals are a type of auxiliary. They are used to indicate an attitude about an action or a state. Most modals can be used when discussing the present, past, or future. However, modals have only two forms. One form is used for the past and the other for the present and the future. For a complete list of modals and their meanings, see page 119.

> (171) They *might be* police. (present)
> (172) Carol *might leave* tomorrow. (future)
> (173) We *might have dialed* the wrong number. (past)

Modals can also be used with the progressive form of some tenses.

> (174) They *should be carrying* guns. (present progressive)
> (175) The students *might have been waiting* in the library. (present perfect progressive)
> (176) Carol *will be going* by plane. (future progressive)

P1 **Modals: Form**

1. Most modals are not used with the word *to*.

   (177) X He wants *to can* speak English.
   (178) He wants *to be able to* speak English.

2. Modals never take a final *s,* even with the third person singular.

   (179) X She *cans* tell you about the exam.
   (180) She *can* tell you about the exam.

3. Never use two modals together.

   (181) X They *might will* come to the party next week.
   (182) They *might* come to the party next week.

4. The verb which follows a modal is always in the base form.

   (183) X She *may goes* next week.
   (184) She *may go* next week.
   (185) X You *should are* studying.
   (186) You *should be* studying.
   (187) X He *must has* left already.
   (188) He *must have* left.

5. Short answers with modals never include the main verb, unless it is *be*. But they always include any other auxiliaries.

   (189) Shouldn't he be here?
   　　　Yes, he *should be.*
   (190) Could they have gotten lost?
   　　　Yes, they *could have.*
   (191) Would we have been on time?
   　　　No, we *wouldn't have been.*
   　　　or
   　　　No, we *wouldn't have.*

6. The negative is formed by putting *not* after the modal auxiliary; the auxiliary *do* (*do, does,* or *did*) is not used.

   (192) X She *does not can* speak English.
   (193) She *can not* speak English.

7. Questions are formed by putting the auxiliary in front of the subject (S); the auxiliary *do* (*do, does,* or *did*) is not used.

(194) X *Does* she *can* speak English?

(195) *Can* she speak English?

8. There are several contractions.

Full Forms: (more formal)	Negatives Contractions: (less formal, to use in conversation)
might not	mightn't
cannot/can not	can't
could not	couldn't
shall not	shan't (unusual in American English)
should not	shouldn't
will not	won't
would not	wouldn't

The affirmative full forms with *will* and *shall* have contractions with *'ll*.

(196) I *shall* return. = I*'ll* return.

(197) They *will* have finished long before his arrival.
= They*'ll* have finished long before his arrival.

The affirmative full forms with *should* and *would* have contractions with *'d*.

(198) He *would* have come earlier if he had known about the problem. = He*'d* have come earlier if he'd known about the problem.

In example 198, the verb forms *have* (simple) and *known* (past participle) help us to determine the full form:

he'd have come = he would have come
he'd known = he had known

The perfect form *have* is sometimes contracted in conversation.

(199) He could*'ve* come. = He could *have* come.

Note: Although the *'ve* sounds like the preposition *of,* it must be written *'ve* or *have* as in example 199.

(200) X He could of come.

9. Sometimes both members of a pair (*will/would, shall/ should, may/might, can/could*) can be used in describing a present or future situation.

(201) present tense form; future situation
Tomorrow, the train *may* be late.
(202) past tense form; future situation
Tomorrow, the train *might* be late.

The two sentences are close in meaning, but the sentence with *might* is less strong, that is, less sure or definite, as would be a sentence with *would, should,* or *could.*

Exercise

If the sentence is correct, write **OK**. If it is not correct, write **X** and correct it.

_OK_ 1. He could do that next week.
_____ 2. They want to can speak English.
_____ 3. He must does all the homework.
_____ 4. She could have done that for you.
_____ 5. Should we have gone?
No, we shouldn't.
_____ 6. They do not might go with us.
_____ 7. Florence can't remember all the new vocabulary words.
_____ 8. Should I speak with Professor Gramer?

MODALS: MEANING

Permission

Both *may* and *can* are used in sentences of permission. Very conservative grammar books say that only *may* expresses permission; however, *can* is common in many situations, except the most formal ones.

Requests for permission

(203) *May* I borrow your eraser?
(204) *Can* I borrow your eraser?

Might and *could* are used for requests that are less direct, more polite, and more formal.

Meanings of Modals

Speaker's attitude or evaluation	Present or future verb forms	Past verb forms
Permission and Ability Permission (requests, statements)	may, can, might, could	
Ability (physical, mental, general)	can, be able to	could
Definiteness (degree of sureness) Possibility	can, may, could, might	may have, could have, might have
Probability (a conclusion, a deduction)	must, should	must have, should have
Certainty (a prediction, agreement, promise)	will (shall), will (shall) have (usual present tense forms)	(usual past tense)
Emphasized certainty	do (does), shall (will)	did
Advisability and Necessity Advisability (choice)	should, ought to, had better, had best	should have, ought to have
Necessity (an obligation, no choice)	be supposed to, must, have to (have got to), need to	had to

(205) *Might* I borrow your eraser?
(206) *Could* I borrow your eraser?

Appropriately, the responses are direct; they require *may* or *can*.

(207) Yes, you *may*.
(208) Yes, you *can*.

Statements of permission

(209) You *may* leave after you finish the test.
(210) You *can* leave after you finish the test.

Q2 Ability

Can is used for present sentences of ability.

(211) physical ability
She *can* run a mile in 5 minutes.
(212) mental ability
He *can* work with very sophisticated computers.
(213) general ability
He *can* read Spanish because he used to live in Mexico.

Could is used for past sentences of ability.

(214) Five years ago she could run a mile in 4½ minutes.

A very common way to discuss ability is with the phrase *be able to*. This phrase has an advantage over *can:* it can be used in all the tenses and forms of other verbs.

(215) They *have been able to* speak English for almost two years.
(216) Mr. Phillips *may be able to* see you this afternoon.

Exercise

Use one of these modals in each blank.

may	might
can	could
be able to	

1. When he was younger, he _could_ play baseball all day long, but now he _can_ play only a few hours.
2. She_____play the piano since she was ten years old.
3. John said to his history professor, "_____I turn in my term paper the day after tomorrow?"
4. _____you tell me the time?

Q3 Definiteness

A speaker can use modals to indicate how sure he is that an action or situation takes place, will take place, or took place. Sureness can be low (possibility), high (probability), or 100% (certainty). In addition, a speaker can emphasize the certainty.

Possibility is the lowest of the levels of definiteness. *Can, could, may,* and *might* are used for present and future situations. *Could* and *might* show a less strong possibility than *can* and *may.*

> (217) These grammar rules *may not* be new to you; nevertheless, you *might* benefit from the review.
> (218) He drives very fast. So he *can* get to Dallas in less than an hour.
> (219) She *could* speak both American and British English, but that is hard to believe.

Perfect forms are used for the past time.

> (220) You *might have* done well on yesterday's test, but I do not know the results yet.

Modals of **probability** indicate a conclusion or deduction, an evaluation based on earlier information. *Must* and *should* are used for present and future conclusions.

> (221) He runs about 10 miles a day. He *should* be ready for the race next month.
> (222) He runs and exercises very hard. He *must* want to win very much.

Perfect forms are used for the past time.

> (223) It is around 11:00. He *must have* finished his morning practice.

Modals of **certainty** indicate a prediction, agreement, or promise. *Will* (sometimes *shall* with *I* or *we*) is used for present and future statements of prediction, agreement, or promise.

> (224) present time prediction
> Whenever a person studies a foreign language, he *will* need a lot of practice.
> (225) future time agreement or promise
> I *will* meet you at the tennis courts at 7:45 tomorrow morning.

Perfect forms indicate completion.

> (226) By the end of next month, they *will have* driven over 5,000 miles.

Usual present- and past-tense forms express the certainty of actions and situations. (See Chapter 3, pages 91 and 94.)

Emphasized certainty indicates very strongly the truth or existence of a situation or activity. It is used to contradict or deny another idea or to remove any doubt about a situation or activity.

Do, does, and *did* with the simple form of the verb show emphasis in the present and past tenses.

> (227) Perhaps you think that I loaf, but I *do* work very hard.
> (228) She is dishonest, but she *does* have a way of making you like her.
> (229) They did not bring any refreshments, but they *did* help us clean up after the party.

Shall (sometimes *will* with *I* or *we*) is used for emphatic agreements, predictions, or promises.

> (230) General MacArthur said, "I *shall* return."

In example 230, *I shall return* is more than just a prediction or a promise; it is a very strong insistence of his intention to return.

The form to use for emphasis is the form not used other times.

Normal	Emphasized
will ——————→	shall
shall ——————→	will

Exercise

Use one of these modals in each blank. Make any necessary changes for time or subject-verb agreement.

can	must	will
could	should	shall
may	might	do

1. I promise that I _____*will*_____ study tomorrow.
2. The windshield is wet. It_____ rained while we were in the movies.
3. It_____ rained, but I do not think so.
4. The food was tasteless, but we_____ like the wine.

5. Certainly he_____be able to run a four-minute mile, despite the unlikelihood of the situation.

6. If you translate the words before you understand the whole sentence, you_____probably be making mistakes.

Q4 Advisability and Necessity

Advisability and **necessity** are related in meaning. They both indicate that there is some reason or motivation for the action or situation. The reason or motivation can come from outside a person—from a law, for example—or from inside a person—from the person's love for someone.

Advisability is not as strong as necessity. It means (1) that there is a benefit to do it, or there is a disadvantage not to do it; but (2) that there is an element of choice whether to do it or not.

Should and *ought to* are used for statements of advisability.

(231) They *should* study at least five hours tonight.
(232) They *ought to* study at least five hours tonight.

Should is used for questions.

(233) *Should* they study tomorrow morning also?

Should have and *ought to have* indicate advisability about a past situation; however, the choice was not to do it.

(234) They *should have* studied last week too, but they went to the beach instead.

Had better and *had best* are used for sentences about present or future advisability; they have the same meaning. They imply a warning of bad results if the advice is not followed.

(235) You *had better* study a lot next week.

Had better and *had best* are not past tense modals.

(236) X She *had best* practice English pronunciation yesterday.

Be supposed to is used for advisability that comes from outside the person.

(237) We *are supposed to* obey all laws, but some laws appear to be silly.

Necessity is stronger than advisability. There is an obligation; there is no feeling of choice whether to do something or not.

Must is a common way of indicating necessity.

(238) A person must have a valid passport in order to travel to foreign countries.

This modal has only a present tense form. Another modal must be used for other tenses.

Have to (less formal: *have got to*) is a common way of indicating necessity because it can be used in all tenses.

(239) A person *has to* have a valid passport in order to travel to foreign countries.

Examples 238 and 239 have the same meaning. Example 240 does not have an equivalent with *must*.

(240) I *have had to* renew my visa several times.

Need (to) is another way of indicating necessity. It can be used in all verb tenses, too.

(241) A person *needs to* have a valid passport in order to travel to foreign countries.
(242) I *have needed to* renew my visa several times.

Note: For negation in sentences of necessity, the negative of *have to* or *need (to)* means that there is no necessity: there is a choice.

(243) When you travel abroad, you *do not have to* carry travelers checks. You can carry money any way that you wish.
(244) She *did not need to* come to the United States to study English. She could have gone to Great Britain or Australia.

The negative of *must* is different: *must not* means that there is no choice. There is the necessity of not doing something.

(245) When you travel abroad, you *must not* be careless with your passport.
(246) She *must not* think that lots of practice is unimportant.

Exercise

Use one of these modals in each blank. Make any necessary changes for time and subject-verb agreement.

should (have)	must
ought to (have)	have to
had better	need (to)
had best	

1. That beaker has acid in it. You _ought to_

   be very careful; you _must_ not spill any of it.

2. In order to solve the problem, they will_____ carry out their own experiments, but they will not _____to use my results.

3. However, they_____look at my results. It might help them find mistakes in their work.

R   CONDITIONAL AND CONTRARY-TO-FACT SENTENCES

Conditional statements have two parts: (1) the cause and (2) the effect or result.

(247) If he goes to Washington, he will see Mary.

(248) If he went to Washington, he would see Mary.

(249) If he had gone to Washington, he would have seen Mary.

(250) If he had gone to Washington last week, he would be here today.

The cause is presented in a subordinate clause beginning with *if,* and the result is presented in an independent clause with a modal auxiliary.

Example 247 is a prediction about a real situation. It has the present tense in the first clause. Example 248 is like a prediction, but the cause and the result are unreal; they are guesses about a situation. It has a past tense verb form in the first clause.

Examples 249 and 250 are statements about a situation that did not happen; sometimes this type of situation is called **unrealized**. It has the past perfect in the first clause.

Example	Cause	Result
251 real	*if*⎫ *when*⎭ + present tense, *goes*	*(then) will, shall, may, can* example: *will see*
252 unreal	*if* + past tense, *went*	*(then) would, should, might,* *could* example: *could visit*
253 unrealized	*if* + past perfect, *had gone*	*(then) would, should, might,* *could + have* example: *would have visited*

(251) real situation
John has already made his plans: he is going to the United States. If he goes to Washington, he will see Mary.
(252) unreal situation
Bill is not sure about his travel plans: he might go to Washington, or he might visit Chicago. If he went to Washington, he could visit Mary.
(253) unrealized situation with cause and effect both in the past
Henry visited Japan instead of the United States last year. If he had gone to the U.S., he would have visited Mary in Washington.
(254) unrealized situation with cause in the past and effect in the present
Ralph is not here today; he is in Washington. If he had gone to Washington last week, he would be here today.

Conditional statements about unrealized situations have two ways of expressing the cause. The examples above show one way: *if* + past perfect. The second way is shown in example 255.

(255) Had he gone to Washington, he would have visited Mary.

The subordinate clause does not have *if*. Instead, the verb phrase has been rearranged as if it were a question. Examples 249 and 255 have the same meaning. The second way is less common and more formal than the first one.

Note: Irregular forms

When the past tense form is used to describe an unreal situation, the verb *be* has special forms to go with *I, he, she,* and *it.*

(256) If $\left\{\begin{array}{l} \text{I} \\ \text{he} \\ \text{she} \\ \text{it} \\ \text{you} \\ \text{we} \\ \text{they} \end{array}\right\}$ were stronger, we could play tennis.

This is the usual form for *you, we,* and *they.*

Contrary-to-fact statements use past and past perfect verb forms, as follows:

Present or future time situation	Past time situation
past tense	past perfect

(257) present time situation
    She talks to Philip as if he were a child.
(258) past time situation
    He treated Claire as if she had been dishonest.

In example 257, Philip is an adult; in example 258, Claire was not dishonest. The sentences contain information that is untrue—contrary-to-fact. Some common introducers of contrary-to-fact information are *as if, as though, suppose (that),* and *wish (that).*

Exercise

Identify the sentences.

    a. real
    b. unreal
    c. past, unrealized

_C_ **1.** If we had added salt, Maurice could not have eaten the soup.

_____ **2.** If he spent more time studying, he would speak English better.

_____ **3.** Had he presented the situation clearly, he might have received a more sympathetic response.

_____ **4.** If we add salt, the soup will be tastier.

Provide the correct verb forms.

5. Even though they are very nervous, they act as if they (be)_____*were*_____confident.

6. If I (be)_____in that position, I would do nothing at all.

7. If she (be)_____with you yesterday, you would not have had any trouble.

Chapter 4
Contents

4 Adjectives and Adverbs

A DETERMINERS

A **determiner** appears in front of the noun in a phrase; and if there are several words in the phrase, the determiner appears before all the other parts of the phrase. Determiners are sometimes optional, sometimes required.

noun phrase

(1) She was going to buy *a* book.

noun phrase

(2) *My* chemistry report was almost 15 pages long.

(3) We were not sure whether to buy

noun phrase

those very long and very unusual sandwiches.

A determiner may appear with an uncountable noun (*that information*) or a plural countable noun (*several people*), but these nouns may appear alone (*information, people*). However, a singular countable noun must have a determiner in front of it within a sentence (*a person,* but not X *person*). (See Chapter 2, page 53.)

Note: In some languages, a determiner is not used when a person's occupation or nationality is identified. However, in English the determiner *a* (or *an*) must be used.

(4)   Ann is a teacher.
(5)   X Ann is teacher.
(6)   John is an Englishman.
(7)   X John is Englishman.

There are a few cases when singular countable nouns appear without determiners in front of them. One of these cases is in discussions of means or methods.

(8)   They went from Tokyo to Calcutta *by plane* and from Calcutta to Bombay *by train*.
(9)   They did most of the work *by hand,* but some of it was done *by computer*.

Notice the following phrases that indicate means or methods: *by mail, through the mail(s), by telephone, on the telephone*.

Another case is in discussions of location.

(10) They are at school.
                in school.
                (at) home.
                at college.
                in town.
                in hospital. (British English)

In these examples, we are discussing a location and its principal use; for example, *They are at college* means that they are in that place because they are college students. When we refer to a particular building or place, but not to its principal use, we use an article.

(11) They are *at the college* visiting their son, who is a student there.

133

Another case is in discussions about seasons of the year.

(12) We were there *in spring*.

The definite article may be used in example 12: *in the spring*.

No article is used in the phrase *at night,* but the other times of the day require an article.

(13) He works at night.
in the morning.
in the afternoon.
in the evening.
during the day.

No article is used in phrases about meals.

(14) We were late *for breakfast*.
(15) There was enough time to discuss our plans *at lunch*.
(16) Did she invite Mary *to dinner*?

A1 **Articles**

There are two articles in English. The **definite article** is *the*. The **indefinite article** is *a* (or *an*). There is only one written form of the definite article: *the*.

Indefinite Article: Form and Meaning

There are two forms of the indefinite article: *a* and *an*. The form to use in a particular phrase depends on the word which follows the indefinite article. If the word begins with a vowel sound, the *an* form is used; if the word begins with a consonant sound, *a* is used.

(17) an elephant
(18) an orange book
(19) a book
(20) a grey elephant

It is important to remember that the deciding factor is the first *sound* of the following word, not the first *letter*. Note the use of *a/an* in the following phrases.

(21) a history book
(22) an hour
(23) a university
(24) an unusual idea

Note: The word *another* may be considered as two words: the indefinite article and *other*. Because of the beginning vowel sound of *other,* the *an* form is used: *an + other.* Two articles can not appear together. We can say and write *another idea* and *the other idea,* but we can not use X *the another idea.*

The indefinite article has the meaning of *one* or *singular;* therefore, it can be used only with singular nouns.

(25) a thought
(26) an idea
(27) a person

It can not be used with an uncountable noun or a plural noun.

(28) X an information (uncountable)
(29) X a police (plural)

Because *another = an + other, another* can not be used with an uncountable or plural noun.

(30) X another information
(31) X another things

Unlike *a/an,* the definite article *the* can be used with any noun.

(32) the thought (singular)
(33) the information (uncountable)
(34) the police (plural)

Exercise
Provide the correct form of the indefinite article: **a** or **an.**

1. ___*a*___ reason
2. _____added reason
3. _____other reason

4. _____hound

5. _____universal principle

6. _____historical principle

7. _____unprincipled person

8. _____umbrella

9. _____apple-red umbrella

10. _____hasty retreat

Exercise

If the article usage is correct, write **OK**. If the article usage is not correct, write **X** and correct the mistake.

___X___ 1. *The* Telephone is a very useful instrument.

_____ 2. We do not use telegrams very often.

_____ 3. A letters will be sent instead of telegrams.

_____ 4. My father is postman.

_____ 5. He delivers the mail by car because he works in the country.

_____ 6. He begins work early in the morning in summer as well as in winter.

_____ 7. Piece of bad news can ruin your whole day.

_____ 8. Good news, on the other hand, can brighten your whole day.

_____ 9. We usually expect that telegram brings bad news.

Definite Article: Meaning

The definite article is used when the noun being referred to in a statement is clear to the sender and the receiver of a message. The article *the* indicates that these people know definitely which person(s), place(s), thing(s), or idea(s) are being discussed.

Sometimes a noun is definite because of grammar, and sometimes the context makes it definite.

Grammar: words, phrases, and clauses that describe a noun can make that noun definite.

(35) adjectives in front of the noun
Did you find any mistakes in the *first three* solutions?

(36) phrase after the noun
     I could not finish all of the questions *on our test.*
(37) clause after the noun
     She returned the dictionary *that I had lent to her.*

The following two examples have different meanings. Example 38 refers to any number of mistakes—one, two, several, etc. Example 39 refers to all the mistakes: the definite article means *all.*

(38) He found mistakes in my term paper.
(39) He found the mistakes in my term paper.

An earlier sentence can make a noun definite.

(40) She bought a television set and a fan at a drugstore near her apartment. However, the fan had to be returned.

In the second sentence, *the* is used because the noun was referred to before.

Context: a noun can be definite because of the common understanding of the people involved in the communication. Because they are living in or thinking about the same situation, they know what to expect there.

(41) There are ten major bodies in the solar system. *The sun* is the biggest and the most important; *the planets* revolve around it. Earth is the most important planet to human beings; *the other planets* are more or less important in relation to their sizes and distances from Earth.

The phrase *the sun* is used because (1) the context of the discussion is clear—the solar system—and (2) there is only one sun in this system. Similarly, *the planets* is used: (1) there is a clear context, and (2) the phrase refers to all 9 of them. And the phrase *the other planets* is used in this same situation to refer to all 8 planets, after Earth is excluded. Example 42 would not be correct in a discussion about the solar system, because there are many moons in the system.

(42) X The moon is 2,160 miles in diameter.

On the other hand, it would be correct in a discussion limited to Earth.

In discussions with comparative or superlative adjectives, we often use the definite article (*the*).

> (43) We have a small car and a medium-size car. We are going to use *the* larger car for our long trip.
> (44) All four of our children can drive, but *the* two youngest ones have not had very much experience.

In examples 43 and 44, *the* is used because there is no other one. In one situation, there are two cars; only one can be larger, so there can not be any other larger one. In the other situation, the number *two* and the superlative form *youngest* eliminate the possibility of any other ones. (See Chapter 4, page 170.)

Exercise

The definite article is underlined several times in this paragraph. Determine why it is used.

   a. grammar: words, phrases, or clauses make the noun definite
   b. grammar: reference to the noun in a previous sentence
   c. context: common understanding of what to find in the situation

1. __*a*__ The university that my brother attends is large.

2. _____ I think that the campus is confusing because it is very big. My brother gave me directions to his dormitory:

3. _____ Park in the north parking lot.

4. _____ Walk two blocks south from the lot.

5. _____ Go past the gymnasium.

6. _____ The dormitory is the tall building with white doors.

Definite vs. Indefinite Articles

The indefinite article refers to any one person, place, thing, or idea when there may be one other or several others. For instance, in discussing the solar system, we might find example 45.

(45) There is a moon near Earth.

Because there are other moons in the context (the solar system), the indefinite article is used. On the other hand, if discussing only Earth, "the moon" would be correct because there is only one in the context of Earth.

The first time a singular noun is used in a conversation or in a written message, it will probably have *a (an)* in front of it.

(46) He saw *a* picture on page 53.

Example 46 should be used if this is the first statement about a picture. The second sentence will have the definite article because the noun has been made definite by the information in the first sentence.

(47) He saw *a* picture on page 53. *The* picture was in black and white.

Exercise

For each sentence, determine why the underlined indefinite article is used.

  a. the first mention
  b. one of several possibilities

_*b*_ **1.** Each state in the United States has _a_ governor.

_____ **2.** The governor of _a_ state is elected by the residents of the state.

_____ **3.** An election can be held anytime during the year.

Exercise

Answer the questions with complete sentences.

1. He bought a hot dog, fried chicken, and a hamburger. Which one did he like best?

    He liked the hamburger best.

2. I have a two-year-old car and a ten-year-old car. Which one is probably more reliable?

3. There is a piece of fried chicken, a large piece of broiled steak, and a piece of bread with butter. Which one(s) could you eat with your hands?

4. Mary has a dictionary and a grammar handbook. Which one will she use to check the use of articles?

5. Which one will Mary use to check the structure of sentences?

General Reference

There are three ways to refer to people, places, things, or ideas in general.

One way to signal general reference is to use the singular form of a noun with the indefinite article.

(48) In our modern society, we use *a computer* quite a lot.

The second way is to use the singular form of a noun with the definite article.

(49) In our modern society, we use *the computer* quite a lot.

The third way is to use the plural form of a noun without a determiner, or an uncountable noun without a determiner.

(50) In our modern society, we use *computers* quite a lot.

(51) In our modern society, we use computer *technology* quite a lot.

These three ways have the same meaning. We are not referring to any one computer or to any group of computers; we are discussing all computers in general.

Exercise

Tell why the underlined noun phrases are used.

a. general reference
b. specific reference

_*a*_ **1.** A grammar book can be a useful

_____ resource for a student

_____ of the English language .

_____ **2.** However, the student must know how to find

_____ information in the book he is using .

The and Proper Nouns

The is generally not used with the following types of proper nouns:

1. Names of people

(52) X We saw the Professor Rosen.
(53) We saw Professor Rosen.

But we use *the Rosens* to mean *the people in the Rosen family.*

(54) We met the Rosens at the movies last night.

2. Holidays, days, months

(55) X The New Year's Day is January 1.
(56) New Year's Day is January 1.
(57) Schools are closed on Saturday and Sunday.
(58) The solstices are in June and December.

However, *the* may be used in discussions of one particular occurrence.

(59) Do you remember the first Sunday we rode our bikes to the state park?

3. Streets

(60) We met at the corner of First Street and Main Avenue.

4. Geographical names

(61) San Francisco
(62) Texas
(63) Australia
(64) Asia

Note: exceptions: *the Hague, the Bronx, the Vatican*

The definite article is used if the name includes an indication of political structure. The words *republic, kingdom,* and *union* indicate the type of structure; but *France* and *Great Britain* do not.

(65) France
(66) the United States
(67) Great Britain
(68) the United Kingdom
(69) the Union of Soviet Socialist Republics

The names of rivers, seas, oceans, and canals have *the*.

(70) the Mississippi (River)
(71) the Dead Sea
(72) the Panama Canal

The names of lakes and mountains do not have *the*.

(73) Lake Titicaca
(74) Mount Everest

Plural geographical names have *the*.

(75) the Netherlands
(76) the United States

5. Names of languages

Names of languages have the definite article only when the word *language* is used directly after it:

(77) X The French is a very beautiful language.
(78) French is a very beautiful language.
(79) The French language is very beautiful.

Exercise

Add the definite article where it is required.

1. English is spoken in *the* Union of South Africa, as well as in Nigeria and Kenya.
2. They introduced us to Pope John.
3. We had arrived in Rome on Tuesday or Wednesday.
4. Flying over Suez Canal and Red Sea was exciting.
5. The airline office was on Broadway, near the Consulate of Soviet Union.

A2 Possessives

The determiner in a noun phrase can be a possessive. It will be a noun with an ending (apostrophe or apostrophe plus *s,* see Chapter 2, page 72) or a possessive adjective—the possessive pronoun form that appears in front of a noun (see Chapter 2, page 75).

(80) *Antonio's* new passport
(81) *immigration officers'* questions
(82) *her* unexpected answer
(83) *their* car

The form of the possessive is not influenced by other words in the noun phrase. The possessive is determined by the possessor. For instance, in example 82, the possessive would still be *her* even if the noun were plural.

(84) *her* unexpected answers

A3 **Demonstratives**

There are four **demonstratives**.

	Uncountable	Countable	
		Singular	Plural
near	this	this	these
far	that	that	those

This and *these* are used with nouns which are near the speaker or writer. The hearer or reader himself may be near or far, but this information is not indicated by the demonstrative.

(85) I think you should read *this book.*

When John says example 85 to Frances, he may be (1) sitting next to her, (2) talking to her on the telephone, or (3) writing a letter that will travel 5,000 miles.

That and *those* are used with nouns which are far from the speaker or writer.

(86) I hope that you read *those* stories I sent you.

In example 86, the speaker or writer is now far from the stories, but we have no information about the location of John when he hears or reads the sentence.

Nearness or farness may be physical; for example, the book may be in John's hands when he uses the phrase *this book.* However, nearness or farness may be a matter of time; for example, perhaps Frances read *those stories* many weeks ago.

Exercise

Circle the correct demonstrative.

1. this/(these) people
2. that/those news
3. this/these page
4. that/those ideas
5. this/these demonstrative

Exercise

Use the correct demonstrative in each blank space.

The rules in the book that I am reading now are easier than the rules in a book that I read last week. _____ rules are short and clear; _____ other rules were much more difficult to understand. _____ book,

which I am reading for my class, has exercises; but
_____ book, which I finished last week, did not
have any. My teacher gave me _____ piece of
advice: read the rules and practice using them.

A4 Indefinite Determiners

The indefinites are used when we do not want to refer to
any special one or ones.

Each and every

These two indefinites occur only with singular nouns.

> (87) Each check had been carefully written.
> (88) The teller counted every dollar slowly.

We understand that example 87 is about all the checks and
that example 88 is about all the dollars. However, *each* and
every are grammatically singular; they emphasize each individual one (see Chapter 2, page 66).

Because they are singular, they can not appear with uncountable nouns or plural countable nouns.

> (89) X every information   (90) X each police

Each can be used alone but *every* can not except in the
phrase *every one of.*

> (91) The teller counted *every one of* them slowly.
> (92) *Each* had been carefully written.
> (93) *Each of* them had been carefully written.
> (94) X The teller counted *every* slowly.
> (95) X The teller counted *every of* them slowly.

Any and some

These indefinites can be used with singular, plural, or uncountable nouns.

> (96) After Tom bought the groceries, there was some
>   change left from the $20.
> (97) After Tom bought the groceries, there wasn't any
>   change left from the $20.

(See Chapter 6, page 255 for more information about the
use of the indefinites.)

A5 Quantifiers

Quantifiers tell us *how much* or *how many*. They may be used as determiners before nouns in a noun phrase, or alone.

1.

Uncountable	Plural Countable
much, more, most	many, more, most
little, less, least	few, fewer, fewest
a little	a few
quite a little	quite a few

The quantifiers *much* and *many* refer to large amounts.

(98) He had not learned *much* useful information in that course.

(99) He had *many* things to learn.

Note: *Much* is not used very often in an affirmative statement; *a lot (of)* or *lots (of)* is used.

(100) He had learned *much* useful information.

(101) He had learned *a lot of* useful information.

The quantifiers *little, a little, few* and *a few* refer to small amounts.

(102) There is *little* time for lunch before the movie.

(103) There is *a little* time for lunch before the movie.

(104) There were *a few* opportunities to practice English.

(105) There were *few* opportunities to practice English.

Little and *few* indicate a small amount, perhaps not enough. *A little* and *a few* indicate a small amount, perhaps enough or close to enough. Therefore, if there is *little time* (example 102), we can not eat lunch; but if there is *a little time* (example 103), we might decide to eat. In examples 104 and 105, if there were *few opportunities* to practice, the students did not have enough practice; but *a few opportunities* means that there were some opportunities, that they were helpful, and there is a positive feeling about the amount.

Another way to consider the meanings of these quantifiers is to look at opposites or negatives.

Positive	Negative
a little	no, none,
a few	nothing

Positive	Negative
enough	little
many	few
much	

(106) Maria contributed *nothing* to the charity; on the other hand, Jacqueline donated *a little* money.

(107) Philip made *many* promises to us, but he kept *few of* them.

Quite a little and *quite a few* mean *much* and *many*. This may seem illogical, because *quite = very;* and *a little* and *a few = a small amount*. Example 108 describes a crowd of people.

(108) *Quite a few* people met him at the airport.

(See Chapter 4, page 170 for comparative and superlative forms.)

2. a lot (of) = lots (of)   plenty (of)
    enough   several (of)

The quantifiers *a lot (of)* and *(lots of)* have the same meaning: *a large amount*. They are used in informal conversation; they usually appear instead of *much* in affirmative sentences. *Enough* indicates a satisfactory amount (but we do not know whether that is a large or small amount); *plenty (of)* means *a large amount,* perhaps more than enough. These five quantifiers can be used with plural countable nouns and with uncountable nouns.

(109) We had *a lot of* time before the plane left.
(110) We had *lots of* time before the plane left.
(111) We had *lots of* books about prehistoric Africa.
(112) We had *enough* books but not *enough* time to do the research report.
(113) We thought that we had *plenty of* books and *plenty of* time.

The quantifier *several* is used with plural countable nouns.

(114) We found *several* opportunities to practice.

The quantifier *enough* sometimes appears after the noun.

(115) We did not have *time enough* to do the research report.

(See Chapter 4, page 165 for information about *enough* as a **de-emphasizer**.)

3. all (of)   both (of)
   half (of)   a number (of)
   one-third (of)

The quantifiers *all (of), half (of), one-third (of),* and other fractions can be used with countable or uncountable nouns.

(116) half the water   (117) half the glasses

However, if there is no determiner, *half* can not be used with the noun.

(118) ✗ half (of) information

Both (of) and *a number (of)* can be used only with countable nouns.

(119) both the glasses   (120) a number of the glasses

When quantifiers are used with pronouns, they require *of.*

(121) We bought *a few of* them.
(122) They had *enough of* it.

Each quantifier should be considered as a unit, even if it is written as two or three words. For instance, example 123 has two grammatical units and two meaning units.

(123) a number of people

grammar: quantifier + noun plural
meaning: *several + persons*

It is important to treat the quantifier as a unit for two reasons. One reason is that the grammar of the noun phrase may affect another part of the sentence, such as the verb.

(124) *A number of* people are waiting outside.

The plural noun *people* is the subject of the sentence, therefore the verb form is *are waiting* instead of *is waiting.* The second reason is the meaning.

(125) *A little* cat hid under the car.
(126) *A little* sugar would improve the flavor.

In example 125, *little* is an adjective describing size. The subject of this sentence has three parts: a determiner (the article *a*) + an adjective (*little*) + a noun (*cat*). In example 126, *a little* is one unit of meaning specifying a quantity.

147

The subject of this sentence has two parts: a determiner (the quantifier *a little*) + a noun (*sugar*).

Quantifiers can be used with a following noun; in this case, they are similar to adjectives.

(127) Did they have *much* time?
(128) Yes, they had *plenty of* time.

In this case, one of the quantifiers required *of;* one did not.

Quantifiers can be used alone; in this case, they are similar to nouns.

(129) Did they have a lot of plants?
    Yes, they had *plenty.*
(130) We bought *a few.*

Exercise

Fill in each blank with one of these quantifiers: **a few, a little, few, little, many, much, quite a few, quite a little.**

1. We use commercial banks because they offer us ___*many*___ services.
2. We can have a checking account and buy travelers checks without_____ expense.
3. Travelers checks are useful when traveling because _____ people refuse to accept them.
4. And they involve_____ inconvenience.
5. It is worthwhile to spend_____ time choosing the best bank for you.

Exercise

The subject (S) of each of the following sentences is a phrase with a quantifier. Underline the complete phrase and circle the correct verb form.

1. A lot of students (travel)/travels abroad to study.
2. Is/are there enough money for everyone to study abroad?
3. One-quarter of the time abroad is/are spent learning a foreign language.
4. One-tenth of the students do/does not succeed.
5. Plenty of determination is/are required to be an international student.

A6 Cardinal numbers

The **cardinal numbers** are the ones used in counting. The cardinal numbers from 0 to 99 follow:

0 zero	10 ten	20 twenty
1 one	11 eleven	21 twenty-one
2 two	12 twelve	22 twenty-two
3 three	13 thirteen	23 twenty-three
4 four	14 fourteen	24 twenty-four
5 five	15 fifteen	25 twenty-five
6 six	16 sixteen	26 twenty-six
7 seven	17 seventeen	27 twenty-seven
8 eight	18 eighteen	28 twenty-eight
9 nine	19 nineteen	29 twenty-nine

30 thirty	40 forty	50 fifty	60 sixty
70 seventy	80 eighty	90 ninety	

Note: In counting, the numeral 0 is read as "zero" or "0." In a sentence, speakers of English usually use *no* rather than *zero. Zero* is used to emphasize the number or to give statistics. *Nothing* is used for sports scores.

(131) No
⎱
Nine ⎰ people had arrived before then.

(132) The score was three to ⎰ zero.
⎱ nothing.

The **compound numbers** have two digits: *21, 37, 55, 98,* etc. They are written with a hyphen between the two parts.

(133) twenty-one
(134) thirty-seven
(135) fifty-five
(136) ninety-eight

Note: Notice the spelling of the parts of *44:*

(137) forty-four

The first part is *forty*—not what we might expect.

The cardinal numbers above 99 are as follows:

149

100   one hundred, or a hundred

1,000   one thousand, or a thousand

1,000,000   one million, or a million

In reading these numbers, we use *one* when we want to be exact or to emphasize the number and when we read data. We use *a* in speaking more generally, less exactly.

    (138) According to the last census, the population of the city is 175,000. ("one hundred seventy-five thousand"; statistical information)

    (139) The police estimated that about 100,000 people attended the parade. ("a hundred thousand" or "one hundred thousand")

Numbers from 1,100 to 9,999 can be read in two ways: (a)____thousand, ____hundred, or (b)____hundred.

    (140) 1,200   a. one thousand, two hundred

                      b. twelve hundred

    (141) 2,340   a. two thousand three hundred forty

                      b. twenty-three hundred forty

It is not usual to write large numbers in words; most often we use figures.

    (142) 56,471

    (143) fifty-six thousand four hundred seventy-one

Note: The compound numbers—the ones from 21 to 99—are the only ones to have hyphens when numbers are written in words.

    (144) X fifty-six-thousand

    (145) fifty-six thousand

The cardinal numbers can appear first in the noun phrase (as determiners) or later, after another determiner.

    (146) Nine people had arrived.

    (147) The first nine people had arrived.

The cardinal numbers can appear with no other word after them; in this case, they are like nouns.

    (148) Eleven people arrived after lunch.

           Nine had arrived earlier.

    (149) The first nine had arrived early.

When the cardinal number refers to part of a larger group, we use a prepositional phrase with *of*.

(150) We had invited 20 people to our party.
     Nine *of our guests* arrived early.

The prepositional phrase must have a determiner and a plural noun to indicate the larger group; therefore example 151 is not correct.

(151) X One of my friend could not come.

The cardinal numbers can appear with pronouns; in this case, we use *of.*

(152) Nine *of* them had arrived early.
(153) The first nine *of* them had arrived early.

Exercise

If the sentence is correct, write **OK**. If the sentence is not correct, write **X** and correct it.

_OK_ **1.** I gave her a dollar and expected forty-five cents change.

_____ **2.** It cost only fifty seven cent.

_____ **3.** About twenty-five-hundred students and teachers came to see the parade.

_____ **4.** One of the people had arrived the day before.

_____ **5.** A thousand them were caught in the snowstorm on the way.

_____ **6.** The other fifteen-hundred or so watched from inside buildings.

A7 **Ordinal Numbers**

The **ordinal numbers** indicate place in an arrangement or order. The ordinal numbers from 1st to 99th are as follows:

1st	first	10th	tenth	20th	twentieth
2nd	second	11th	eleventh	21st	twenty-first
3rd	third	12th	twelfth	22nd	twenty-second
4th	fourth	13th	thirteenth	23rd	twenty-third
5th	fifth	14th	fourteenth	24th	twenty-fourth
6th	sixth	15th	fifteenth	25th	twenty-fifth
7th	seventh	16th	sixteenth	26th	twenty-sixth
8th	eighth	17th	seventeenth	27th	twenty-seventh
9th	ninth	18th	eighteenth	28th	twenty-eighth
		19th	nineteenth	29th	twenty-ninth

30th thirtieth	50th fiftieth	70th seventieth
40th fortieth	60th sixtieth	80th eightieth
		90th ninetieth

Form

1. Most of the ordinal numbers are formed by adding *-th* at the end of the cardinal number: *ten + th = tenth*. The ending *-eth* is added to *thirty, forty,* etc.; and the final *y* is changed to *i: thirtieth, fortieth,* etc.
2. The compound ordinals (those with two digits)—*21, 33, 62, 96,* etc.) are written with hyphens.
3. The ordinal figures are combinations. They have numerals (*1, 2, 30, 85,* etc.) and the last two letters of the written ordinal number. For example, the ordinal is *21st,* because *twenty-first* ends in the two letters *-st.*

Note: Ordinal numbers are not written with small raised circles.

(154) X 22°
(155) 22nd

22° means ''22 degrees'' in measurements of temperature or angles.

4. Notice the following irregular forms:
    a. *First* and *second* are completely unexpected: they have no relation to the cardinal numbers *one* and *two.*
    b. *Third, fifth,* and *twelfth* are irregular in pronunciation and spelling.
    c. *Eighth* and *ninth* have irregular spellings (not X *eightth* and X *nineth,* as we might expect).
5. The cardinal numbers above *99th* are as follows:

100th	one hundredth
1,000th	one thousandth
1,000,000th	one millionth

Exercise

Complete the ordinal figures by adding two letters.

1. 101 _st_
2. 32___

3. 46_____

4. 55_____

5. 73_____

Write, in words, the corresponding ordinal numbers.

6. 101 _____ *one hundred first* _____

7. 67 _____

8. 44 _____

9. 79 _____

10. 200 _____

B **ADJECTIVES**

B1 **Adjectives: Meaning**

Adjectives are words, phrases, and clauses that describe. They answer the questions *which one(s)?* and *what kind(s)?*

(156) He bought an electric typewriter.

In example 156, the adjective *electric* tells us what kind of typewriter it was.

B2 **Adjectives: Place and Form**

An adjective appears before the principal noun in a noun phrase, that is, in front of the noun that it describes.

Adj.   Noun

(157) brown eyes

Adj.   Noun

(158) a forty-watt bulb

Adj.   Adj.   Noun

(159) the large wooden crate

Note: One-word adjectives do not appear after the noun.

Noun   Adj.

(160) X eyes brown

Note: An adjective can appear without a noun, in the following construction: *the* + Adj. This construction means *the people who are;* for example, *the rich* means *the people who are rich.*

153

Note: Adjectives can also appear in phrases with indefinite pronouns (see Chapter 4, page 144). In such phrases, the adjective comes after the pronoun.

(161) They needed *someone smart* to solve the problem.

(162) There was *nothing funny* about the accident.

Most adjectives can appear after the verb *be* and other linking verbs, as in example 164 (see Chapter 1, page 11).

(163) She looks old.

(164) Her eyes are brown.

Some adjectives can appear only in front of a noun.

(165) That was his principal idea.

(166) X His idea was principal.

Other adjectives like this are *chief, main, only, outright, same,* and *very*.

Some adjectives have different meanings in these two places.

(167) He is an old friend.

(168) My friend is old.

Example 167 refers to a friend that I have known for a long time; there is no information about his age. In contrast, example 168 says that my friend is old; it says nothing about how long we have been friends. Other adjectives like this are *certain, clear, definite, late, particular, plain,* and *true*.

An adjective has only one form. This form is not affected by the nouns it describes: there are no masculine, feminine, neuter, singular, or plural adjective forms.

(169) X others things (plural form of adjective with plural form of the noun)

Example 169 is incorrect, because adjectives do not have endings to signal the meaning of plural, the way that nouns do. Adjectives change forms only to signal the meanings of comparative and superlative (see Chapter 4, page 170).

Exercise

Underline each one-word adjective.

1. Often, new residents and international students in the United States are not comfortable about using checks.
2. Checks are often used for purchases instead of cash.

3. We use checks for large payments when it might be unsafe to carry money.
4. For example, I pay the monthly rent by check, and I wrote a big check for my last car.
5. Checks are useful because they give us permanent receipts of our expenditures.

B3 Adjective-Equivalents

In addition to one-word adjectives, there are **adjective-equivalents**. These words, phrases, and clauses describe nouns and are used in the same way as adjectives.

Adjectives and Prepositions

It is often difficult to determine which preposition should follow a particular adjective; for example, is it *accustomed to* or *accustomed with*? Appendix G shows adjectives and their accompanying prepositions. Some adjectives can be followed by several prepositions and prepositional phrases. Sometimes, the prepositions indicate different meanings; sometimes, they do not.

Exercise

Complete each sentence, using one of these words and the correct preposition that goes with the word.

parallel	homesick	interested	perpendicular
different	impatient	independent	sick

1. If two lines meet in a 90° angle, we say that one line is _perpendicular to_ the other.
2. Ivan is not happy living abroad; he is_____ his own country.
3. I understand that she is bored with school. I have not been able to find anything that she is_____.
4. Alan is not at all like Louis; in fact, he is completely _____his brother.
5. You must learn to relax and take your time; you should not be so_____very young children.
6. If line AB is_____line CD, they will not intersect.

155

7. The United States started as a colony, but now it is _____Great Britain.

8. Of course, they did not come to school: they are both _____a bad case of the flu.

Other Adjective-Equivalents

1. Adjective clauses

An adjective clause is a relative clause that describes a noun. An adjective clause comes after the noun it describes.

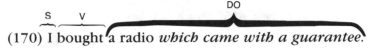

(170) I bought a radio *which came with a guarantee.*

In example 170, the direct object is made up of an article (*a*) + the principal noun (*radio*) + an adjective clause that describes the typewriter (*which came with a guarantee*).

2. Verb forms

Participles (verb + – *ing*) and infinitives (*to* + verb) can be used to describe nouns. They appear after the nouns which they describe.

(171) The man *paying for the typewriter* is my roommate.

The noun *man* is described by the participle phrase *paying for the typewriter.*

(172) A good typewriter *to buy* is one that is not very heavy.

The noun *typewriter* is described by the infinitive *to buy.*

3. Prepositional phrases

A prepositional phrase can be used to describe a noun or noun-equivalent. A prepositional phrase comes after the noun that it describes.

(173) He decided to buy the typewriter *with a guarantee.*

The noun *typewriter* is described by the prepositional phrase *with a guarantee.* (See Chapter 4, page 54.)

4. Adverbs

A noun can be described by an adverb. The adverb (or adverb phrase) comes after the noun which it describes. (See Chapter 4, page 161.)

(174) He chose the typewriter *over there*.

The adverb phrase *over there* describes the noun *typewriter* and provides information as to which one.

5. Nouns-as-adjectives

Any noun in English can be used to describe any other noun. The noun-as-adjective comes in front of the noun which it describes.

(175) He did not buy an *expensive typewriter* cover.

The adjective *expensive* and the noun *typewriter* describe the noun *cover;* they provide information about what kind.

Exercise

Underline the adjective equivalents and identify them.

    a. an adjective clause
    b. a participle phrase
    c. an infinitive phrase
    d. a prepositional phrase
    e. an adverb
    f. a noun-as-adjective

1. __*a*__ When she walked out of the store <u>where she bought the computer</u>, she realized that she had
2. _____ locked her car keys in the car.
3. _____ She decided that the thing to do was to call a
4. _____ garage nearby.
5. _____ The man answering the phone said that he could
6. _____ send someone to help her in about half an hour.
7. _____ Because it was raining, he told her to wait inside the computer store.
8. _____ The result of this delay was that she had to rush
9. _____ to meet her friends who had invited her to have lunch with them.

Participial Adjectives

There are pairs of adjectives used to describe a feeling that is the result or reaction in a situation. The – *ing* form is

157

used for the cause or reason for the reaction, and the – *ed* form is used for the person(s) with the feeling or reaction.

(176a) That research interests John.
(176b) the cause of the interest:
That research is *interesting* (to John).
(176c) the person with the reaction:
John is *interested* (in that research).

Note: Do not let the tense or form of the verb confuse you in choosing the correct adjective form.

(176d) That research interested John.

In spite of the verb form in example 176d, we still describe the research as *interesting* and John as *interested*.

These adjective pairs come from verbs that describe reactions to a situation. Some of them are: *amaze, arouse, bore, enervate, excite, exhaust, frighten, interest, intrigue, invigorate, please, refresh, satisfy, shock, stun, suit, surprise,* and *tire.*

Exercise

If the sentence is correct, write **OK**. If it is incorrect or does not say what the user intended to say, write **X** and correct it.

_X_ **1.** Phillip told us, "I am very ~~interesting~~ *interested* in computers."

____ **2.** After we had watched for three hours of the day, we decided that it was very boring.

____ **3.** Certainly, after that long play we were very boring.

Fill in the correct adjective form.

4. I am sure that they were (exhaust) *exhausted* after all that (tire) *tiring* work.

5. Some of us were (amaze) ; others were just (surprise) ; but all of us were (please) with the very (satisfy) news.

B4 **Order of Parts of a Noun Phrase**

Different kinds of structures can be used in a noun phrase. It is very unusual to have many of them together because it is difficult to understand a long, complicated phrase. When two or more of these structures occur, they appear in the following order:

Pre-determiner	Determiner	Adjective	Noun	Adverb	Prepositional phrase	Adjective, Participle, or Infinitive phrase
all (of) both (of) some (of)	article possessive demonstrative indefinite quantifier cardinal number ordinal number	size general age shape color adjective from proper noun noun-as-adjective				
all (of)	the two	red	books	over there	near the lamp	that have low gas mileage
both (of)	fewer	big American	cars			costing more than $10
some (of)	any	good	bottle		of wine	
	the first	old	person			to arrive in Chicago

159

```
                                    noun
          general  age   shape  color  as adj.  noun
```
(177) Both of the nice old square red leather bags were
his.

```
          general  age   color   noun as adj.   noun
```
(178) The cheap old black aluminum wire was thrown
away.

Exercise

Arrange each list to make a noun phrase to form a correct
sentence.

1. Clark decided to buy   about astronomy
                           book   *that expensive*
                           expensive   *book about*
                           that   *astronomy.*

2. Therefore, he could not buy   books
                                  that I had showed
                                  him
                                  the
                                  two

3. budget
   for this month
   his   allowed him to buy   book
                                               costing more
                                                   than $25
                                               new
                                               one

4. He has to wait until he has saved enough
                                  from his part-time
                                    job
                                  for his library
                                  money
                                  to buy additional
                                    books

C   ADVERBS

C1   Adverbs: Meaning

Adverbs are words, phrases, and clauses that modify sentences, adjectives, or other adverbs. They answer questions such as *how, how long, how often, when, where, why, to what extent.* They can also tell the speaker's or writer's attitude about a statement.

(179) Mark often buys things on sale.

In example 179, the adverb *often* provides information about how often the action takes place.

Note: Adverbs can also function as adjectives; that is, they can describe nouns. (See Chapter 4, page 157.)

C2   Adverbs: Place and Form

Adverbs can appear in several different places in a sentence depending on their use in that sentence. For example, a **de-emphasizer** will probably appear next to the word it modifies. A **sentence modifier** will probably appear at the beginning of the sentence it modifies. And some adverbs can appear in several different places in the sentence, depending on the meaning and emphasis that the user of the sentence wants to provide. (See Chapter 6, page 272.)

An adverb has only one form, except when signalling comparative or superlative. (See Chapter 4, page 170.)

Exercise

Underline each one-word adverb and identify its meaning.

    a. how
    b. how long
    c. how often
    d. to what extent
    e. when
    f. where
    g. why

_a_ **1.** Mark waited impatiently while the clerk looked at his driver's license.

_____ **2.** He wondered why the clerk worked so slowly.

_____ **3.** He had arrived at the store early in order to avoid crowds.

161

_____ **4.** Although he rarely shopped in bargain stores, he had decided to go to this one.

_____ **5.** When he arrived there, he found long lines.

_____ **6.** He was angry to have to wait long in line.

_____ **7.** But he was happy that he was finally out of the store.

C3 **Adjective and Adverb Pairs**

Many adverbs are related to adjectives in meaning, and they are similar in form. A common way to form adverbs is to add – *ly* to adjectives.

Adjective	**Adverb**
forceful	forcefully
quick	quickly
sensible	sensibly
simple	simply

(180) He was very happy.
(181) He sang happily.

In some cases, the adjective form is exactly like the adverb form. A few examples are: *deep, low, far, near, fast, early, hard, high, late, long.*

Note: Some words ending in – *ly* are not adverbs. For example, *friendly* is an adjective.

(182) Sam has a very friendly smile.

Friendly is an adjective; it modifies the noun *smile.*

Exercise

Choose the adjective or adverb and circle the correct word.

1. He is a good/well worker. He works especially good/ well under pressure.
2. I hope that she does not work so quick/quickly that she becomes careless/carelessly.
3. They speak English very rapid/rapidly, and sometimes they are impatient/impatiently when I do not understand.

C4 **Adverb-Equivalents**

In addition to one-word adverbs, there are **adverb-equivalents**. These words, phrases, and clauses appear in the same grammar structures as adverbs; and they signal the same meanings that adverbs do.

1. Adverb phrases

An **adverb phrase** is made up of an adverb and a word, phrase, or clause.

(183) adverb plus clause

Adv. Clause

He ran so fast that he was out of breath.

(184) adverb plus prepositional phrase

Adv. Prepositional phrase

They arrived sometime after four o'clock.

2. Adverb clauses

An adverb clause is added to a sentence and functions like an adverb.

S V Adv.

(185) They arrived before the weather got very bad.

In example 185, the adverb clause provides information about *when.*

Commonly an adverb clause comes before or after the necessary parts of a sentence.

3. Prepositional phrases

A prepositional phrase can be used as an adverb-equivalent.

(186) They arrived *before the storm.*

The prepositional phrase provides information about *when.* (See Section 4, page 167.)

4. Nouns

Nouns can be used as adverbs to tell *when, how often,* or *how long.*

(187) He arrived *Monday.*
(188) He takes a vacation *every year.*
(189) He works *five days a week.*

5. Infinitive and participle phrases

Infinitives (*to* + verb) and participles (verb + *– ing*) can be used as adverbs.

163

(190) *To draw* the line accurately, she measured the distance twice.

(191) By *holding* the edge firmly, she could draw the line easily.

In example 190, the infinitive phrase *to draw the line accurately* provides information about why. And in example 191, *by holding the edge firmly* provides information about how. (See Chapter 1, page 20.)

Exercise

Identify the meanings of the underlined phrases.

  a. how
  b. how long
  c. how often
  d. when
  e. where
  f. why
  g. to what extent

___*d*___ 1. When Marco arrived in the United States, he was surprised to some degree by introductions.

_____ 2. At their first meeting, Americans say, "How do you do?"

_____ 3. Men shake hands, but quite often women do not.

_____ 4. In order to answer "How do you do?" they say "How do you do?" or "I'm happy to meet you."

_____ 5. When meeting people they know well , they do not shake hands.

_____ 6. Hand-shaking is reserved for people who do not meet regularly at all.

_____ 7. At a party, a person does not greet everyone.

_____ 8. According to their customs, Americans greet only the people that they will have a conversation with.

_____ 9. Marco was also surprised that Americans do not go around and say good-bye to everyone as they leave a party .

C5 Emphasizers and De-Emphasizers

One use of adverbs is to modify an adjective or another adverb. Adverbs can (1) emphasize and increase meanings or (2) de-emphasize and decrease meanings.

Emphasizers	De-emphasizers	
quite so too very	enough rather relatively somewhat indeed	Formal: for use in writing and speaking
a most really (as. . .) as can be	a bit a little kind of pretty sort of	Informal: for use in speaking
awful real		Very informal: for use in very casual speech

Emphasizers and **de-emphasizers** show that the meaning of the adjective or adverb is especially strong or weak.

> (192) The typewriter was good.
> (193) The typewriter was very good.
> (194) The typewriter was good enough.

Example 193 indicates the high quality of the machine: the meaning of *very good* may be close to *excellent.* In contrast, example 194 indicates that the machine was satisfactory, but nothing more.

Most of the (de-)emphasizers appear in front of the adjectives or adverbs that they modify; *indeed, enough,* and *as can be* appear in back of them.

> (195) X The typewriter was enough good.

(See Chapter 5, pages 190-191, 198, 202, 226, and 243 for more information on the use of *too* and *so* as emphasizers and clause combiners.)

Note: When *too* is used as an emphasizer with an adjective or adverb, it means "excessively."

> (196) Mark did not buy the largest typewriter because it was too expensive.

In example 196, we see that the cost of the typewriter was

a problem: Mark could not buy it or did not want to buy it because of the great expense.

The emphasizer *too* does not have the same meaning as *very*. Logically, example 197 is possible, but example 198 is not. However, we could add information, as in example 199; this statement says it was a bad idea to stay indoors.

(197) The weather was very nice.
(198) X The weather was too nice.
(199) The weather was too nice to stay inside and study.

Informally, *too* may have the same meaning as *very*, especially in negative sentences that give advice.

(200) Don't spend too much money on a machine.
(201) Don't spend very much money on a machine.

Examples 200 and 201 have the same meaning; 200 should be limited to informal conversations.

Note: In conversation, *a most* has the meaning of *very*.

(202) It was a most enjoyable party.
   (= It was a very enjoyable party.)

Example 202 does not mean the same as *the most enjoyable party*.

C6 Sentence Modifiers

Sentence modifiers are words and phrases that indicate the user's attitude or belief about a statement.

(203) Mark bought a very expensive typewriter. Actually, it was a wise purchase, because he needed special features for his job.

Some common sentence modifiers are: *actually, as a matter of fact, indeed, naturally, of course,* and *(un)fortunately*. Sentence modifiers usually come at the beginning of a sentence. They are set off from the rest of the sentence with commas. (See Chapter 7, page 288.)

Exercise

Underline the emphasizers, de-emphasizers, and the sentence modifiers. Then identify them.

   a. emphasizer
   b. de-emphasizer
   c. sentence modifier

_b_ __1.__ Marco was <u>rather</u> amused when he shook hands with the American.

_____ __2.__ Of course, he expected to shake hands when they met.

_____ __3.__ But he was a little surprised that the American gripped his hand so hard.

_____ __4.__ Actually, Marco knew what to expect because friends had prepared him.

_____ __5.__ But he was quite surprised when it happened.

C7 Adverbs of Place, Manner, and Time

__1.__ Adverbs of place tell _where._

(204) He bought a new shirt _in a department store._
(205) They were having a sale _there._
(206) _There_ they were having a sale.

These adverbs can appear either at the end of the clause or at the beginning (see Chapter 6, page 258). But they do not appear in the middle of a clause.

(207) X They were having _there_ a sale.

__2.__ Adverbs of manner tell _how._

(208) He paid for the shirt _in cash._
(209) He counted his change _carefully._
(210) _Carefully_ he counted his change.

These adverbs can appear at the end of the clause or at the beginning.
Short one-word adverbs of manner can appear in front of the main verb.

(211) He _carefully_ counted his change.

But they can not appear between a verb and an object or object complement.

(212) X He counted _carefully_ his change.

__3.__ Adverbs of time tell _when, how long,_ or _how often._

(213) He went shopping _yesterday._
  (_yesterday_ = when)
(214) He looked at different shirts _for half an hour._
  (_for half an hour_ = how long)
(215) He tried one on _from time to time._

(216) *From time to time* he tried one on.
(*from time to time* = how often)

These adverbs, as in examples 213, 214, 215, and 216, can appear at the end of the clause or at the beginning. (See Chapter 6, page 258.)

Short adverbs of frequency (how often) and adverbs of indefinite time (*first, next, later, afterwards, just,* etc.) can also appear in front of the main verb.

(217) He *usually* spends a lot of time shopping.
(218) We have *just* bought a new television set.

They appear after the verb *be* when it has only one word.

(219) They are never late.
(220) They have never been late.

But they can not appear between a verb and an object or a complement.

(221) ✗ He spends *usually* a lot of time shopping.

Short, one-word adverbs of definite time can not appear in front of a main verb.

(222) ✗ He *yesterday* went shopping.

Adverbs of frequency tell how often an event takes place. The following list shows some of them arranged in order, from the most often to the least often.

100% of the time	always
	almost always
	most of the time
	usually
	frequently
	often
	sometimes
	occasionally
	once in a while
	seldom
	hardly ever
	rarely
	almost never
0% of the time	never

4. Place, manner, time
If two of three of these adverbs are used at the end of

a clause, they appear in the following order: place, manner, time.

(223) We met him *there yesterday.*

(224) We went *there by bus yesterday.*

Any long or complicated adverb usually appears at the end of the clause.

(225) We met him *yesterday next to the big post office downtown.*

Exercise

If the sentence is correct, write **OK**. If there is an error in adverb usage, write **X** and correct the error.

<u>OK</u>   **1.** John bought two size **Large** shirts at the sale.

_____ **2.** He buys usually size **Medium** shirts.

_____ **3.** He tried on at the store several shirts on Monday.

_____ **4.** Then he had to choose the two which fit him best.

_____ **5.** He slowly examined each shirt.

_____ **6.** First he looked to see if it fit well.

_____ **7.** He inspected then the workmanship.

_____ **8.** He chose quickly the shirts that he wanted to buy.

_____ **9.** He did not care if he spent in that store a lot of money.

_____ **10.** On Monday he spent almost $50.

Exercise

Add the adverbs and adverb-equivalents to the ends of the sentences. Use the following order: place, manner, time.

1. I am going shopping. downtown, tomorrow afternoon

I am going shopping downtown tomorrow afternoon.

2. A friend of mine and I are going. by car, there

3. We expect to finish our work. early, here

4. We can arrive. before one o'clock, if we drive fast, there

5. We both want to be. back here, before six

C8 Adverb-Substitutes

Like pronouns, **adverb-substitutes** refer to an antecedent:

169

they point to an earlier unit of meaning in the sentence, composition, or conversation. (See Chapter 2, page 59.)

(226) We arrived at the airport at 3:00 in the morning.
We had to wait *there* until 5:00.
(227) They could wait only until 7:00 p.m.
They would have to leave *then*.
(228) He drove at night. *Thus* he avoided a lot of traffic.

Example	Adverb Substitute	Tells
226	there	where
227	then	when
228	thus	how, in what way

D   THE COMPARATIVE AND SUPERLATIVE OF ADJECTIVES AND ADVERBS

When we compare two nouns or noun-equivalents, we use the **comparative forms** of adjectives. There are also comparative forms for adverbs.

When the comparison involves more than two, we use the **superlative forms** of adjectives or adverbs. For example, we can say that one car is the biggest one on the street or that one idea is the best of the five which were presented at a meeting.

When the adjective or adverb is not used as a comparative or a superlative, it is called the **positive form**.

Positive	Comparative	Superlative
big	bigger	the biggest
forcefully	more forcefully	the most forcefully

D1   Comparative and Superlative: Form
How to make comparative and superlative forms

Adjectives and adverbs follow the same rules when they become comparative and superlative forms. To form the comparative, either add the ending *-er* after the positive form or add the word *more* in front of it.

$$\text{Positive} \quad + \quad \begin{array}{c} \textit{-er} \\ \textit{more} \end{array} \quad = \quad \text{Comparative}$$

high	+	*-er*	=	*higher*
expensive	+	*more*	=	*more expensive*

To form the superlative, either add the ending *-est* after the positive form or add the word *most* in front of it.

Positive	+	*-est* *most*	=	Superlative

high	+	*-est*	=	the *highest*
expensive	+	*most*	=	the *most expensive*

The superlative also requires *the*.

How to decide between the endings (-er and -est) and the words (more and most)

The comparative and superlative forms follow the same rules for selecting an ending or a separate word. The important issue is the number of syllables in the positive form. If the positive form of the adjective or adverb is pronounced with one syllable, the endings *-er* and *-est* are used.

Positive	Comparative	Superlative
high (1 syllable)	*higher*	*highest*
fast (1 syllable)	*faster*	*fastest*

If the positive form has three or more syllables, the words *more* and *most* are used.

Positive	Comparative	Superlative
expensive (3 syllables)	*more expensive*	*most expensive*
reasonable (4 syllables)	*more reasonable*	*most reasonable*

The following types of two-syllable adjectives can use either way to become comparative and superlative forms:

1. final *-y: funny, happy* (but *earlier*, not ✕ more early)
2. final *-ow: hollow, narrow*
3. final *-le: gentle, able*
4. final *-er, -ure: clever, obscure*
5. *common, polite, quiet*

All other two-syllable adjectives and adverbs use *more* and *most*.

171

Positive	Comparative	Superlative
sadly	*more sadly*	*most sadly*
abrupt	*more abrupt*	*most abrupt*

Note: If you can not decide between an ending (*-er* and *-est*) and a word (*more* and *most*) for a two-syllable word, use a word; your chances are better for making a correct choice, and incorrect forms will not sound very bad.

Sometimes, adding *-er* or *-est* requires a spelling change. Turn to Appendix A for the correct rule.

Doubling the final consonant
big + er = bigger

Changing the final y to i
happy + est = happiest

Canceling the final e
pale + er = paler

Note: Example 229 is incorrect because it has two indications of the comparative: the word *more* and the adjective + *er*.

(229) X Mexico City is more higher than San Francisco.

There are some irregular comparative and superlative forms, for example, *worse* formed from *bad + er*. Turn to Appendix F.

Exercise

Complete the chart of adjective and adverb forms.

Positive	Comparative	Superlative
1. slow	*slower*	*slowest*
2. backward		
3.		quietest
4.	more quiet	
5. progressive		
6. capable		
7. slyly		
8. recalcitrant		
9. near		
10. overt		

D2 Comparative Meaning: Similarity

Statements of comparison can be used in order to show similarities; frequently, we use an adjective or adverb with *as . . . as*.

(230) Her typewriter cost $500, and my typewriter cost $500. Her typewriter is *as expensive as* mine.
(231) She types *as fast as* I do.

Note: Some grammarians insist that a comparison with the phrase *as . . . as* must be limited to affirmative sentences and that a negative sentence requires *so . . . as*. Both of these forms are correct, although the phrase with *so . . . as* is more formal and less frequently used.

(232) Her typewriter is *not as expensive as* mine.
(233) Her typewriter is *not so expensive as* mine.

D3 Comparative Meaning: Difference

Statements of comparison are used to show differences; frequently, we use an adjective or adverb and *than*.

The comparative form (*-er* or *more*) emphasizes and increases the meaning of an adjective or adverb when two persons, places, things, or ideas are compared.

(234) Marie types 65 words per minute, but Paul types 75 words per minute.
Paul types *faster than* Marie.
(235) Her typewriter is *more expensive than* his.

Another form is used in order to de-emphasize and decrease the meaning: *less* + the positive form of the adjective or adverb.

(236) His typewriter is *less expensive than* hers.

Note: Although the construction with *less* is a type of comparative, we do not use the comparative form of an adjective or adverb.

(237) X Marie types less *faster* than Paul.
(238) Marie doesn't type as fast as Paul.

Note: Comparative structures are not formed with *that*.

(239) X Marie types less fast *that* Paul.

Exercise

Complete each sentence with a comparative form of the adjective or adverb; or use the comparative of a quantifier.

1. Marie is home today because she's sick, but Ronald is in the hospital. Ronald must be _(sick) sicker than_ Marie.
2. Jose received his passport in three days, while Alonso waited almost two weeks. Jose had to wait ___(long)___ Alonso did.
3. A watch made of steel is much ___(practical)___ one made of gold and diamonds.
4. A personal check for $50 is not ___(convenient)___ a travelers check for $50.
5. I learn new vocabulary words___(slowly)___ I learn new grammar rules.

D4 Comparative Meaning: Parallelism

The comparative form of an adjective or adverb tells us that the message is about two persons, places, things, or ideas. The second one is introduced by the word *as* (*as . . . as* or *so . . . as*) or the word *than*.

Incomplete Comparisons

The speaker or writer must state both people, things or ideas which are being compared, unless it is clear within the context of the conversation. Without such a statement, the message may be unclear as in example 240.

(240) This cereal tastes better.

Example 240 is unclear because we do not know what the cereal is being compared to. Does the cereal taste better than another cereal, better than it used to taste, or better than cardboard?

Example 241 shows another type of ambiguity.

(241) I like Mary more than Paul.

This sentence has two possible meanings. It may mean,

(242) I like Mary more than I like Paul.

or

(243) I like Mary more than Paul likes Mary.
        I like Mary more than Paul does.

Parallelism

When making comparisons it is important to compare two things of the same type. For example, what is being compared in example 244?

(244) X The distance from New York to London is less than Honolulu.

Obviously the writer of this sentence did not mean to compare a city to a distance—but that is what he or she said. Example 245 presents the comparison clearly.

(245) The distance from New York to London is less than the distance from New York to Honolulu.

When two things can logically be compared they are called **parallel**. Logical parallelism is supported by grammatical parallelism. For instance, the comparison in example 245 has the following two parts, and the parts have the same grammatical structures:

(246) noun   prepositional phrase
     the distance   from New York to London
     the distance   from New York to Honolulu

The comparison in example 247 is not logically clear and not grammatically parallel.

(247) X Alice's typewriter was more expensive than Paul.

This sentence presents a comparison between the price of a typewriter and the price of a person. The following two sentences present the comparison with correct parallelism.

(248) Alice's typewriter was more expensive than Paul's typewriter (was).
(249) Alice's typewriter was more expensive than Paul's (typewriter was).

Parallelism and Form of Pronouns

The choice of pronoun forms can affect the meaning of the comparison.

(250) I like Mary more than *he*.
(251) I like Mary more than *him*.

The choice of the subjective case *he* or the objective case *him* depends on the meaning of the statement. This is clearer if we look at the more complete statements.

175

(252) I like Mary more than *he* likes Mary.
(253) I like Mary more than I like *him*.

The choice of the pronoun form *his* is the correct one in the following comparison:

(254) Alice's typewriter is more expensive than *Paul's*.
(255) Alice's typewriter is more expensive than *his*.

The pronoun form *he* could be used only in a discussion of buying Paul, and the pronoun form *him* could not be used at all.

Expand the statement in order to determine the correct form of the pronoun to use (see examples 252 and 253). It is clear which forms of the pronouns should be used because the meaning of the statement is clear. (See Chapter 2, page 62.)

Note: Some people always use the objective case form of pronouns after *as* and *than*.

(256) X He types as fast as *me*.
(257) X But he can not type faster than *her*.

This usage is informal and often confusing. In order to determine the pronoun to use, expand the statement.

(258) He types as fast as *I* (type).
(259) But he can not type faster than *she* (types).

Note: The phrase *as . . . as can be* does not present a comparison. This phrase should be considered as an emphasizer. (See Chapter 4, page 165.)

Note: Although we are discussing many typewriters, the comparative form *more expensive* is correct in the following example.

(260) This typewriter is more expensive than any other in the store.

We are comparing two typewriters at a time: this typewriter and typewriter #2, this typewriter and typewriter #3, etc.

Exercise

If the sentence is correct, write **OK**. If there is a mistake in parallelism, write **X** and correct the mistake.

____X____ **1.** Alan's bank is much closer than Mary. *Mary's*

_____ **2.** Mary has to travel about two miles more than Alan.

_____ **3.** It is less important to learn grammar rules than to practice the language.

_____ **4.** It is less important to learn grammar rules than practicing the language.

_____ **5.** Did they meet Robert sooner than she?

Exercise

Expand the sentences in order to make the parallelism very clear.   *I spoke to*

1. I spoke to him earlier than ᵥher.
2. I spoke to him earlier than she.
3. This jacket looks better with these pants than those.
4. Did Rafael do better or worse on the test than Antonio?
5. Rafael studied as long as Antonio.

D5 Superlative Meaning

The **superlative form** is used when the evaluation involves three or more people, places, things, or ideas: one is different from the others. ·

The superlative form (-*est* or *most*) emphasizes and increases the meaning of an adjective or adverb.

> (261) Marie types 65 words per minute, Paul types 75 words per minute, and Ann types 80 words per minute. Ann types (the) *fastest* of the three typists.
> (262) IIcr typewriter is the *most expensive* one that I've ever seen.

Another form is used in order to de-emphasize and decrease the meaning: *least* + positive form of the adjective or adverb.

> (263) Paul's typewriter is the *least expensive* of those that he saw.

The superlative form of an adjective or adverb joins two parts of a statement: (1) the one that is superlative and (2) all those that were included in the evaluation. For instance, example 263 includes (1) Paul's typewriter and (2) all the typewriters that he saw.

In order to be clear, a superlative statement must provide both pieces of information. If a statement does not have

177

both pieces, the receiver of the message may be confused.

(264) John types (the) *fastest*.

Does example 264 involve an evaluation of John and other people? Which other people?

Exercise

Complete each sentence, using superlative forms.

Length			
	inch	=	2.54 centimeters
	foot	=	12 inches
	meter	=	1.094 yards
	yard	=	3 feet

1. An inch is (short) *the shortest* length of the four in the chart.

2. _____ is _____ (long) _____ one in the chart.

Weight			
	gram	=	0.035 ounce
	kilo	=	2.2 pounds
	ounce	=	31.1 grams
	pound	=	16 ounces

3. A kilo is _____ (heavy) _____ of the four weights shown in the chart.

4. _____ is the _____ (light) _____ one in the chart.

Quantity			
	liter	=	1.06 quarts
	pint	=	0.47 liter
	quart	=	2 pints

5. A _____ of milk will be_____
   (expensive) _____ of the three quantities shown.

E PREPOSITIONAL PHRASES

E1 Prepositional Phrases: Form

A prepositional phrase has two parts: a preposition and an object of the preposition.

The preposition is the first part of the prepositional phrase. It can be a simple one-word preposition or a complex preposition with two, three, or four parts.

Prepositional phrase

(265) He leaves his house *at* 7:30 each morning.

Prepositional phrase

(266) He leaves then *because of* his long trip.

Prepositional phrase

(267) He lives in a suburb *in spite of* his long commute.

E2 Simple and Complex Prepositions

Simple Prepositions (and some complex alternates)

aboard	about	above
across	after	against
along	alongside (of)	amid F
amidst F	among	amongst F
apropos (of) F	around	as
at	atop F	barring F
before	behind	below
beneath	beside	besides
between	beyond	but
by	concerning	considering
despite	down	during
except (for)	excluding	following
for	from	in
including	inside (of)	into
less	(un)like	minus
near	notwithstanding F	of
off (of)	on	onto
opposite	out (of)	outside (of)
over	past	per
pending F	plus	regarding
round (about)	since	than I
through	throughout	till
to	toward(s)	under
underneath	until	unto F
up	upon F	versus
via W	with	within
without		

F = very formal
I   = very informal
W = written only

Complex Prepositions

Complex prepositions are made up of two, three, or four separate words; however, they should be considered as one unit: all the parts must be used. For example, *because of* is a complex preposition.

(268) X He leaves then *because* the long trip to work.

Example 268 is incorrect: *because* is not a preposition; therefore, it can not be at the beginning of a prepositional phrase.

according to	across from	along with
apart from	as for	as to
aside from	away from	because of
but for	by means of	by way of
down from	due to	except for
in accordance with	in addition to	in aid of
(in) back of		in case of
in care of	in / on > behalf of	in favor of
in front of		in need of
in place of	in charge of	
in relation to	in lieu of	in / with > regard to
in (the) face of	in quest of	
instead of		
on top of	in respect < of / to	in spite of
together with	in view of	insofar as
	next to	on account of
	owing to	regardless of
	up to	for the sake of

Object of the Preposition

The second part of a prepositional phrase is the object of the preposition. The object of the preposition is a noun or noun-equivalent. (See Chapter 2, page 57.)

noun

(269) She does not trust answers from machines.
(270) She does not trust answers from

Noun phrase

over-confident people who respond very quickly.

The object of a preposition can be an entire clause.

Clause

(271) She is interested in what others have considered.

The object of a preposition can be a gerund (the simple form of the verb + *-ing*).

Gerund phrase

(272) She is interested in learning new ideas.

The object of a preposition can be a pronoun (see Chapter 2, page 61).

(273) She is interested in *them*.

Note: A pronoun *object* of a preposition is an *object* form (see Chapter 2, pages 61-62). The object forms are *me, you, him, her, it, us,* and *them;* they are used regardless of the number of objects in the phrase.

Examples 274, 275, and 276 are incorrect.

(274) X To *I*, it seemed like a good idea.
(275) X To John and *I*, it seemed like a good idea.
(276) X It seemed like a good idea to Alice and *he*.

Exercise

Put parentheses around the prepositional phrases.

1. (In the United States) university students can choose the courses that they want to take.
2. In addition to the courses required for a major field, there are others called "electives."
3. Students choose their courses before each semester.
4. They choose among the required courses.
5. Along with them, students choose a few electives.
6. Some students are careless about choosing electives.
7. They may choose from a wide variety of courses that interest them.

8. They should think about what they need for graduation.
9. Toward the end of their education, they may not have chosen the required courses.
10. There may not be much that they can do about it and they will not be able to graduate on time.

E4 **Prepositional Phrases: Uses**

Prepositional phrases have the same uses as adjectives and adverbs: they answer questions like *which one(s)*, *what kind of*, *how, how often, when, where, why, to what extent.*

Because prepositional phrases are units, the noun or pronoun object can not be the subject of a verb.

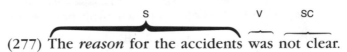

(277) The *reason* for the accidents was not clear.

In example 277, the verb form is *was* because it agrees with the noun *reason,* which is singular. Example 278 is not correct: the verb agrees with the wrong noun; the noun *accidents* is part of the prepositional phrase *for the accidents.*

(278) X The *reason* for the accidents were not clear.

Exercise

Underline the prepositional phrases and identify each one as an adjective-equivalent (**adj.**) or an adverb-equivalent (**adv.**).

adv 1. On Monday morning, Alexis arrived in class late.
_____2. It was his first class of the day.
_____3. He walked into class, but said nothing.
_____4. Going to the nearest desk, he sat down.
_____5. He tried not to interrupt the activity of the class.
_____6. After he put his books under his desk, he opened his notebook in front of him.
_____7. In American classrooms, a late student does not say anything when arriving.
_____8. A student next to him can quickly tell him what has happened.
_____9. After class, he can get more complete information about what he missed.

F **ADJECTIVES AND ADVERBS:
SPECIAL PROBLEMS**

1. *Actual* and *actually*

These words do not mean *now, at this time, at the present time;* they mean *real, true, really, truly.*

> (279) Do not think only of the purchase price of the car. The *actual* cost also includes maintenance, insurance, and fuel.
>
> (280) The car may only cost $3,000, but you may actually have to pay twice that amount when you include upkeep and insurance.

2. *In time* and *on time*

On time means *at the indicated moment.*

> (281) The plane left *on time*—exactly at 9:30, as the schedule indicated.

In time means *before the indicated moment.*

> (282) Fortunately, we had gotten to the airport *in time.* The heavy traffic had delayed us, but we did not miss our flight.

Frequently, *in time* is used to mean that there was enough time to do something before an indicated time.

> (283) We got to the airport *in time* to pick up our tickets before our scheduled departure.

3. In compound adjectives consisting of a number and a countable noun, notice the differences in form of the number and the following countable noun.

> (284) The book cost ten dollars.
>
> (285) It was a ten-dollar book.

When we want to use a compound adjective (example 285) instead of a number followed by the plural form of the countable noun (example 284), the form changes: a number, a hyphen, and a singular form of the noun (see Chapter 7, page 277).

4. *Downtown* and *(at) home*

The adverb *downtown* does not appear with a preposition.

> (286) They had to commute downtown to work.

The following phrases do not occur: ✗ *at downtown,* ✗ *in downtown,* ✗ *to downtown.*

To answer where, use *at home* or *home.* To answer where to, use *home* (not ✗ *to home*).

> (287) He was *(at) home* when I called him.
> (288) He went *home* because he was sick.
> (289) ✗ He went *to home* because he was sick.

5. Measurement with and without *per*

The preposition *per* is used for statements of measurement and distribution.

> (290) They traveled 500 miles *per* day.
> (291) It cost $5.00 *per* pound.

The same type of statement can be made without *per,* but with a determiner in front of the noun.

> (292) They traveled 500 miles *each* day.
> (293) It cost $5.00 *a* pound.

Exercise

If the sentence is correct, write **OK**. If it is incorrect, write **X** and correct it.

_____✗____ **1.** He lived in Ottawa before; actually *now* he is living in Miami.

_____ **2.** I arrived on campus on time to have breakfast before my 9:00 class.

_____ **3.** After buying a fifty-five-dollar book, he had just enough money to get home.

_____ **4.** Did you go shopping to downtown?

_____ **5.** No one ever expected gold to be $750 an ounce.

Chapter 5
Contents

Chapter 5

5 *Combining Sentences*

A *SIMPLE SENTENCES*

Some sentences in English have only one clause. These are called **simple sentences**. For example, the first two sentences in this paragraph are simple sentences.

A clause that can stand alone as a complete and correct sentence is called an **independent clause**. We can write it with a capital letter at the beginning and a period, question mark, or exclamation point at the end.

Exercise

There are 10 simple sentences in the passage. Indicate them with beginning capital letters and appropriate end punctuation.

~~a~~ A university is a group of colleges many universities have a college of arts and sciences and a college of engineering colleges sometimes have other names two examples are a graduate school and a school of medicine universities are usually large

the size of a school is important to a student some students prefer large schools others prefer small schools which do you prefer each student must answer this important question

B **COMPOUND SENTENCES**

A **compound sentence** contains two or more independent clauses. Each of the clauses could be a separate, simple sentence; the writer or speaker has brought the clauses together because the ideas are connected or related in some way.

> (1) We observe many national holidays, and we celebrate a few religious ones, too.

Example 1 has two thoughts about holidays. We could put them into separate sentences, with a period after *holidays* and a capital letter at the begining of the next sentence.

The ideas in a compound sentence are equal in importance; we know this because each one is expressed as an independent clause. (If the speaker or writer wants to indicate that one idea is more important than another, he will use a **complex sentence**. See Chapter 5, page 210.) When two ideas or clauses are equal in importance, they are called **coordinate**.

B1 **Compound Sentences: Form**

A compound sentence has three features:

1. Two or more independent clauses
2. A coordinate conjunction (for example, *and* or *but*) or a semicolon between the independent clauses
3. A comma after each clause, except before a semicolon or at the end of the sentence (where there is a period).

> (2) Independence Day is a national holiday, but Easter is a religious holiday.
> (3) Independence Day is a national holiday; Easter is a religious holiday; New Year's Day is neither national nor religious.

Example 2 has two independent clauses. They are connected with the coordinate conjunction *but*; there is a comma after the first clause. Example 3 is also a compound sentence. It has three independent clauses connected with semicolons; there are no commas in this sentence. (See also Chapter 7, page 279.)

Exercise

Punctuate the following sentences. Use a comma or semi-

189

colon in each compound sentence. Do not add punctuation to simple sentences.

1. In the U.S., we celebrate religious and national holidays, but there are more national ones.
2. The biggest religious holiday is Christmas (December 25) the biggest national one is Independence Day (July 4).
3. Most holidays have typical celebrations or observations.
4. We have a large feast on Thanksgiving (in November) and we remember the dead on Memorial Day (in May).
5. We celebrate New Year's with a party on December 31 and we often spend January 1 resting.
6. Independence Day is a day for picnics and other outdoor activities.
7. Some holidays are always on a particular day of the week the others change days.
8. For example, Labor Day is the first Monday in September and Thanksgiving is the fourth Thursday in November.
9. We celebrate Labor Day on a three-day weekend and Thanksgiving Day gives some people a four-day weekend.
10. Some holidays are celebrated all over the country but some are observed only regionally.

B2 Compound Sentences: Coordinate Conjunctions

Ideas are brought together in a compound sentence because they are related. There are four different relationships that coordinate conjunctions in compound sentences signal to the reader or hearer.

Meanings	Coordinate conjunction
1. addition	*and*
	not only . . . but { *also* ... *too*
2. choice	*or*
	either . . . or
	nor
	neither . . . nor

Meanings	Coordinate conjunction
3. contrast	*but*
	yet
4. cause-and-effect or result	*for* (cause)
	so (effect or result)

In order to make the message clear, the speaker or writer will use the coordinate conjunction which shows his idea clearly.

> (4) Today is a holiday, *and* we are in school.
> (5) Today is a holiday, *but* we are in school.

Examples 4 and 5 are correct in grammar and punctuation. However, it is more difficult to understand the speaker's point in example 4 because it is hard to see the connection between the two ideas expressed. Because holidays are not school days, the connection between the two ideas is clearly expressed with *but*, not with *and*.

Note: The coordinate conjunctions *not only*, *neither*, and *nor* are negatives. Since they appear at the beginning of a clause, that clause must have a rearranged word order (see Chapter 6, page 254).

> (6) *Not only* is there a parade this afternoon, but there is also a fireworks display tonight.
> (7) *Neither* have the armies stopped their fighting, *nor* have they agreed to discuss a cease-fire.

Note: The coordinate conjunctions *so* and *for* must come after the ideas that they explain.

> (8) X For it was snowing, there was no parade.
> (9) There was no parade, *for* it was snowing.

Exercise

Make compound sentences. Use the coordinate conjunctions that show the relationships clearly, and use correct punctuation. Use **and**, **or**, **but**, or **so**.

1. We tried to make plane reservations for our vacation. It was too late. *We tried to make plane reservations for our vacation, but it was too late.*

2. We could not get plane reservations. We discussed traveling by car.

3. It would be less comfortable to travel by car. We would not be able to spend as much time at our destination.
4. We could change our minds and decide to take our vacation in July. We could postpone it until later in the year.
5. We discussed it all day Sunday. We could not come to a final decision.

Exercise

Make compound sentences, using the coordinate conjunctions that show relationships clearly. Use **not only** . . . **but also**, **either** . . . **or**, **yet**, or **for**.

1. Each person will bring something. It would be too expensive for one person to provide refreshments for everyone.
2. David will make his famous popcorn. He will bring soft drinks.
3. Many people volunteered to bring food. Not many offered to bring drinks.
4. Some will have to change their minds. We will not have enough to drink.
5. We will have too much to eat. We will have too little to drink.

B3 Compound Sentences: Ellipsis

Sometimes there is information that is repeated in a compound sentence.

(10) My classmates went to the parade, and I went to the parade.

Because we feel that there is unnecessary repetition of information in example 10, we restate the sentence.

(11) My classmates and I went to the parade.

This process is called **ellipsis**. Ellipsis is the shortening of a sentence by the elimination of repeated information. When ellipsis is done correctly, the sentence is shorter, but the full meaning is still clear. Thus a reader or listener could expand the sentence and reconstruct the longer one.

(12) The result must be equal to or greater than 90%.

Example 12 is a shortened sentence. Because the ellipsis was done correctly, we can expand the sentence.

(13) The result must be equal to 90%, or it must be greater than 90%.

In addition to the type of ellipsis shown in example 12, there is another type of ellipsis, shown in example 14. (See Chapter 5, page 198.)

(14) My classmates went to the parade, and I did, too.

Compound Structures

One important use of shortening is to make a simple sentence from a compound sentence.

(15) compound sentence
It was cold, and it was very windy.
(16) simple sentence after removing repeated information
It was cold and very windy.

When ellipsis results in a simple sentence, the sentence will have a **compound structure**; that is, there will be a list of two or more items. The compound structure can be the subject, the verb, the predicate, objects, prepositional phrases, or any other structure.

(17) compound subject
My classmates and I went to the parade.
(18) compound predicate
After the parade, we *went to a restaurant and ate lunch*.
(19) compound verb
We *waited and talked* until the end of the parade.
(20) compound direct object
We met *Annette and her sister* at the restaurant.
(21) compound prepositional phrases
We discussed going *to the movies or to a restaurant*.

Coordinate Conjunctions

Compound structures consist of (1) lists of two or more items, (2) coordinate conjunctions, and (3) sometimes commas.

1. Each list has items of equal importance (which is why the structure is considered compound).
2. A coordinate conjunction joins the items in a list or joins two items, as in example 22.

(22) I needed a raincoat *or* an umbrella.

Some coordinate conjunctions appear in pairs, as in example 23.

(23) I needed *either* a raincoat *or* an umbrella.

The coordinate conjunctions that are used in compound structures are: *and/or, (both . . .) and, not only . . . but also, (either . . .) or, (neither . . .) nor, but,* and *yet.* When the list has more than two items, we have only one conjunction, which is between the last two items.

(24) I took gloves, a hat, *and* a muffler.

Note: It is possible to have several conjunctions in a list, but it is unusual.

(25) I wore gloves and a hat and a muffler.

Example 25 would be used when a person wants to stress that he wore many things: the repeated *and* makes the list seem very long.

3. When the compound structure is a list of three or more items, it is called a **series**. A series is made up of a coordinate conjunction between the last two items and commas between the other items (see Chapter 7, page 282).

(26) I wore gloves, a hat, *and* a muffler.

You can also write the series without a comma before the coordinate conjunction.

(27) I wore gloves, a hat *and* a muffler.

Both examples are correct. Choose one style or the other, but be consistent.

Note: Example 28 is not correct.

(28) X We went to a restaurant, and ate lunch.

The list is not a series, since it has only two items. Therefore, the use of a comma is incorrect.

Note: There is no comma after the items in a series.

(29) X I wore gloves, a hat, and a muffler, when I went out this morning.

Example 29 is incorrect; the comma is not used after the series of three items.

Exercise

These sentences have been shortened by ellipsis. Expand them, reconstructing the longer compound sentences. Use correct punctuation in the compound sentences.

1. They wanted to go there early, but I did not.

   They wanted to go there early, but I did not want to go there early.

2. They wanted to go there early and stay for the whole parade.
3. I had a slight cold and did not want it to get worse.
4. I was going to a party that evening, and Kay was, too.
5. We would go downtown early, but stay only two hours.

Exercise

Use ellipsis to shorten these compound sentences. Write simple sentences with compound structures. Use correct punctuation.

1. The fireworks were supposed to start at dusk, and they were supposed to last for an hour. *The fireworks were supposed to start at dusk and last for one hour.*
2. We knew that it would be crowded, and we knew that we would have to be there early if we wanted good seats.
3. David drove to my house, and Teresa drove to my house.
4. I drove my car, and I took them to the university.
5. People met at the faculty parking lot, they met near the gymnasium, or they met next to the bookstore.
6. They talked for a little while, and then they formed car pools to get to the fireworks.
7. We saved money, and we saved a little time.
8. We drove fewer cars, and we spent less money for gasoline.
9. We drove a few cars, but we spent a lot of time searching for parking places.
10. Our trip to the fireworks was cheaper than it might have been, and it was more pleasant than if we each had gone alone.

195

B4 **Parallelism**

When a compound sentence is shorted by ellipsis, there is a new, simple sentence with a list. As we saw in Chapter 5, page 193, that list has two or more items joined with a coordinate conjunction. A coordinate conjunction is used because the items in the list are equal in importance.

Grammar structure helps the reader or hearer to understand that the items in a list are equal. The items should have the same grammar structure: all nouns, all adverbs, all predicates, all prepositional phrases, etc. The use of the same grammar structure is called **parallelism**.

> (30) X I like parties and to read good books for relaxation.

Example 30 is not correct, because it does not have grammatical parallelism where it should. The compound direct object (DO) has two parts, *parties* and *to read good books,* joined by the coordinate conjunction *and.* But the first item is a noun; the second one is an infinitive phrase. Example 31 has correct grammatical parallelism.

> (31) I like to go to parties and to read good books for relaxation.

One way to check parallelism is to take the items out of the sentence and to write them in a regular list.

> (32) I like   1. parties   for relaxation.
>   2. to read good books

This way it is easier to see that the items in the list are not parallel.

Exercise

Check the parallelism in these sentences. If necessary, rewrite each sentence for yourself, putting the items in a regular list. If the items are grammatically parallel, write **OK**. If the sentence is incorrect, write **X** and correct it.

___X___ **1.** She liked to play tennis, swimming, and television

She liked to play tennis, swim, and
soap operas.

watch television soap operas.

_____ **2.** After the lecture, we went to the library, the cafeteria, and to our dormitory.

_____ **3.** Andre knew that Thanksgiving is in November and that Memorial Day is in May.

_____ **4.** We had to learn the major holidays, their dates, and how they are celebrated for our test.

_____ **5.** We had to learn the major holidays, their dates, and their celebrations for our test.

_____ **6.** We had to learn what the major holidays are, when they occur, and how they are celebrated for our test.

_____ **7.** Typically, we eat breakfast in the morning, having lunch around noon, and dinner at six.

_____ **8.** The evening meal is called either "dinner" or "supper."

B5 Compound Subjects and Subject-Verb Agreement

When a sentence has a compound subject, it is especially important to check the subject-verb agreement. For example, when two or more items are joined with *and,* or *not only . . . but,* the subject is plural, and so is the verb.

(33) Not only my books but also my calculator *were* found in the auditorium.

(34) Clarice and Diane *are* not going to the parade.

Note: Sometimes *and* connects several parts of one idea. In this case, the verb is singular because the meaning of the subject is singular.

(35) The analysis and evaluation of reports of UFOs *is* very difficult.

In example 35, there is one process which includes both analysis and evaluation.

When the coordinate conjunction expresses a choice (*or* or *nor*), the last item is the one to use to determine subject-verb agreement.

(36) My *roommates are* going to drive to the parade.

(37) My roommates or *Frank is* going to drive to the parade.

(38) My roommates, Frank, or *I am* going to drive to the parade.

197

Some people feel that such sentences sound strange. They use another type of ellipsis to avoid such sentences, keeping the information separated in different clauses (see Chapter 5, page 198).

Exercise

Circle the correct verb form.

1. You, I, or both of us together am/are going to have to fix this dent.
2. When Frank lent us his car, he said that you and I was/were responsible for it.
3. Either you or Paul has/have damaged the car, because I have not driven it.
4. Both you and Paul is/are careful drivers; nevertheless, the car needs repairing.
5. Neither you nor Paul admits/admit damaging the car.

B6 Compound Sentences: Ellipsis in the Second Clause

Ellipsis can be used to shorten a compound sentence by removing repeated information from the second clause.

(39) compound sentence with repeated information
My classmates went to the parade, and I went to the parade.
(40) compound sentence without repeated information
My classmates went to the parade, and I did, too.
(41) compound sentence without repeated information
My classmates went to the parade, and so did I.

Although the sentence has been shortened, it is still a compound sentence. Therefore, it has a comma after the first independent clause.

This type of ellipsis is used when we present a comparison, a contrast, or a choice between two actions or situations. For instance, in examples 40 and 41, we are presenting the similarity between my classmates' action and mine. In this type of sentence, the first clause is not affected. It is the second clause that is shortened by ellipsis.

Note: When the second clause is shortened with *so,* the auxiliary comes before the subject. Compare examples 40 and 41 (see Chapter 5, page 202).

There are three important pieces of information in the second part of these sentences:

1. A coordinate conjunction that presents the meaning between the clauses;
2. An indication of which person(s), place(s), thing(s), or idea(s) are involved;
3. An indication of whether the second action or situation is like or unlike the first one.

The coordinate conjunctions in shortened compound sentences signal three meanings:

Meanings	Coordinate Conjunctions
1. Comparison: similarity	*and* *neither...nor* *nor*
2. Contrast: dissimilarity	*but* *yet*
3. Choice	*or* *either...or*

The second and third pieces of information are expressed in a short clause called a **tag statement**. A tag statement has a subject plus an auxiliary verb or a form of the verb *be;* if it is negative, it also has *not* or *n't*. A tag statement is formed like this:

$$\text{Subject(S)} \ (\text{or } \textit{there}) \ + \ \left\{ \begin{array}{l} \text{Vaux} \\ \textit{be} \end{array} \right\} \ + \ \left\{ \begin{array}{l} \textit{not} \\ \textit{n't} \end{array} \right\}$$

(42) We thought there was a fire, but there wasn't.

A tag statement is a short version of a complete statement sentence; it is part of the sentence pattern. We look at the complete statement sentence in order to decide how to form the correct tag statement.

The subject in a tag statement is a noun or a noun-equivalent.

(43) Our class went to the parade, but *David* did not.
(44) Our class went to the parade, and *theirs* did too.

Sometimes a tag statement is a short form of a statement with the expletive *there* (see Chapter 6, page 267). In this case, the expletive *there* is used in the subject position.

199

(45) We did not think that there would be any snow, but there was.

The verb form in a tag statement is one of the following: *is, am, are, was, were, have, has, had, do, does, did, will, would, shall, should, can, could, may,* or *might.*

To form sentences with tag statements, follow the steps below.

1. If the verb has 2 or more words, divide the sentence after the first word in the verb phrase.

   (46) I'm going to the party, and you are too.

2. If the verb has only one word and if the word is a form of the verb *be,* divide the sentence after the verb.

   (47) Marie is a good student, but Fran isn't.

3. If the verb has only one word, and the word is not a form of the verb *be,* divide the sentence after the subject and look at the tense of the verb and the meaning of the subject.

   a. If the verb is in the past tense, add the auxiliary *did* after the subject.
   (48) They told me to go, and I did.
   b. If the subject is *he, she, it,* or an equivalent, add the auxiliary *does* after the subject.
   (49) Tom thinks he works hard, but he *doesn't.*
   c. In all other cases, add the auxiliary *do* after the subject.
   (50) Tom thinks the work is hard, and I do too.

If the statement is negative, *not* or *n't* will follow the verb form.

   (51) They've skiied but we haven't.
   (52a) I had a good time, and Marie had a good time too.

Does Step 1 apply to 52a? No, it does not; the verb does not have 2 or more words. Does Step 2 apply? No, it does not; the one-word verb is not a form of the verb *be.* Does Step 3a apply? Yes, it does; the verb is in the past tense.

   (52b) I had a good time, and Marie *did* too.

The second clause may also have other words to make the comparison, contrast, or choice clear.

(53)   He cannot do it for you today, but he can tomorrow.

Example 53 has the adverb *tomorrow* so that the contrast between the situations in the two clauses is clear.

Exercise

Put in appropriate coordinate conjunctions to show the relationship between the two clauses.

1. Some banks are open on Saturday mornings, __but__ mine is not.
2. Some banks are open late on Friday evenings, _____ mine is too.
3. We need some money. _____ you can cash a check today, _____ I can tomorrow.
4. Samantha has not decided whether to open a checking account, _____ has Edgar.
5. Samantha does not have a checking account, _____ I do.

Exercise

Complete the tag statements.

1. Paul began studying English last year, but I __didn't__.
2. I have studied English for three years, and Jose _____ too.
3. I am not in Jose's class, but Paul _____.
4. Paul knows English fairly well, and Jose _____ also.
5. I would not expect a student to be in an intermediate-level class after one year of study, yet Paul _____.
6. Either Jose does not study very much, or Paul _____.
7. Jose practiced English when he visited Toronto, and we _____ too.
8. There are many opportunities to practice it there, but there _____ at home.
9. I do not speak it very comfortably, but they _____.
10. Paul and Jose will study in the United States, and I _____ too.

B7 Compound Sentences: Comparison With Ellipsis

When the sentence expresses a comparison, the comparison may be shown two ways: (1) the coordinate conjunction *and;* and (2) an emphasizing word in the second clause.

(54) I had a good time, *and* Marie did *too.*

The emphasizing words reinforce the fact that the two situations are similar. Another use of these words is to emphasize information in the second clause. This is done with inverted word order (*and so did Marie*). Emphasizing words and their uses are shown in the following chart and are illustrated in examples 55, 56, 57, and 58.

	Usual Word Order	Inverted Word Order
Affirmative clauses	*too, also*	*so*
Negative clauses	*either*	*neither*

(55) affirmative clauses; usual word order: *too* or *also* comes at the end of the clause
I had a good time, and Marie did *too.*

(56) affirmative clauses; inverted word order: *so* comes at the beginning of the clause
I had a good time, and *so did Marie.*

Note: With inverted word order, subject (S) comes at the end of the sentence (see Chapter 6, page 257).

(57) negative clauses; usual word order: *either* comes at the end of the clause
Phil did not have a good time, and Alice didn't *either.*

Note: The negative meaning *either* is different in meaning and placement from the choice *either.*

(58) negative clauses; inverted word order: *neither* comes at the beginning of the clause
Phil did not have a good time, and *neither did Alice.*

The inverted word order emphasizes the meaning of negation (see Chapter 6, page 255).

Note: When the negative word *neither* is used in a comparison, the verb after it is affirmative. Example 58 has *did* (instead of *didn't,* as in example 57).

Exercise

Combine the independent clauses to make a compound sentence. Use **and** and the emphasizing word given, and use ellipsis in the second clause. Also use correct punctuation.

1. This exercise is about ellipsis. The next one is about *This exercise is about ellipsis, and the next one is too.* ellipsis. *too*

2. This exercise will take only a few minutes. The next one will take only a few minutes. *so*
3. I do not mind doing exercises. Marsha does not mind doing exercises. *neither*
4. I do not mind doing exercises. Marsha does not mind doing exercises. *either*
5. I can finish quickly. Marsha can finish quickly. *too*

Exercise

Combine the independent clauses to make a compound sentence. Compare or contrast the two actions or situations, using **and** or **but**. Use ellipsis in the second clause. Use negative and emphasizing words where necessary.

1. An inch is a measure of length. A pound is a measure of weight. *An inch is a measure of length, but a pound is not.*

2. An ounce is less than a kilo. A pound is less than a kilo.
3. A liter of gasoline is not cheap. A gallon of gasoline is not cheap.
4. A month is a measure of revolution of a heavenly body. A year is a measure of revolution of a heavenly body.
5. A quart of milk costs less than a dollar. A gallon of milk costs more than a dollar.
6. The metric system does not take long to learn. The English system takes long to learn.
7. They do not need to learn the English system. We need to learn the English system.
8. John has not studied the metric system. He will study the metric system.

9. I have been encouraging John to study. Albert has been
encouraging him to study.

Compound Sentences with Semicolons: Form

When two clauses are connected with a semicolon, the writer is indicating that the two ideas are closely related. However, it may not be clear to the reader how they are related,
because the meaning relationship is not explicitly stated.

(59) Thanksgiving Day is near the end of November;
there are many parades then.

Example 59 is correct in grammar and punctuation. It would
be clearer if the reader knew the meaning relationship between the two parts. Examples 60 and 61 show two
possibilities.

(60) Thanksgiving Day is near the end of November;
nevertheless, there are many parades then. (In spite
of the cold weather, there are parades.)

(61) Thanksgiving Day is near the end of November;
therefore, there are many parades then. (There are
many parades, because Christmas is not far away.)

In compound sentences with semicolons, we can show
the relationship between ideas with **sentence connectors**
or **transitions**. These words and phrases provide a connection between ideas.

Transitions can appear at the beginning, middle, or end
of a clause. The strongest and clearest place is at the beginning, because it is logical to put the transition word between
the two ideas that are connected. So *nevertheless* and
therefore appear before the second clause in examples 60
and 61. When transitions are used within clauses, they are
separated with one or two commas (see Chapter 7, page
288).

(62) Thanksgiving Day is near the end of November;
there are, *therefore,* many parades then.

Note: When short sentence connectors occur at the beginning or end of a clause, they often appear without commas.

(63) We met at Fred's house; *then* we drove downtown.

Note: A transition can also be used after a period at the
beginning of the next sentence. Although it connects the
ideas in two sentences, grammatically the sentences are
separate.

(64) Thanksgiving Day is near the end of November. *Nevertheless,* there are many parades then.

Exercise

The following compound sentences are missing punctuation. The ideas are connected with transitions (the transitions are underlined). Punctuate the sentences, using semicolons and commas.

1. National and religious holidays are serious in other words they are not mainly for fun. *National and religious holidays are serious; in other words, they are not mainly for fun.*

2. Some other holidays are meant for fun we celebrate them therefore with parties.

3. New Year's Eve (December 31) is mostly for adults on the other hand Halloween (October 31) is for children.

4. Some holidays are designed for specific members of the family we can name Mother's Day and Father's Day in particular .

5. Some people think that these holidays are for the family on the contrary I think they are primarily for business.

6. They are designed to increase purchases for example Father's Day makes people go out and shop in June.

7. June is not an active business month as a matter of fact it is six months away from the most active month for purchases.

8. We all know the reasons for such holidays nevertheless we observe them.

9. They provide reminders for us specifically they remind us to show our love.

10. As a result the business community is happy we are happy too.

B9 Compound Sentences with Semicolons: Meaning Connections

Meanings	Sentence connectors
1. Addition	*also, besides, furthermore, in addition, moreover, too*

Meanings	Sentence connectors
2. Choice	at the same time, else, on the other hand, otherwise
3. Comparison	in the same way, likewise, similarly
4. Contrast	however, in contrast, notwithstanding, on the other hand
5. Correction	instead, on the contrary, rather
6. Dismissal	anyhow, at any rate, in any case, nevertheless, regardless, still
7. Effect or Result	accordingly, as a result, consequently, hence, in that case, therefore, thus
8. Emphasis or Reinforcement	actually, as a matter of fact, indeed, in fact
9. Example	for example, e.g., for instance, in particular, specifically
10. Manner or Means	in that way, thus
11. Place	farther, further, nearby
12. Purpose or Reason	in order to
13. Restatement or Summary	in other words, namely, that is, i.e.
14. Time or Sequence	after a while, afterward(s), before, earlier, first (second, third, etc.), later, meanwhile, next, previously, then

Note: The abbreviations *e.g.* (= for example) and i.e. (= *that is*) are from Latin. They are used in formal writing.

Exercise

Make compound sentences, using semicolons. Show the meaning connections clearly. Use **therefore, for example**, **regardless**, or **meanwhile** in each sentence.

1. We were washing the car. They were mowing the lawn.
   We were washing the car; meanwhile they were mowing the lawn.
2. It started to snow. We decided to stay until the end of the football game.
3. Baseball is a very popular sport in the U.S. In some cities, 50,000 people attend each game.
4. The New Year's Eve party lasted until 6:00 a.m. We decided to stay in bed all day the next day.
5. Some holidays are very popular with children, because they become the center of attention. On Halloween they dress up in costumes.

Exercise

Keep the sentences grammatically separate, but show meaning relationships clearly. Use the sentence connectors **in other words**, **on the contrary**, **in that way**, or **on the other hand**.

1. My friends and I decided to watch the championship game together. We could visit and not miss the most important game of the season. *My friends and I decided to watch the championship game together. In that way we could visit and not miss the most important game of the season.*

2. We could stay home to watch the game comfortably on television. We could go out to the stadium to catch the excitement.

3. We decided to stay home. We chose comfort over excitement.

4. We did not have as much fun. We did not have cold feet and hands.

5. The home team didn't have a good day. They lost 50-0.

B10 Compound Sentences: Common Mistakes

1. One common mistake in writing compound sentences is a **comma splice**. A comma splice occurs when the writer joins two independent clauses with only a comma. (See Chapter 7, page 279.)

    (65) X There was a big parade, we had a good time.

2. Another common mistake in writing compound sentences is a **run-on sentence** or a **fused sentence**. A run-on sentence occurs when the writer does not see that a sentence is made of two ideas of equal importance; the sentence is written as if it had only one independent clause.

    (66) X There was a big parade we had a good time.

3. There are three ways to show the connection between ideas of equal importance. Use one of these ways to correct a comma splice or a run-on sentence.

    (67) comma plus coordinate conjunction (Chapter 5, page 189)
        There was a big parade, *so* we had a good time.
    (68) semicolon (Chapter 5, page 189)
        There was a big parade; we had a good time.
    (69) separate sentences (Chapter 5, page 189)

There was a big parade. *We* had a good time.

Exercise

If the sentence is correct, write **OK**. If the sentence is not correct, identify the mistake: a comma splice (**cs**) or a run-on sentence (**r**).

___*r*___ 1. Americans use first names a lot sometimes this surprises learners of English.

_____ 2. Although first names are used a lot, this does not mean that Americans are friendlier than other people.

_____ 3. They might not know each other well, perhaps they have just met.

_____ 4. The use of a person's last name shows respect the person is older or more important than the speaker.

_____ 5. But the use of the last name also shows that there is a lot of distance between the people.

_____ 6. On the other hand, using first names seems to show that the people are not far apart.

_____ 7. Therefore, they can meet as equals, they can work together.

_____ 8. We must choose either respect and distance or equality it is sometimes a hard choice.

B11 Proportional Statements

Proportional statements are often used as proverbs in English. They are used in order to state an idea that is felt to be a basic truth. For instance, if one person mentions that there are very many people at a party, another person can respond with example 70. Or in a discussion about the building of a bridge, someone comments on the completion of the project; example 71 would be appropriate.

(70) The more, the merrier.
(71) The sooner, the better.

Proportional statements are made of two parts. Each part uses a comparative adjective, adverb, or quantifier; there is a comma between the parts. The meaning relationship is that one part increases or decreases in proportion to the increase or decrease of the other. Example 71 is a reduced version of example 72.

(72) The sooner this bridge is finished, the better it will be for the economy of the region.

Exercise

Match the proportional statements with the situations. Make an appropriate comment or reaction.

    a. The sooner, the better.
    b. The darker the color, the sweeter the fruit.
    c. The more you pay, the more you get.
    d. The bigger they are, the harder they fall.
    e. The more, the merrier.

1. Tom: I'm very disappointed with this shirt, even though I got it on sale.
Claire: When you buy something cheap, you have to remember this: _____ *c* _____.

2. Alberta: It's hard to choose good produce at the store.
Andy: Just remember: _____.

3. Ann: Let's get this job finished. I'm getting bored and tired.
Sue: Yes, let's finish. _____.

4. Philip: Ask them to ride with us. _____.
Alan: How many people can you get in your car?

5. _____. When a worker loses his job, a few people know it; but when a president loses his job, the whole country feels it.

C   COMPLEX SENTENCES

C1   Complex Sentences: Form

Some sentences in English have two types of clauses; these sentences are called **complex sentences**. A complex sentence is a combination of an independent clause and a dependent clause. It is not possible to separate the clauses into different sentences, because a dependent clause can not stand alone as a sentence and must always be connected to an independent clause.

(73) compound sentence: 2 independent clauses with
    , but
    She was tired, but she walked up to the third floor.
(74) complex sentence: independent clause and
    dependent clause

> She walked up to the third floor although she was tired.

(75) compound sentence: 2 independent clauses with a semicolon

> He arrived after 7:00; therefore, we did not have enough time to eat dinner.

(76) complex sentence: dependent clause and independent clause

> Because he arrived after 7:00, we did not have enough time to eat dinner.

Unlike the clauses in a compound sentence, the two clauses in a complex sentence are not equal in importance. Dependent clauses are also called **subordinate clauses**.

The verb tense in the independent clause may influence the verb tense in the dependent or subordinate clause (see Chapter 5, page 228).

Exercise

These sentences have two clause patterns. Some of the sentences have two clauses of equal importance; write **compound**. Write **complex** for the remaining sentences which have one independent clause and one dependent clause.

compound 1. The numbering of floors in a building may seem strange to you at first, but it is not hard.

_____ 2. The ground floor is the floor that you enter directly from the street.

_____ 3. The ground floor is also called the first floor; the floor above the ground floor is the second floor.

_____ 4. The basement is the floor which is under the ground floor.

_____ 5. When you take an elevator three floors up, you are on the fourth floor.

_____ 6. In many other countries, the ground floor is not the first floor; in this country it is.

_____ 7. In those countries, people will arrive on the third floor when they take an elevator three floors up.

_____ 8. You should remember that all floors above ground have numbers.

_____ **9.** Sometimes we do not use the number 13, so that the numbering is not always consecutive.

_____ **10.** Because some people consider the number 13 unlucky, the floors in some tall buildings go from 12 to 14.

C2 **Complex Sentences: Uses of the Dependent Clause**

A dependent or subordinate clause takes one of the parts in the pattern of the independent clause. The dependent clause can be a noun-equivalent (Chapter 2, page 57), an adverb-equivalent (Chapter 4, page 155), or an adjective-equivalent (Chapter 4, page 162).

1. A **noun clause** answers the questions *who(m)* or *what.*

S   V   DO

(77)   Mary knows the answer.

S   V   DO

(78)   Mary knows that a meter is longer than a yard.

What does Mary know? She knows *the answer;* she knows *that a meter is longer than a yard.*

2. An **adverb clause** answers questions like *how, how long, how often, when, where, why,* or *to what extent.*

S   V   Adv.   Adv. clause

(79)   They arrived late because the weather was bad.

Why did they arrive late? They arrived late *because the weather was bad.*

Note: When an adverb clause appears in front of the independent clause, there is a comma after the dependent clause (see Chapter 7, page 285).

(80) Because the weather was bad, they arrived, late.

3. An **adjective clause** answers the questions *which one(s)* or *what kind(s).*

S   V   DO   Adj. clause

(81) He bought a typewriter which was guaranteed.

Which typewriter did he buy? He bought one *which was guaranteed.*

Note: An adjective clause comes after the noun (*typewriter* in example 81) that it describes.

Exercise

Underline each dependent clause and identify its use. Put in a comma if it is required.

adj: adjective clause
adv: adverb clause
noun: noun clause

adj. **1.** People <u>who come from other countries</u> may not
noun know <u>that in the U.S. there is a different idea about being on time.</u>

_____ **2.** If they arrive late they might not realize that they're being judged.

_____ **3.** On the other hand, Americans may not realize
_____ that they are too early when they use their idea of being on time.

_____ **4.** Is your culture's idea of being on time different from the one that is used in the United States?

_____ **5.** Do not be surprised if you receive an invitation with a beginning time and an ending time.

_____ **6.** If you arrive about thirty minutes after the beginning time, that is all right.

_____ **7.** And it is all right if you leave about 45 minutes
_____ after the time which is given as the ending time.

C3 Complex Sentences: Form of the Subordinate Clause

A statement can be used as the subordinate clause in a complex sentence. The subordinate clause is connected to the independent clause with a **subordinate conjunction.** This type of conjunction appears at the beginning of the subordinate clause.

Except for the subordinate conjunction, there is no other grammar signal of a subordinate clause: word order is not changed.

(82) A meter is about 39 inches long.

(83) He figured out that a meter is about 39 inches long.

In example 83, the subordinate conjunction is *that,* and the subordinate clause follows it.

Note: There are two choices for the form of a noun clause with the subordinate conjunction *that.* One choice is shown in example 83: *that,* expressed in writing and in speech. The other choice is shown in example 84: *that* is not used.

(84) He figured out a meter is about 39 inches long.

The following chart shows four relationships and some examples of the subordinate conjunctions that signal them.

Meanings	Adverb subordinate conjunctions
1. Cause	*as, because, provided (that), since, unless, whereas*
2. Contrast	*although, even if, even though, though*
3. Purpose or Reason	*in order that, so (that)*
4. Time or Sequence	*after, as, as soon as, before, each/every time (that), once, until, while*

Note: Do not use two conjunctions in one sentence to show the same relationship.

(85) X Although it was expensive, but we bought it.

Adverb clauses appear before or after the other parts of the independent clause. For instance, in examples 86 and 87, the adverb clause is *after he found the number of inches in a meter.*

(86) After he found the number of inches in a meter, he finished the problem.

(87) He finished the problem after he found the number of inches in a meter.

Although both arrangements are correct, you can see that each one emphasizes different information in the sentence (see Chapter 6, page 272).

Exercise

Combine the clauses into a complex sentence. Use a subordinate conjunction **although, because, before, so that.**

1. It was very sunny. It was quite cold. *although it was very sunny, it was quite cold.*
2. It was cold and rainy. We decided to stay inside all day.
3. We packed our bags Thursday night. We could leave early Friday morning.
4. Paul had studied English for two years. He went to Australia.
5. Paul had studied English for two years. He could read it very well.
6. Paul had studied English for two years. He could not speak it very well.
7. The winter ended in March. We had many bad snowstorms.
8. We had bought some wood. We could build fires in our fireplace.
9. We had bought some wood. We did not use our fireplace very often.
10. We had bought some wood. The price of wood went up.

C4 Complex Sentences: Indirect Questions

When a question is in an independent clause, it is called a **direct question** (example 88); in a dependent clause, it is called an **indirect question** (example 89).

(88) Are you going?
(89) John wants to know if you are going.

Direct and indirect questions have different word orders and different punctuation.

A yes/no question in an independent clause has three distinctive signals (see Chapter 1, page 22):

1. Question word order (see Chapter 1, page 22.)
2. Rising intonation
3. A question mark as end punctuation

(90) *Does* Jack have a car?

A yes/no question in a dependent or subordinate clause does not have any of these signals. The one signal for the indirect yes/no question is the subordinate conjunction *if* or *whether*.

(91) I must know *if* Jack has a car.

Less formal indirect questions have a second signal: the words *or not*. This phrase can be used with either of the subordinate conjunctions; but *whether* allows two possible word orders, while *if* allows only one.

(92) I must know whether or not Jack has a car.
(93) I must know whether Jack has a car or not.
(94) I must know if Jack has a car or not.

This form of yes/no indirect question presents the two choices for the answer: affirmative or negative.
Another choice question is shown in example 95.

(95) I must know if Mary has a car or a motorcycle.

This sentence comes from these sentences:

(96) I must know something. Does Mary have a car or a motorcycle?

Strictly speaking, the direct question is not a yes/no question: it calls for an information answer. However, the indirect question is formed as if it were a yes/no question.

A wh-question in an independent clause has three signals (see Chapter 1, page 19):

1. A question word or phrase at the beginning
2. Question word order
3. A question mark as cnd punctuation

(97) *What* kind of car *does* Jack have*?*

A wh-question in a dependent or subordinate clause has only one of these signals: a question word or phrase at the beginning.

(98) I must know *what* kind of car Jack has.

The end punctuation can be a period as in example 98 or a question mark as in example 99.

(99) Do you know what kind of car Jack has?

Note: A very common mistake is to use question word order in a subordinate clause.

(100) X I must know what kind of car does Jack have.

It is important to remember that the only signal of a question in a subordinate clause—an indirect question—is the introductory word, *if, whether,* or a wh-word.

Exercise

Make sentences that have indirect questions. Use appropriate end punctuation according to the purpose of the independent clause: a period after a statement and a question mark after a question.

1. Find out. Is a liter bigger than a quart?

   Find out if a liter is bigger than a quart.

2. Do you know? Is a liter bigger than a quart?
3. I would like to know this. Is a liter bigger or smaller than a quart?
4. Do you know this? Why has the class started late every day this week?
5. The police want to know this. Who telephoned them about the loud party?
6. They want to find out this information. What are the possibilities of an earthquake here?
7. It would be helpful for you to decide this. At what time of day do you prefer to study?
8. What difference does it make if I decide this? At what time of day do I prefer to study?
9. How can they find out this information? Whom did you speak to after the movie last night?
10. What are your thoughts about this? How can we improve the chances for peace? How can we decrease the occurrence of epidemics?

C5 **Complex Sentences: Wh- Subordinate Clauses**

Uses

Including indirect questions, there are many dependent clauses that begin with wh-words. They are used as noun-equivalents, adjective-equivalents, and adverb-equivalents. Some clauses can be used as two or three different types of equivalents. For instance, examples 101, 102, and 103 have the same wh- subordinate clause.

    (101) noun clause
        I would like to know where John is living now.

(102) adjective clause
>She went to the apartment where John is living now.

(103) adverb clause
>We decided to meet where John is living now.

Form: The wh- signal

Indirect questions and other subordinate clauses beginning with wh-words all have only one grammatical signal: a wh-word or phrase at the beginning.

(104) adjective clause with *whose*
>They were congratulating Mary Ann, whose essay had won the first prize.

(105) noun clause with *how*
>They did not know how hard she had worked on it.

(106) adverb clause with *when*
>When she heard the news, she was surprised and happy.

Question word order is not used in this form.

(107) X They did not know how hard had she worked on it.

C6 Complex Sentences: Adjective Clauses

Form

In order to understand the meaning and form of an adjective clause, we can separate it from the independent clause and make it into an independent clause.

(108) complex sentence with adjective clause
>They were congratulating Mary Ann, whose essay had won the first prize.

(109) two separate sentences
>They were congratulating Mary Ann.
>Her essay had won the first prize.

The sentences in example 109 can be combined because (1) they are related and (2) the relationship is shown by the words *Mary Ann* and *her*.

The process of combination involves substitution; a new word or phrase replaces a word or phrase in an independent clause. This replacing word is called a **relative pronoun**.

The process of making a sentence with an adjective clause has three steps:

1. Substitute a relative pronoun.
2. Move the relative pronoun to the beginning of the clause, if it is not already there. You may move other words in the new wh- phrase too.
3. Put the adjective clause right after the noun that it describes.

Step 1: Substitute possessive *whose* for *her*.
(110a) They were congratulating Mary Ann.

whose
~~Her~~ essay had won the first prize.

Step 2: No move is necessary (110b).

Step 3: Put new clause into independent clause.
(110c) They were congratulating Mary Ann, whose essay had won the first prize.

Step 1: Substitute *which* for *the topic*.
(111a) The topic was the one she liked.

which
We had advised her not to choose ~~the topic.~~

Step 2: Move *which* to the beginning.
(111b) The topic was the one she liked.
which we had advised her not to choose

Step 3: Put new clause into independent clause.
(111c) The topic which we had advised her not to choose was the one she liked.

When the relative pronoun is part of a phrase, there are two possibilities: to move just the pronoun or to move the whole phrase.

Step 1: Substitute *which* for *the topic*.
(112a) The topic was the one she liked.

which
We had warned her about ~~the topic.~~

Step 2: Move *which* to the beginning.
(112b) The topic was the one she liked.
which we had warned her about

Step 3: Put new clause into independent clause.
   (112c) The topic which we had warned her about was the one she liked.

Step 2: Move entire phrase to the beginning.
   (113b) The topic was the one she liked.
        about which we had warned her

Step 3: Put new clause into independent clause.
   (113c) The topic about which we had warned her was the one she liked.

Relative Pronouns

	People	Places, things, and ideas	Either
Subject	who	which	that
Object	whom	which	that
Possessive	whose	of which whose	-----

Relative pronouns refer to people or to places, things, and ideas. *That* can substitute for any noun; however, the subordinate clause must be restrictive (see Chapter 5, page 224).

Whom and which can substitute for any object in a sentence. *That* can substitute for any object also, but it must be the first word in the dependent clause.

   (114) The topic that we had warned her about was the one she liked.
   (115) X The topic about that we had warned her was the one she liked.

If the relative pronoun is not the very first word in the clause, *that* cannot be used; another pronoun must be used, for instance, example 116.

   (116) The topic about which we had warned her was the one she liked.

Sometimes it is possible to omit the relative pronoun in the dependent clause (see Chapter 5, page 225).

Whose is the possessive form for people. For other nouns, *of which* and *whose* are used.

(117) He bought a car the color of which I hated.
(118) He bought a car whose color I hated.

Some very formal grammar rules say that only *of which* can be used for places, things, and ideas. However, in written and spoken English, we find *whose* used very commonly in less formal sentences.

In addition to the relative pronouns which substitute for nouns or noun-equivalents in a clause, there are relatives that substitute for adverbs or adverb-equivalents.

Meanings	Relative Pronouns
1. Manner or Degree	*how*
2. Place	*where*
3. Purpose or Reason	*why*
4. Time	*when*

Note: *What* can be used at the beginning of a noun clause, as in example 119.

(119) What he told you is probably true.

But *what* is not a relative pronoun: it cannot connect an adjective clause to an independent clause. Therefore, example 120 is incorrect.

(120) X We can believe all what he tells us.

The adjective clause requires a relative pronoun.

(121) We can believe all that he tells us.

Two problems in adjective clauses

1. *Who* or *whom* in a subordinate clause

Who/whom has two jobs in a complex sentence. It is sometimes difficult to decide whether to use *who* or *whom* in a subordinate clause. One job is to connect the dependent or subordinate clause to the independent clause. The other job is to fill a position in the dependent clause. *Who* is the subject form; use it to indicate the subject (S) in the clause. *Whom* is the object form; use it when the position is to indicate someone or something that is not the subject. The entire wh- clause fills a position in the independent clause, but that position is unimportant in the choice of *who* or *whom*.

(122) *who* is subject (S)

$$\overset{\text{S}}{\overbrace{}}\ \overset{\text{V}}{\overbrace{}}$$

I did not know *who* was there.

(123) *whom* is direct object (DO)

$$\overset{\text{DO}}{\overbrace{}}\ \ \ \ \overset{\text{V}}{\overbrace{}}$$

I did not know *whom* he saw.

In examples 122 and 123, the subordinate clauses are direct objects (DO) of the verb *know*. However, within the noun clauses, *who* is the subject (S) of the verb *was,* and *whom* is the direct object (DO) of the verb *saw.*

In examples 124, 125, and 126, there is the same clause pattern in the subordinate clause: S V Adv. Therefore, *who*—the subjective case form—is used.

(124) noun clause subject (S) of *is*

$$\overset{\text{S}}{\overbrace{}}\ \overset{\text{V}}{\overbrace{}}$$

Who was there is important information.

(125) noun clause object

$$\overset{\text{DO}}{\overbrace{}}$$

He asked us *who* was there.

(126) adjective clause

$$\overset{\text{Adj. clause}}{\overbrace{}}$$

We spoke to the assistant director *who* was there.

It is unimportant whether the subordinate clause is a subject, an object, or an adjective; we do not use *whom* in any of the three examples.

Note: When you are determining whether to use *who* or *whom,* it is important to separate the use of the entire dependent clause from the use of *who/whom* inside the dependent clause. However, this can take some time. If you are rushed and do not have the time to think about the grammar structure of the sentence, you should use *who;* it is the form most often used even though it is sometimes grammatically incorrect.

2. Repeated information

Adjective clauses are also called **relative clauses**; they are formed with relative pronouns, which substitute for a word or phrase in the subordinate clause. The relative pronouns are the same as the wh- information question words.

In the process of forming an adjective clause, a word or phrase is removed, and a relative pronoun is substituted. Examples 127, 128, and 129 show this removal by substitution (see Chapter 5, pages 217-218).

Step 1: Substitute for possessive form.

whose

(127) ~~Her~~ essay had won the first prize.

Step 1: Substitute for time.

when

(128) She learned the results in the dormitory last night.

Step 1: Substitute for place.

where

(129) She learned the results in the dormitory last night.

After the substitution in Step 1, the clauses have the following forms:

(127a) *whose* essay had won the first prize
(128a) she learned the results in the dormitory *when*
(129a) she learned the results *where* last night

Example 130 shows a complex sentence with the adjective clause in example 129a: Steps 2 and 3 have been completed.

(130) Mary Ann went to the dormitory, *where* she learned the results last night.

Example 131 is incorrect, because *where* has been added, but *in the dormitory* has not been removed.

(131) X Mary Ann went to the dormitory, *where* she learned the results in the dormitory last night.

Similarly, example 132 is incorrect: *that* was added, but *him* was not removed.

(132) ✗ He is the man *that* I know him.
(133) He is the man *that* I know.

The mistake is clear if we apply the following test:

1. Use a wh-word for the relative.
2. Change the subordinate clause into a question.

Step 1: Use *whom* (= *that*).
    (134a) ✗ He is the man *whom* I know him.

Step 2: Make a question.
    (134b) ✗ *Whom* do I know him?

Example 134b shows clearly that there is a repetition in the clause, while 135b shows that there is no repetition.

Step 1: Use *whom* (= *that*).
    (135a) He is the man *whom* I know.

Step 2: Make a question.
    (135b) *Whom* do I know?

Exercise

Write **who** or **whom** in each blank.

whom **1.** Paul Johnson is the man _____ you must see.
_____ **2.** Can you tell me _____ he is?
_____ **3.** Yes, he's right over there. He is the tall man with _____ those two women are talking.
_____ **4.** Yes, he's right over there. He is the tall man _____ is showing those two women the map.
_____ **5.** While you're here, be careful about _____ you see and _____ talks to you.
_____ **6.** Is _____ I see and _____ talks to me any of your business?
_____ **7.** Yes, it is. You should not talk to every person _____ you meet.
_____ **8.** I will see _____ I wish to see.

Exercise

If the complex sentence is correct, write **OK**. If it is not correct, write **X** and correct it.

_✗_ **1.** It was my first visit to New York, where many of my mother's relatives have been living there.

223

_____ **2.** Do you know anyone whose car we can borrow?

_____ **3.** Do you know anyone who his car we can borrow?

_____ **4.** Baseball has specific rules that everyone should know them.

Restrictive and Non-Restrictive Adjective Clauses

When an adjective clause is put into a sentence, it has one of two purposes:

1. to identify the noun that it follows
2. to provide more information about the noun, but not to identify it

(136) Yesterday afternoon I spoke to my father, who lives in Florida.

The adjective clause in example 136 provides information about the noun that it describes, but it does not serve the purpose of identification, because a person has only one father. Similarly, example 137 has an adjective clause which does not identify; it provides additional information about the country.

(137) In our discussion of big countries, someone mentioned Canada, which has an area of about 3,852,000 square miles.

These adjective clauses do not identify, because the identification is clearly done by the words *my father* and *Canada*.

On the other hand, some adjective clauses have the purpose of identification.

(138) Yesterday afternoon I spoke to a friend who lives in Florida.
(139) In our discussion of big countries, someone mentioned a country which has 3,852,000 square miles.

In these examples, the adjective clauses identify the friend and the country. This purpose is verified if the adjective clause is removed from the sentence.

(140) Yesterday afternoon I spoke to a friend.

Because of the lack of identification, we might ask, "Which

one did you talk to?'' But this question would not occur as a response to example 141.

(141) Yesterday afternoon I spoke to my father.

The adjective clauses that identify are called **restrictive clauses**; the adjective clauses that do not identify are called **non-restrictive clauses**. Non-restrictive clauses are indicated by commas (see Chapter 7, page 285) as in examples 136 and 137. Examples 138 and 139, which do not have commas, contain restrictive clauses.

Sometimes a non-restrictive clause appears after a noun that need not be identified or distinguished because its name does this. For example, we would not use a restrictive clause after *the countries in North America* or *Mr. and Mrs. Johnson*. Other times, a non-restrictive clause appears after a noun that has been identified in an earlier statement or is identified because of the topic of the conversation.

(142) in a discussion of the earth
The moon, which revolves around the earth, is responsible for our eclipses of the sun.
(143) in a discussion of the solar system
The moon which revolves around the earth is responsible for our eclipses of the sun. The moons which revolve around Mars are not responsible for these eclipses.

In certain sequences, it is possible to omit the relative pronoun:

1. when the adjective clause is restrictive
2. when the relative pronoun appears alone at the beginning of the adjective clause
3. when the relative pronoun substitutes for an object in the subordinate clause

For instance, examples 144 and 145 show the two possibilities.

(144) The topic that we had warned her about was the one she liked.
(145) The topic we had warned her about was the one she liked.

The sentences have the same meaning; the one with the relative pronoun is more formal than the one without it.

225

Example 146 is incorrect because the adjective clause is non-restrictive; the comma shows this clearly.

    (146) X He bought a new car, he paid for in cash, from
          my brother Sal.
    (147) He bought a new car, which he paid for in cash,
          from my brother Sal.

Example 148 is incorrect because the relative pronoun does not appear at the very beginning of the adjective clause.

    (148) X That is not the man to I gave the tickets.
    (149) That is not the man to whom I gave the tickets.

Example 150 is incorrect because *who* does not substitute for an object; it substitutes for the subject of *earns*.

    (150) X He is a man earns a lot of money.
    (151) He is a man who earns a lot of money.

Exercise

Put in commas where they are needed.

Our school newspaper had printed part of a speech by the President of the University who wants to develop our athletic program. Two students who were against this development wrote a letter to the editor of the newspaper. The editor who agreed with them was unsure what to do. He did not want to offend the man who headed the school. On the other hand, he felt an obligation to the students who attended the school. It took him a long time to resolve this conflict which had come about very quickly.

Exercise

Where possible, cross out relative pronouns.

1. Traveling is an experience that I can recommend to you.
2. On our vacation, we went to several countries where people speak English.
3. It is good to practice with people who speak English as their native language.
4. I was glad to meet people that I could talk to.
5. I spoke to people with whom I could use only English.

C7 **Complex Sentences: Cause and Effect**

1. *so* and *such*

The emphasizers *so* and *such* frequently require a subordinate clause to complete their meaning. For instance, example 152 is not clear.

> (152) X That particular assignment was so difficult.

The adjective *difficult* is emphasized, but *so* means that the reader will know the result of the difficulty. The meaning is completed in example 153.

> (153) That particular assignment was so difficult that only three of us could finish it.

The meaning relationship between the clauses is cause-and-effect or result. The independent clause presents a condition that causes or allows the result which is presented in the dependent clause.

The emphasizer *so* points out the adjective (example 153) or adverb (example 154) that is central to the relationship.

> (154) They spoke so quickly that we could understand only about half of what they said.

The emphasizer *such* points out the noun that is central to the relationship (example 155).

> (155) He told us such lies that we would never be able to trust him again.

2. *so that* and *in order that*

These conjunctions join two clauses in the same way that the emphasizers *so* and *such* do. The independent clause presents a condition, and the dependent clause presents an effect or result of that condition.

> (156) They spoke slower so that we could follow the conversation.
> (157) We asked questions in order that they would remember that we were there.

Exercise

Complete the statements of cause-and-effect or result. Use **so . . . that, such . . . that,** or **so that.**

1. It was _such_ a hard test _that_ we did not have time to finish.
2. We arrived early _____ we could begin on time.
3. We wrote _____ much _____ we almost ran out of space in the test book.
4. We had been _____ tense _____ we had not eaten breakfast.

227

5. After the test, we went to a movie _____ we could relax.

REPORTED SPEECH AND SEQUENCE OF TENSES

Reporting Speech

When we tell what someone has said or written, we often use a complex sentence.

> (158) In his letter, David says that he found a roommate to share his apartment.

In example 158, the verb *says* indicates that there is a report of someone's words; the direct object is a noun-equivalent, the noun clause *that he found a roommate to share his apartment.* David's exact written words (his **direct speech**) were "I found a roommate to share my apartment." (Quotation marks show that the words are the exact words that David used. See Chapter 7, page 289.)

In a complex sentence of reported speech, there are three important parts:

1. A **reporting verb** in the independent clause indicates that the sentence is a report of someone's words. Some common reporting verbs are: *admit, (dis)agree, announce, answer, complain, deny, explain, promise, report, say, teach, tell,* and *write.*
2. Pronouns may have to be changed when direct speech is changed into reported speech. For example, when David writes his letter, he uses *I* and *my;* however, the reporting has *he* and *his.* In addition, adverbs may require changing. For example, in his letter David may write *here* or *today,* but the reporting may require *there* or *yesterday.*
3. Verb tenses may have to be shifted when direct speech is changed into indirect speech. This shift is sometimes called **sequence of tenses**.

Sequence of Tenses

If the verb of the independent clause is in the present tense, there is no shift of the tense in the subordinate clause. On the other hand, if that verb is in the past tense, there is a shift of tense in the subordinate clause, as follows:

Direct speech	Indirect speech after a past tense verb in the independent clause
Present tense ———⟶	Past tense
Present Perfect ———⟶	Past Perfect
Past tense ———⟶	Past Perfect

The following examples show the application of sequence of tenses in reporting speech from this conversation:

David: "I found a roommate to share my apartment."
Helene: "You are lucky. I have been looking for one since January."

Present tense verb in the independent clause

> (159) In his letter, David *says* that he found a roommate to share his apartment.
> (160) In her letter, Helene *writes* that David is lucky; she has been looking for one since January.

Past tense verb in the independent clause

> (161) David *told* Helene that he had found a roommate.
> (162) Helene *said* that he was lucky; she had been looking for one since January.

In order to produce the correct sequence of tenses, we distinguish present tense verbs from past tense verbs; no other distinctions are important. Therefore, we make the following classification of the common ways of expressing future time:

Present	will (do)	be going to (do)
Past	would (do)	$\begin{Bmatrix} \text{was} \\ \text{were} \end{Bmatrix}$ going to (do)
Past Perfect	would have (done)	had been going to (do)

> (163) direct speech
>   Helene said, "I will continue my search."
> (164) reported speech: present tense *will* shifted to past tense *would*
>   Helene said that she would continue her search.

Other modal auxiliary verbs are like *will;* they have similar tense forms:

229

can (do)   may (do)   shall (do)
could (do)   might (do)   should (do)
could have (done)   might have (done)   should have (done)

(165) direct speech
      Mary Lu said to Helene, "I think I can help you.
      I met a new student who was going to look for
      a place to live."
(166) reported speech:
      present tense shifted to past tense
         think ———> thought
      present tense shifted to past tense
         can ———> *could*
      past tense shifted to past perfect
         met ———> *had met*
      past tense shifted to past perfect
         was going to ———> *had been going to*

      Mary Lu said that she thought she could help
      Helene. She had met a new student who had been
      going to look for a place to live.

Statements of Unchanging Situations

There is a potential problem with some statements that are put into dependent clauses with shifted verb tenses. These are statements about situations that do not change; for example, the statement that "the earth is round" is a statement of an eternal truth. If such a statement has a verb shifted to the past perfect or past, there may be an unintended change in meaning also.

The past tense verb form is used to describe situations that were true at some past moment, but that may not be true at the present time (see Chapter 3, page 94). Thus a sentence like example 167 sounds strange to many speakers of English.

    (167) X Yesterday, the young boy found out that the
         earth *was* round.

Sometimes the present tense is used in the subordinate clause.

    (168) Yesterday, the young boy found out that the earth
         is round.

Exercise

Combine the two clauses.

1. Last week Diane and I decided to get married. Yesterday I wrote to my parents that . *Yesterday I wrote to my parents that last week Diane and I decided to get married.*
2. The Johnsons have a party almost every week. Paula does not realize that . . .
3. The Johnsons are having a party on Tuesday. She did not know that . . .
4. Mrs. Johnson offers a drink only once. I saw that . . .
5. Americans do not think it's impolite to accept a drink the first time it's offered. I found out that . . .

Exercise

Complete the statements. Use information from this conversation.

Phyllis: I like your jacket.
Raymond: Thank you. It's new. I got it last week.
Phyllis: May I ask where you got it? I have been looking for a nice birthday gift for my brother.

1. When Phyllis says that *she likes his jacket* she is offering a typical American compliment.
2. Raymond answered that _____
   and that _____.
3. Raymond's answer that _____
   and that _____ is also typical.
4. Phyllis wanted to know where Raymond had bought the jacket because _____.

D1 Reported Imperatives

Form

Verbs such as *advise, ask* (= *request*), *demand, direct, forbid, insist, move* (= to make a formal motion in a meeting), *prefer, propose, recommend, request, require, suggest,* and *urge* are used when reporting imperatives.

   (169) Rachel *insisted* that we finish the work before next month.

  It is also possible to report imperatives by using words such as *necessary, important,* or *a good idea.*

231

(170) It is *important* that we do it.

(171) It is *a good idea* that he not be late.

Many imperatives have no expressed subject; they have **you-understood** (see Chapter 1, page 34). Other imperatives have an expressed subject.

(172) Be on time for the meeting.

(173) Alice, bring potato chips and dip.

When an imperative is put into subordinate clauses, it is necessary that the subject be expressed.

(174) He insists that *you* be on time for the meeting.

(175) They suggested that *Alice* bring potato chips and dip.

The verb form in a reported imperative is the simple form (sometimes called the **base form** or the **infinitive without** *to*) (See Chapter 1, page 32). For instance, the verbs in examples 172 and 173 are *be* and *bring*. When imperatives are reported, the same verb forms are used. The negative of the verb in a subordinate imperative is formed with *not*.

(176) It is important that sick people *not* go out in bad weather.

Meaning

The resulting complex sentence is a report; that is, it tells about a situation involving an imperative. However, when the verb in the main clause is in the present tense, the sentence may be an imperative. For instance, example 177 may be an imperative, and example 178 is a command.

(177) It is advisable that she remain in the hospital for another two or three days.

(178) I insist that you tell them the results of the experiments.

Consider the following two sentences, both of which are correct.

(179) It is important that Alice is here.

(180) It is important that Alice be here.

Example 179 is not an imperative; it is a report of information, as in example 181.

(181) Alice is here. That is important information for us to know because it affects our plans.

Example 180 is an imperative; it can be restated as in example 182.

>(182) Tell Alice that she must be here.
>>We need her in order to finish this job.

Note: Imperatives may be reported in question sentences, too.

>(183) Is it a good idea that they ask so many questions?

Exercise

Complete the statements.

1. We watched the game because Bill insisted that _we watch it_____.

2. She will review the English verb tenses because it is necessary that _____.

3. We adjourned the meeting after Paul moved that ____

_____.

4. They arrived late even though Professor Smith requested that_____.

5. If you think that we should postpone the discussion, propose that _____.

6. Yesterday the test _____

because the printed instructions said that it was important that the test be started at 9:00 a.m.

7. He was more polite because his parents insisted that

_____.

D2 **Reported Exclamations**

Form

When an exclamation is reported, there is no change of word order. The only part of the clause to look at carefully is the verb: the verb tense may change. This is another example of the sequence of tenses (see Chapter 5, page 228).

>(184a) actual words used: direct speech or writing in present tense
>>How sweet American food *is*!
>(184b) present tense verb in the independent clause
>>He usually *notices* how sweet American food *is*.
>(184c) past tense verb in the independent clause

Yesterday he *noticed* how sweet American food *was.*

(185a) actual words used: direct speech or writing in past tense
What an interesting meal that *was!*

(185b) present tense verb in the independent clause
When he thinks of his visit, he *remembers* what an interesting meal that *was.*

(185c) past tense verb in the independent clause
When he thought of his visit, he *remembered* what an interesting meal that *had been.*

Meaning

The resulting sentence is a report; that is, it is not an exclamation itself. It is a report of someone's exclamation; therefore, the end punctuation is a period, not an exclamation point.

Note: Exclamations may be reported in question sentences, too.

(186) Did he notice how sweet American food is?

Exercise

Complete the statements. Use the exclamations from this conversation.

Yvonne: What a good idea it was to study in the United States! We can practice our English every day.

Edward: Yes, I agree. How interesting it is to be able to think in another language!

1. Yvonne has realized *what a good idea it was to study in the United States* .

2. She wrote a letter to her parents and told them _____

_____ .

3. Edward is telling Yvonne _____ .
4. He wrote to his brother, telling him _____

_____ .

E **SENTENCE FRAGMENTS**

When we consider independent and dependent clauses in sentences, we have four possibilities. In addition, there is a common sentence error: a **sentence fragment**. A sentence fragment is a dependent clause used as a sentence.

One Clause

A simple sentence has one clause; the clause is independent (see Chapter 1, page 3).

(187) A university is a group of colleges.

Sometimes a dependent clause is written like a sentence. This is a mistake: each correctly written sentence must have at least one independent clause.

(188) X Because a dependent clause is not a sentence.

More Than One Clause

There are three types of sentences with more than one clause. A compound sentence has two or more independent clauses, but no dependent clauses (see Chapter 5, page 189).

(189) A university is a group of colleges; with several colleges, a university is large.

A complex sentence has one independent clause and one or more dependent clauses. (Example 190 has one independent clause and two dependent clauses (the dependent clauses are in italics).

(190) *Although she was tired,* she walked up to the third floor *because she wanted the exercise.*

A compound-complex sentence has (1) two or more independent clauses and (2) one or more dependent clauses.

(191) She was tired, but she walked up to the third floor because she wanted the exercise.

Exercise

Identify the sentences.

    a. Compound sentence
    b. Complex sentence
    c. Compound-complex sentence
    d. Simple sentence
    X Sentence fragment

_d_ **1.** The idea of being on time varies from culture to culture.

_____ **2.** In the United States, a student is late if he arrives after the scheduled beginning of a class.

_____ **3.** Because we consider that a 9:00 class begins exactly at 9:00, a 9:10 arrival is late.

235

_____ **4.** If a student arrives within five or ten minutes before the appointed time.

_____ **5.** Anyone who has an appointment should arrive at least five or ten minutes before the appointed time.

_____ **6.** Although the person may not see you at the appointed time.

_____ **7.** People usually arrive at the appointed time for a lunch or dinner, but they arrive thirty minutes to one hour after the announced time for a party.

_____ **8.** Arriving one hour after a party begins is all right; on the other hand, arriving two hours after is considered impolite.

F ## *OTHER TYPES OF COMBINED SENTENCES*

F1 ## **Apposition**

Apposition is a way of combining ideas in order to identify or describe. (See Chapter 7, page 285.)

> (192) We discussed the problem with Andrew Sanders, a lawyer.

Example 192 provides additional information about Andrew Sanders. This information does not appear as part of the same clause as the first seven words of the sentence. Apposition is like renaming: the person, place, thing, or idea is (1) named and (2) identified or described.

The naming and/or the identifying can be single words, phrases, or clauses. For instance, the appositive in example 193 is a clause, the information after *his suggestion*.

> (193) We rejected his suggestion that we stop working at 5:00.

Appositives are either **restrictive appositives** or **non-restrictive appositives**. Non-restrictive appositives appear with commas, as do non-restrictive adjective clauses (see Chapter 5, page 224).

Exercise

Underline the appositives and put in commas where they are needed.

1. Dr. Thomas, our chemistry professor, announced a test for next Tuesday.

2. My cousin Bill had arrived, but my cousin Alice had not.
3. They carefully considered her proposal a dramatically new way to reroute traffic.
4. The most popular holiday in the U.S. in December is Christmas Day December 25.
5. New York the largest city in the United States is on the East Coast.

F2 **Participles**

Usually the *-ing* forms of verbs are used with the auxiliary verb *be* (see Chapter 3, page 98). However, V-*ing* can be used to combine ideas. It can be used as an adverb-equivalent (see Chapter 4, page/163), an adjective-equivalent (see Chapter 4, page 156) or a noun-equivalent (see Chapter 2, page 57).

When *-ing* verb forms are used without *be,* they do not indicate present or past tense (see Chapter 3, pages 91 and 94) or simple or progressive activity (see Chapter 3, pages 91 and 101). The only verb meaning is indicated by perfect (*having* + past participle) and non-perfect forms.

(194) Having done her homework, Beverly watched television.
(195) Doing her homework, Beverly watched television.

The perfect form indicates that one situation or action has taken place before another; in example 194, Beverly did her homework before she watched television. The non-perfect form indicates that the situation or action is taking place at the same time as another; in example 195, Beverly did her homework and watched television at the same time.

Because it is a verb form, a V-*ing* can appear in phrases with adjectives, adverbs, and nouns. For instance, in example 196, *buying* has a direct object (DO): *the coat.*

(196) The young man buying the coat is my brother-in-law.

In example 197, *studying* has an adverb: *hard.*

(197) Studying hard is not one of Paul's favorite activities.

The negative of V-*ing* is made with *not.*

(198) Not having done her homework, she decided to miss class.

Present Participles as Adverb-Equivalents

A present participle can function as an adverb-equivalent. For instance, example 199 has a participle.

> (199) Feeling very hungry, he also bought some hamburgers.

The participle phrase *feeling very hungry* provides the information why. We can think of this construction as a shortened form of an adverbial clause.

> (200) Because he was feeling very hungry, he also bought some hamburgers.

An introductory adverb present participle phrase is separated from the rest of the sentence in which it appears by a comma.

> (201) X Feeling very hungry he also bought some hamburgers.

Exercise

Make the first sentence into a present participle phrase. Join it to the second sentence to show an adverb meaning. Use a comma.

1. She does not know the correct formula.
   She hopes that the professor will call on someone else.

   Not knowing the correct formula, she hopes that the professor will call on someone else.

2. He converted inches into centimeters earlier.
   Then he could finish the problem.
3. Annette wanted to try many different foods.
   Annette ordered corn-on-the-cob.
4. Ivan was unaware that there are several ways to have corn.
   Ivan did not order corn-on-the-cob.
5. Ivan decided to leave corn for the cows.
   Ivan ordered spinach.

Present Participles as Adjective-Equivalents

A present participle can function as an adjective-equivalent. For instance, example 202 has a participle phrase: *buying the coat* describes *man*.

> (202) The young man *buying the coat* is my brother-in-law.

We can think of this construction as a shortened form of an adjective clause.

> (203) The young man *who is buying the coat* is my brother-in-law.

As an adjective-equivalent, a present participle appears after the noun that it describes.

Exercise

Combine each pair of sentences. Make the first sentence into a participle phrase. Add the participle phrase to the second sentence to function as an adjective-equivalent.

1. The man is ordering a hot dog with sauerkraut and chili.
   Look at that man.

   Look at that man ordering a hot dog with sauerkraut and chili.

2. Americans eat fried chicken with their hands.
   Have you ever seen Americans?
3. The students are not studying English.
   Do you know many students?
4. The party begins after 6:00 p.m.
   A party is considered a cocktail party.
5. The tourists are standing near the Statue of Liberty.
   You can see some tourists.

Present Participles as Noun-Equivalents

The *-ing* verb form that functions as a noun-equivalent is called a **gerund**. For instance, example 204 has a gerund as the subject (S) of the verb *is*.

> (204) *Studying* is not one of Paul's favorite activities.

The subject of a gerund is expressed as a possessive form (see Chapter 2, page 72).

> (205) Paul's studying hard surprised everyone.
> (206) His studying hard surprised everyone.

Exercise

Combine each pair of sentences. Make the first sentence into a gerund phrase. Replace the underlined subject in the second sentence with the gerund phrase.

1. I opened a checking account.
That took about an hour.

Opening a checking account took about an hour.

2. People travel to foreign countries.
It can be fun and educational.

3. Americans call the ground floor the first floor.
Some people are confused by that.

4. Anne arrived an hour late.
They considered it very impolite.

5. She had not telephoned us.
We were surprised about it.

Past Participles as Adjective-Equivalents

Usually the past participle forms of verbs are used with auxiliary verbs (*have, be,* or *get*). However, they can be used to combine ideas. They can be used as adverb-equivalents or as adjective-equivalents.

Because they are verbs, past participles can appear in phrases with adjectives, adverbs, and nouns. For instance, in example 207, *baked* has an adverbial prepositional phrase: *at home.*

(207) Bread baked at home is usually delicious.

The negative of a past participle or past participle phrase is made with *not.*

(208) Bread not baked at home may be old and stale.

As stated above, a past participle can function as an adjective-equivalent. For instance, example 209 has a past participle phrase: *made in bakeries* describes *bread.*

(209) Some bread made in bakeries is very sweet.

We can think of this construction as a shortened form of an adjective clause; we remove the subject and the verb form of *be.*

(210) Some bread that is made in bakeries is very sweet.

As an adjective-equivalent, a past participle appears after the noun that it describes.

Exercise

Combine each pair of sentences. Change the first sentence into a past participle phrase. Join it to the second sentence to function as an adjective-equivalent.

1. A man was seen near the house. The man left very quickly. *The man seen near the house left very quickly.*
2. The police were surprised at the lack of clues. The police could not investigate the crime easily.
3. A man was found dead in the living room. The man was quite old.
4. A man was left for dead upstairs. The man was somewhat younger than the other one.
5. Some silver was stolen that afternoon. The silver was found in a pawnshop.

F3 Infinitives

Often infinitives occur after other verb forms (see Chapter 3, page 112). However, infinitives—with and without the infinitive marker *to*—are used to combine ideas. They can be used as adverb-equivalents (see Chapter 4, page 163), adjective-equivalents (see Chapter 4, page 156), and noun-equivalents (see Chapter 2, page 57).

Infinitives do not indicate present or past tense (see Chapter 3, pages 91 and 94). They do indicate the meanings of perfect (*to have* + past participle) and non-perfect and the meanings of simple and progressive (*to be* and V-*ing*).

> (211) Yesterday John told Elizabeth that she was lucky to have bought the jacket for only $100.
> (212) Yesterday John told Alice that she was lucky to buy the jacket for only $150.

The perfect form indicates that one situation or action has taken place before another; in example 211, Elizabeth had bought the jacket before John spoke to her. The non-perfect form indicates that the situation or action takes place at the same time as another; in example 212, Alice bought the jacket yesterday, the day when John spoke to her.

> (213) It was a good idea to be studying when the professor walked in.

241

(214) It was a good idea to stand up when the professor walked in.

The progressive form indicates that the activity is in progress. In example 213, the studying had begun before the moment of the professor's arrival; it was going on at that moment. The simple form does not indicate an activity in progress. In example 214, the standing up began at the time of the professor's arrival.

Because an infinitive is a verb, it can appear in phrases with adjectives, adverbs, and nouns. For instance, the clause in example 215 has an infinitive with a noun direct object (DO) and an adverb prepositional phrase.

V: Inf.   DO   Prep. phrase: Adv.

(215) to buy the jacket for only $150

The subject of an infinitive is in the object form (see Chapter 3, page 113). At the beginning of a sentence, the subject has *for* in front of it.

(216) He asked her to buy the jacket.
(217) For her to buy the jacket, she had to save for six months.

The negative of an infinitive is made with *not* before the infinitive marker *to*.

(218) I decided not to buy the jacket.

Whenever possible, it is a good idea not to separate the *to* from the simple verb form. When they are separated, the result is called a **split infinitive**.

(219) X I decided to not buy the jacket.

Infinitives as Adverb-Equivalents

An infinitive can function as an adverb-equivalent. For instance, example 220 has an infinitive phrase: *to convert kilos into pounds.* The infinitive phrase tells why or how.

(220) To convert kilos into pounds, we multiply by 2.2.

We can make the meaning clearer by adding words.

(221) In order to convert kilos into pounds, we multiply by 2.2.

An introductory adverb infinitive or infinitive phrase is separated from the rest of the sentence with a comma.

(222) X To convert kilos into pounds we multiply by 2.2.

As an adverb-equivalent, an infinitive can modify an adjective or other adverb. Example 223 has an infinitive phrase: *to buy the coat* gives the reason for her happiness.

(223) She was happy to buy the coat.

When it is a modifier, an infinitive comes after the adjective or adverb that it modifies.

The emphasizer *too* often requires the addition of information after the adjective or adverb that it emphasizes. For instance, example 224 is not clear.

(224) X That particular assignment was too difficult.

The adjective *difficult* is an emphasizer, but *too* means that there is a result from the difficulty. The meaning is completed in examples 225 and 226.

(225) That particular assignment was *too* difficult for me to do myself.
(226) That particular assignment was *too* difficult to do.

The meaning relationship is cause-and-effect or result. The independent clause represents a condition that prevents the effect or result which is presented in the infinitive. The emphasizer *too* points out the adjective (examples 225 and 226) or adverb (example 227) that is central to the relationship.

(227) They spoke *too* quickly for us to understand them.

The meaning relationship can be restated, as in example 228.

(228) They spoke quickly. Because of that, we could not understand them.

Similarly, the emphasizer *enough* often requires additional information to make an idea clear.

(229) X Her car is big *enough*.
(230) Her car is big *enough* for six people to ride in.

The meaning relationship is also cause-and-effect or result. The independent clause presents a condition that allows or causes the result which is presented in the infinitive. The emphasizer *enough* points out the adjective (example 230), adverb (example 231), or noun (example 232) that is central to the relationship.

(231) You speak clearly *enough* for us to understand.
(232) He has *enough* money to buy a new car.

The meaning relationship can be restated, as in example 233.

(233) He has money. Because of that, he can buy a new car.

Exercise

Change the adverb clause into an infinitive phrase.

1. If we learn a foreign language, we learn a foreign culture.

   To learn a foreign language, we learn a foreign culture.

2. If you study English, you must read about English-speaking countries.
3. If you buy something very expensive, pay with a check.
4. If you carry a lot of cash, you must be asking for trouble.
5. If you are considerate of people in the new culture, you must always be on time.

Exercise

Combine the sentences. Use **too** or **enough** and an infinitive.

1. This silk shirt is expensive. We can't buy it.

   This silk shirt is too expensive for us to buy.

2. This cotton shirt is large. You could wear it.
3. When he goes shopping, Alan is impatient. He will not try on several garments.
4. When I go shopping, I am slow. I don't buy everything that I need.
5. I have patience. I can try on many garments.

Infinitives as Adjective-Equivalents

When an infinitive is used as an adjective-equivalent, it appears after the noun that it describes.

(234) These are the courses for you to take this semester.

The infinitive phrase *for you to take this semester* tells which courses.

Note: We might expect to have a direct object (DO) pronoun after some infinitives.

(235) ✕ These are the courses for you to take them this semester.

However, there is no DO after it; *the courses* is the direct object of the verb *to take*.

Infinitives as Noun-Equivalents

An infinitive or infinitive phrase can function as a noun-equivalent in a clause pattern.

(236) To learn grammar rules is not difficult.
(237) Our friends wanted us to bring some potato chips.

Example 236 has an infinitive phrase as the subject (S) of the verb *is*. Example 237 has an infinitive as the direct object (DO) of the verb *wanted*. The pronoun *us* is used to make clear who would bring the potato chips.

Exercise

Change the first sentence into an infinitive. Use the infinitive as a noun-equivalent in the second sentence. Add a pronoun where necessary.

1. One should know a little about money changing. It is a good idea *to know a little about money changing* when traveling abroad.
2. She should try new foods. Do not force _____.
3. She should try new foods. _____ would require a major change in her personality.
4. Let's play cards tonight. He invited _____.
5. I finish this exercise quickly. I hope _____.

F4 Dangling Modifiers

Often phrases with *-ing* or *-ed* participles, infinitives, and absolutes do not contain all the information that would be found in a complete clause pattern. Examples 238, 239, and 240 do not indicate who or what is doing the action, that is, the subject (S) of the verb.

(238) studying for the English test
(239) hit by a truck
(240) to make a good impression

When these phrases are combined with independent clauses, we do not lack any information; the modifier appears next to the word, phrase, or clause that it describes.

245

For instance, example 241 is clear. We know who is studying, because the participle phrase appears next to *Marie*.

(241) Studying for the English test, Marie decided to go to the library.

On the other hand, example 242 is logically impossible.

(242) X Studying for the English test, the library was a good place for Mary to go.

This sentence says that the library was studying; the participle phrase appears next to the thing that it describes — *the library*.

Examples 243 and 244 are correct and logical, but they show different information.

(243) Hit by a car, Alexander's bicycle could not be used.

(244) Hit by a car, Alexander could not use his bicycle.

Example 243 says that a car hit the bicycle and damaged it. Example 244 says that a car hit Alexander and injured him so that he could not ride. Example 245 is not logically possible.

(245) X To make a good impression, a coat and tie should be worn.

Who or what is making a good impression? A coat and a tie?

Exercise

If the sentence is logical, write **OK**. If the sentence is not logical, write **X** and circle the noun that should appear side-by-side with the modifier.

__X__ 1. To learn a foreign language, a sense of humor is needed by (every student.)

_____ 2. Living in another country, unusual customs may surprise you.

_____ 3. Understanding cultural differences, you will be ready for strange events.

_____ 4. Ready for these surprises, a person can adjust more easily to the new culture.

_____ 5. Observed carefully, a person can deal with cultural differences in a reasonable way.

Chapter 6
Contents

6 Rearrangement of Sentence Patterns

INTRODUCTION

This chapter deals only with statements. It presents the ways that sentence patterns can be changed in order to give additional information or emphasize different parts of the sentence.

A NEGATION IN THE VERB

One of the most common rearrangements of the parts of a sentence is **negation**.

(1) They arrived at the start of the game.
(2) They *did not arrive* at the start of the game.
(3) The room was empty.
(4) The room *was not* empty.

In examples 2 and 4, the verb is negated; the subject stays the same.

A1 Form of Negation in the Verb

The verb is usually negated with the word *not*. If the verb has two or more words, insert the word *not* after the first word of the verb.

(5) affirmative statement

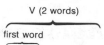

first word

They *have* finished the exam.
(6) negative statement: ADD *not*
They have *not* finished the exam.
(7) affirmative statement

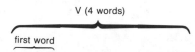

first word

He *should* have been finishing then.
(8) negative statement: ADD *not*
He should *not* have been finishing then.

If the verb has one word and if it is a form of *be,* insert the word *not* after the verb.

(9) affirmative statement

V

be

She *is* in Chicago today.
(10) negative statement: ADD *not*
She is *not* in Chicago today.

If the verb has one word and that word is not a form of *be,* it is necessary to change the verb and add *did, does,* or *do* before inserting *not.*

a. If the verb is in the past tense, add *did* and change the verb to the simple form (also called the **base form** or the **infinitive**).

affirmative statement

(11) They went to school in Boston.

Step 1: ADD *did* and CHANGE *went* to *go.*
(11a) They *did go* to school in Boston.
Step 2: negative statement: ADD *not*
(11b) They did *not* go to school in Boston.

b. If the subject is *he, she, it,* or an equivalent, add *does* and change the verb to the simple form.

affirmative statement
v
⌢

(12)   She likes the cold winters.

Step 1: ADD *does* and CHANGE *likes* to *like.*
(12a) She *does like* the cold winters.
Step 2: negative statement: ADD *not*
(12b) She does *not* like the cold winters.

c. In all other cases, ADD *do,* but DO NOT CHANGE the form of the verb.

affirmative statement
v
⌢

(13)   They prefer a smaller city.

Step 1: ADD *do,* but DO NOT CHANGE *prefer.*
(13a) They *do prefer* a smaller city.
Step 2: negative statement: ADD *not*
(13b) They do *not* prefer a smaller city.

Note: In British English it is common to negate the verb *have* the same way as *be.* Therefore, the sentence *I didn't have enough money for a new car* would be expressed as *I had not enough money for a new car.*

Full Forms and Contractions

When we negate a verb it is possible to use the **full form** of the word *not,* or the short form *n't* called the **contraction**. A contraction is a shortened form of the verb plus the word *not.*

(14) full form: have not finished
     contraction: haven't finished
(15) full form: is not
     contraction: isn't
(16) full form: does not like
     contraction: doesn't like

Note: One contraction cannot be attached to another contraction.

(17) full form of *not* with full form of *is*
     She is *not* in Chicago.

251

(18) contraction of *not* with full form of *is*
    She is*n't* in Chicago today.
(19) contraction of *not* with contraction of *is*
    X She *'sn't* in Chicago today.

In example 19, the contraction of *not* cannot be used, because the verb is already a contraction. The correct forms are shown in examples 18 and 20.

(20) full form *not* with contraction *'s*
    She's *not* in Chicago today.

Contractions occur very often in spoken English. They also occur in informal written English. Because they are so frequent, the learner of English as a second language should learn to understand and use them. However, it is important to remember that in formal written English, contractions are generally not appropriate. If the learner cannot decide whether to use contractions or full forms, he should use the full forms.

B **NEGATIVE ADVERBIALS OF FREQUENCY**
The most common method of negation is to add the word *not* to the sentence. However, there is another common method: to add a **negative adverbial of frequency**. Adverbials of frequency tell how often. Some of these adverbials are *never, seldom,* and *rarely* (see Chapter 4, page 168).

(21) affirmative statement
    They went to movies during the week.
(22) negative statement: add *never*
    They *never* went to movies during the week.
(23) negative statement: add *seldom*
    They *seldom* went to movies during the week.

When these adverbials of frequency occur in a sentence, the meaning of the sentence is negative. Structurally, however, a statement with *never* is like a statement with *always;* therefore, no adjustment is required when the negative meaning is added this way.

(24) He never arrives on time.
(25) He always arrives on time.

Exercise

Change the affirmative sentences to negative sentences, inserting *not*. Use full forms in sentences 1-5 and, if possible, contractions in sentences 6-10.

1. Marcia buys her clothes in small shops.
   Marcia does not buy her clothes in small shops.
2. Many people are like her.
3. They might prefer the convenience of a shopping mall.
4. We like the large size of a department store.
5. Better service is provided in small shops.
6. Some shoppers have tried both big and small stores.
7. You have plenty of time to shop for shoes.
8. It's difficult to choose between two nice pairs.
9. I should be a sensible consumer.
10. Paul Rutledge is buying the first pair of jeans he sees.

Exercise

Change these affirmative sentences to the negative, adding *never*.

1. Alice shops at sales.
   Alice never shops at sales.
2. She has saved a lot of money.
3. Good quality merchandise is cheap.
4. You can get something for free.
5. Last year, we had luck at sales on kitchen appliances.

Exercise

Change these sentences from the negative to the affirmative.

1. My wife and I do not like to gamble.
   My wife and I like to gamble.
2. We have never bet on horse races.
3. She wouldn't think of playing bingo.
4. And I can not play cards very well.
5. Last Thanksgiving, we did not go to Las Vegas.
6. As a matter of fact, we rarely go away for a winter vacation.
7. We didn't have good luck.
8. She never had good luck.
9. She did not beat the one-arm bandits.
10. In addition, I did not win at cards all weekend long.

B1 **Negation at the Beginning of a Sentence**

The speaker or writer can start a sentence with a negative word or phrase if he wants to emphasize the negation in the sentence. This rearrangement involves two parts of the sentence: the negation and the verb. The negative part of the sentence is moved from its usual place and put at the beginning. Then the verb is changed to the question word order (see Chapter 1, page 14).

(26) usual arrangement

> S   V
> He was not on time once.

(27) negation rearrangement
Not once was he on time.

(28) usual arrangement

> S   V
> We rarely go to movies during the week.

(29) negation rearrangement
Rarely do we *go* to movies during the week.

(30) usual arrangement

> S   V   DO
> He could solve only two problems correctly.

(31) negation rearrangement
Only two problems could he *solve* correctly.

The negation rearrangement is also used in a clause introduced with *neither* or *nor*.

(32) We have not done such a thing, *nor would* we consider it.

However, this rearrangement is not used when the negation is in the subject.

(33) Not one person knew the answer to the question.

Exercise

Rearrange each sentence so that the negative word appears at the beginning.

1. She never even thinks of doing such things.

Never does she even think of doing such things.

254

2. Many Americans rarely eat spicy food.
3. They can be fooled only once in a while.
4. I rarely ate any.

C   USE OF THE NEGATION REARRANGEMENT

This rearrangement of the usual order of parts of a sentence is used to emphasize the negation. As with exclamations (see Chapter 1, page 38) it is not used often since having too many of these sentences together decreases their strength. Because the feeling of a negation rearrangement is similar to the feeling of exclamatory sentences, examples 34 and 35 could be written with exclamation points at their ends.

(34) Not once was he on time!
(35) Only two problems could he solve correctly!

Exercise

Respond to these sentences very emphatically in the negative, using the instructions given.

1. Is it true that you saw some of the questions before the test day? *Not one question did I see!*

    Response about yourself: change *some* to *not one*.
2. Does your roommate usually do his share of the cleaning in the apartment?

    Response about your roommate: begin with a negative adverbial.
3. They never discussed their work in my class. What about in your class?

    Response about them: move the negative.
4. I would say that all of the participants were happy about the results.

    Response about the participants: change *I* to *Only Mario and Sheila*.

D   INDEFINITES

In Chapter 6, page 249, we looked at negation of the verb. We saw that it is usually done with the word *not* or a contraction. We also saw negation using a negative adverbial of frequency.

Negation in a sentence can also occur in the subject (S), the indirect object (IO), the direct object (DO), or an adverbial (adv.)

$$\overbrace{\textit{Not one person}}^{\text{S}} \quad \overbrace{\text{finished}}^{\text{V}} \quad \overbrace{\text{the test.}}^{\text{DO}}$$

(36) *Not one person* finished the test.

$$\overbrace{\text{The teacher}}^{\text{S}} \quad \overbrace{\text{gave}}^{\text{V}} \quad \overbrace{\textit{no one}}^{\text{IO}} \quad \overbrace{\text{a passing grade.}}^{\text{DO}}$$

(37) The teacher gave *no one* a passing grade.

$$\overbrace{\text{They}}^{\text{S}} \quad \overbrace{\text{have noticed}}^{\text{V}} \quad \overbrace{\textit{nothing}}^{\text{DO}} \quad \text{in the food.}$$

(38) They have noticed *nothing* in the food.

$$\overbrace{\text{He}}^{\text{S}} \quad \overbrace{\text{could find}}^{\text{V}} \quad \overbrace{\text{an honest man}}^{\text{DO}} \quad \overbrace{\textit{in no country.}}^{\text{Adv.}}$$

(39) He could find an honest man *in no country*.

Typically, the negative nouns or noun-equivalents and adverbials have the word *not* or *no*.

There are also common negative pronouns and adverbials. They are called **indefinites** because they do not refer to specific people, objects, or places. Each indefinite has three forms: a negative, an affirmative, and a non-assertive.

Affirmative	Non-assertive	Negative
some	any	no
someone	anyone	no one
		none
somebody	anybody	nobody
something	anything	nothing
somewhere	anywhere	nowhere
someplace	anyplace	no place
sometime	anytime	no time
some more	anymore	no more

An indefinite alone can indicate the negation in a sentence; examples 37 and 38 show the negative forms *no one* and *nothing*. Examples 40 and 41 show the corresponding affirmative sentences.

(40) The teacher gave *someone* a passing grade.
(41) They have noticed *something* in the food.

The non-assertive forms are used when there is a negative before the indefinite in the sentence.

(42) The teacher did *not* give *anyone* a passing grade.
(43) They have *not* noticed *anything* in the food.

Note: Remember that the non-assertive forms—with *any*—are used only when there is a negation earlier in the sentence. Notice the answers to the following question:

(44) What did you see in the garden?
        I did not see anything.
        I saw nothing.
        Nothing.

It is not possible to give the one-word answer "Anything" because there is no negative in that short answer.

(45) affirmative sentence

    V   IO   DO   S   V   IO   DO

        Ask me a question, and I will tell you a lie.
(46) negative sentence
        Ask me *no* question, and I will tell you *no* lie.

Note: Grammatically correct sentences have only one negative word in each clause.

(47) X The teacher did *not* give *no one* a passing grade.
(48) X The teacher did *not* give *no one no* passing grade.

Exercise

If the sentence is correct, write **OK**. If it is incorrect, write **X** and correct it.

OK **1.** Paul gave not one cent to charity last year.

_____ **2.** He didn't give nothing?

_____ **3.** When I was younger, my family never went nowhere on vacation.

_____ **4.** Anyone did not answer the question.

_____ **5.** (It was a school holiday. Who did you see in the classroom?)
        Anybody.

E **SUBJECT-VERB INVERSION**

The subject and verb of a sentence may be inverted to show a connection with a preceding statement and/or to focus the reader's or hearer's attention on the information in the subject.

There is a special case of rearrangement when (1) the verb indicates a position or motion and (2) the tense is the simple present or the simple past. Under these two conditions, there is an inversion of the subject and the verb.

(49) basic arrangement

S V Adv.

The bus is here.

(50) inversion rearrangement

Adv. V S

Here is the bus.

Many times when we invert the subject and the verb the resulting sentence sounds literary or poetic, as in example 52. Therefore you should be careful when you use this type of rearrangement.

(51) basic arrangement

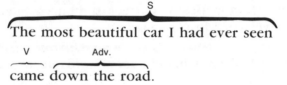

S

The most beautiful car I had ever seen

V   Adv.

came down the road.

(52) inversion rearrangement

Adv.   V

Down the road came

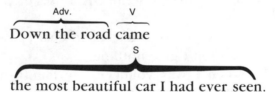

S

the most beautiful car I had ever seen.

This rearrangement does not involve question word order (Chapter 1, page 16) or the use of an expletive *there* (Chapter 6, page 266) or *it* (Chapter 6, page 269). There is a simple switching of positions of the subject and the verb.

In example 53, there is no rearrangement of subject and verb.

S V

(53) There it is.

One of the results of this inversion (examples 50 and 52) is to focus attention on the important, new information in the subject (S). However, in example 53, the pronoun *it* does not indicate anything important or new. Therefore, example 54 is not correct English.

(54) X There is it.

Exercise

Rearrange these sentences, if appropriate and possible. Put the adverbial or subject complement at the beginning of the sentence.

1. A tall stone gate stood at the end of the driveway.

   At the end of the driveway stood a tall stone gate.

2. The somewhat smaller house was to its left.
3. The limousine turned into the driveway.
4. It came to the front steps.
5. Two impressive dogs came out of the car.
6. Their owner stopped near the tall rose bushes.
7. The driver walked into the house.

F   PASSIVE VOICE

F1   Form of the Passive Voice Rearrangement

Another rearrangement of the parts of a sentence is called **passive voice**. In passive voice, a direct object (DO) or indirect object (IO) moves into the subject position, and the subject (S) moves out—either to the end of the sentence or it is eliminated entirely. (Verbs that occur in sentences with objects are called **transitive verbs**. See Chapter 1, page 5.)

Examples 55, 56, and 57 show the basic arrangement (called **active voice** because the subject specifies the doer of the action) and various passive voice rearrangements.

(55) active voice arrangement

   S   V   DO
   Elaine saw Alex.

(56) passive voice rearrangement: DO in subject position
   Alex was seen by Elaine.

(57) active voice arrangement

```
         S     V    IO       DO
```
Elaine gave Paul a new shirt.

(58) passive voice rearrangement: IO in subject position
Paul was given a new shirt by Elaine.

(59) passive voice rearrangement: DO in subject position
A new shirt was given to Paul by Elaine.

(60) active voice arrangement

```
        S         V     DO      OC
```
The people elected Truman President in 1948.

(61) passive voice rearrangement: DO in subject position
Truman was elected President by the people in 1948.

Note: The verb *have* can appear in the active voice, but it can not appear in the passive voice rearrangement when it means *to possess*.

(62) active voice arrangement

```
       S    V    DO
```
Bill had a book.

Subject and Object

Move the doer of the action(s) to the end of the sentence, adding the preposition *by*. If the S is a pronoun, change it to the object pronoun form.

```
          S        V      DO
```
(63)   Elaine might see Alex.

(64a) _____might see Alex by Elaine.

Move an object into the subject position. If it is a pronoun, change it to the subject form.

(64b) Alex might see_____by Elaine.

Change the verb to the passive voice form. (See Chapter 6 page 261.)

(64c) Alex might be seen by Elaine.

Some active sentences have two possible subjects in the passive.

```
        S    V   IO      DO
```

(65) She gave Paul a new shirt.

In this sentence both the direct object *a new shirt* and the indirect object *Paul* can be made the subjects of a passive sentence.

(66) DO as subject

A new shirt was given to Paul by her.

(67) IO as subject

Paul was given a new shirt by her.

Notice that when the DO is put into the subject position we added a preposition, *to*. This helps to make the meaning more clear. Other DO's take other prepositions.

(68) They bought her a book.
(69) A book was bought for her by them.

There is one more step that can be taken. Since one of the uses of the passive voice rearrangement is to avoid naming the doer of the action, it is possible to take out the prepositional phrase entirely. For example, with the passive voice we have the choice of either of the following two sentences:

(70) Paul was seen by Elaine.
(71) Paul was seen.

Verb

A passive voice verb has a form of the verb *be* and a past participle, the third principal part of the verb. To change an active verb into a passive one, follow these 5 steps:

1. Put the verb *be* in front of the main verb (the last verb form if the verb has several words).
2. Make the verb *be* agree in form with the main verb.
3. Change the main verb into its past participle form (if it is not already in that form).
4. If the new verb is negative, check to see if it has the correct form; if it does not, adjust it.
5. Check to see if the new subject of the clause and the new verb agree; if they do not, adjust the verb form.

The following chart shows how these steps work when they are applied to the following verbs: *might see, gave,*

Steps in changing an active verb to a passive verb

ACTIVE VOICE	Elaine *might see* Alex.	She *gave* Paul a shirt.	His classmates *made* him very happy.	They *didn't give* him a book.	The new highway *is creating* traffic jams.
1. Put *be* in front of main verb.	might *be* see	*be* gave	have *be* made	did not *be* give	is *be* creating
2. Make *be* agree with form or tense of main verb.	might *be* see (*see* = simple form)	{was / were} gave (*gave* = past tense)	have *been* made (*made* = past participle)	did not {was / were} give (*did give* = past tense)	is being creating
3. Change main verb to past participle.	might be *seen*	{was / were} *given*	have been *made* (no change)	did not {was / were} *given*	is being *created*
4. Adjust negative verb.				{was / were} not given	
5. Adjust subject-verb agreement.	might be seen	*was* given (because S = Paul)	*has* been made (because S = He)	was not given (because S = He)	*are* being caused (because S = Traffic jams)
PASSIVE VOICE	Alex *might be seen*.	Paul *was given* a shirt.	He *was made* very happy.	He *wasn't given* a book.	Traffic jams *are being created*.

have made, did not give, and *are causing.* The active-voice verbs and the passive-voice verbs are in the same tense; the only difference is the added past participle.

Note: Informally, the passive voice can be expressed with *get* instead of *be.*

(72) She was killed in an automobile accident.
(73) She got killed in an automobile accident.

Exercise

Change these sentences to the passive voice, if possible. If the doer of the action is not important information, do not use a phrase with *by.*

1. People can buy clothes in shops or in department stores.
Clothes can be bought in shops or department stores.
2. Many people prefer department stores for convenience.
3. They can find a large selection of styles, sizes, and prices there.
4. In addition, the entire selection is in one place.
5. You do not need transportation from one place to another.
6. Louis has located a good men's shop.
7. It carries a good selection of styles and colors.
8. His friends are buying a lot of clothes there also.
9. Because of all of their purchases, the owner will earn a good income.

Exercise

Change these passive voice sentences to the active voice.

1. Cultural exchanges between countries are encouraged by many governments. *Many governments encourage cultural exchanges between countries.*
2. Music from all around the world can be heard by the people in one country.
3. The best aspects of their country's art are being shown by the best performers.
4. In September, the paintings on loan from Japan were seen by over 75,000 people.
5. Popular music is appreciated by both professionals and amateurs.
6. Cultural exchanges have been arranged by large museums for a long time.
7. They can not be afforded by small museums.

263

8. Funding for international exchanges should be provided by national governments.
9. Such undertakings can be supported by tax revenues.

F2 Uses of the Passive Voice Rearrangement

In the passive voice rearrangement of parts of a sentence, we can emphasize or de-emphasize some of the information. This arrangement allows us (1) to have a new subject in the sentence, (2) to avoid naming the doer of the action, or (3) to put new, important information last in the sentence.

1. To have a new subject in the sentence

The subject of a clause is what is discussed or commented on; it is the topic of thought. Often, the topic of the discussion is also the doer of the action in the sentence.

(74) Marie went downtown to buy a gift for Paul.
     She bought him a book on modern architecture.

Because we are talking about Marie and her activities, *Marie* and *she* are the subjects of the two sentences.

On the other hand, the topic of the discussion may be the receiver of the action or the receiver of benefits of the action.

(75) Paul kept busy during the party.
     He was given many gifts to open.

In these sentences, we are talking about Paul; therefore, *Paul* and *he* are the subjects. However, in the second sentence, Paul does not do any action: he is the receiver of the gifts.

2. To avoid naming the doer of the action

There are times when we do not want to say who did the action. Maybe we do not know; perhaps that is not important information; or it might be embarrassing to name the person. This rearrangement allows us to eliminate the phrase with *by* plus the doer of the action. There is a subject in the new sentence, so the sentence is grammatically complete.

(76) The man was killed after midnight.

We may use example 76 if we do not know the killer, or if we do not wish to name him, or if the doer of the action is not important information in this particular discussion.

> (77) The satellite was put into orbit successfully after several delays.

3. To put new, important information last in the sentence

If we want to, we can create a feeling of suspense or surprise by putting the expected information last. If the new, important information is the name of the doer of the action, we can use the passive voice rearrangement to put that information last.

> (78) A five-year-old child baked the birthday cake.
> (79) The birthday cake was baked by a five-year-old child.

Examples 78 and 79 both describe the same action: there are the same doers of the action, and there is the same result. However, there is a difference in emphasis.

> (80) What does the proverb "People who live in glass houses shouldn't throw stones" mean?

A question like example 80 can be difficult to form and to understand. The very long subject (11 words) separates the two parts of the verb, the auxiliary *does* and the main verb *mean*. The passive voice rearrangement allows us to put the important information—the eleven-word subject— in the last position in the sentence. This rearrangement also means that the entire verb occurs together and is easier to remember and understand.

> (81) What is meant by the proverb "People who live in glass houses shouldn't throw stones"?

Exercise

For each pair of sentences, identify the reason for using the passive voice in the second sentence.

> a. to have a new subject in the sentence
> b. to avoid naming the doer of the action
> c. to put new, important information last in the sentence

1.   a. When my car was in the parking lot, another car hit it.

_6_ b. When my car was in the parking lot, my car was hit.

2.   a. Last night in the parking lot, a boat hit my car.

_____ b. Last night in the parking lot, my car was hit by a boat.

3.   a. We had not seen that movie; someone was showing it downtown.

_____ b. We had not seen that movie; it was being shown downtown.

4.   a. When we were cleaning up, I broke her 2,000-year-old vase.

_____ b. When we were cleaning up, her 2,000-year-old vase was broken.

5.   a. At the end of the play, we found out that Mrs. Forsham had left the baby.

_____ b. At the end of the play, we found out that the baby had been left by Mrs. Forsham.

G *EXPLETIVE THERE*

Any of the clause patterns discussed previously can be used to introduce new information in a discussion. In addition, **expletive** *there* can be used when the new information is the subject of the sentence.

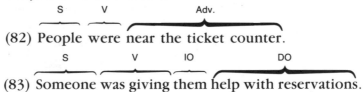

           S   V   Adv.

(82) People were near the ticket counter.

           S   V   IO   DO

(83) Someone was giving them help with reservations.

Another way to say these sentences is shown in examples 84 and 85.

    (84) *There* were people near the ticket counter.

    (85) *There* was someone giving them help with reservations.

G1 **Form of the Rearrangement with the Expletive *There***

There are two steps in this rearrangement. The first step

is to move the subject (S) after any auxiliaries and the verb *be*. The second step is to add the expletive *there* in the subject position. The expletive *there* has no meaning; it is used only to fill the subject position in the sentence.

            S   V

(86)   People were near the ticket counter.
Step 1: Move S after auxiliaries and *be*.

            S   be

(87a) _____were *people* near the ticket counter.
Step 2: Add *there* in the subject position.

(87b) *There* were people near the ticket counter.

          S   V

(88)   Someone had been giving them help with reservations.
Step 1: Move S after auxiliaries and *be*.

        S   Vaux   be

(89a) _____had been *someone* giving them help with reservations.
Step 2: Add *there* in the subject position.

(89b) *There* had been someone giving them help with reservations.

This rearrangement can be difficult. One reason for the difficulty is the agreement between the verb and the subject. In example 87b, for instance, the verb is *were* because it must agree with the subject *people,* which is plural.

The second difficulty is that the expletive *there* is used as the subject when question word order is used. In question word order, a verb form appears before the subject in the clause pattern. Examples 90 and 91 show the yes/no questions that correspond to statements in examples 87b and 89b.

(90)   Were *there* people near the ticket counter?
(91)   Had *there* been someone giving them help with reservations?

And tag statements use *there* in the subject position.

(92)   Yes, there were.

Chapter 6

G2 Use of the Rearrangement with the Expletive *There*

Sentences with the expletive *there* are used to point out the existence of someone or something. This rearrangement allows the speaker or writer to focus attention on the subject (S). New, important information usually comes last in a sentence. If this information is the subject, this rearrangement means that the hearer or reader will find it at the end of the sentence. Important information is put last, and the subject position is filled with an expletive, a word with a grammar role but with no meaning.

Exercise

Change each sentence, using *there* to present the new information in the subject.

1. A parade was going by at the time.

   There was a parade going by at the time.

2. Some drunk people were dancing in the street.
3. All evening, thunder had been sounding off and on.
4. Eye-witnesses are giving contradictory stories.
5. A lot of people are unsure about what happened.

Exercise

Change these sentences to yes/no questions.

1. There is a reason to doubt his word.

   Is there a reason to doubt his word?

2. There were many people standing by the post office.
3. There had been no reliable eye-witnesses.
4. There might have been a distracting noise in the next block.
5. There are doubts in the minds of all of the officials.

Exercise

Add **has been** or **have been**.

1. There __*has been*__ a little news about the accident.
2. There_____an article in the local newspapers.
3. There_____a few short news bulletins on television.

4. There_____quite a lot of rumors.
5. There_____no confirmed report.

H EXPLETIVE IT

Another rearrangement of the basic order in sentences allows us to put an important and complicated subject (S) at the end of the clause. For instance, examples 93 and 94 are both correct.

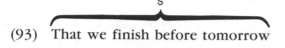

(93) That we finish before tomorrow

is very important.

(94) It is very important that we finish before tomorrow.

Example 93 has the basic arrangement: S V SC. Example 94 has the same three meaning units, but they are in a different order.

H1 Form of the Rearrangement with the Expletive *It*

The subject (S) is moved after the other parts of the sentence; and the empty *it* is put into the subject position: *it* V SC S.

When the empty *it* is used in this rearrangement, it is sometimes called an **expletive**. An expletive is a word which has no meaning and is used to fill the subject position in a sentence.

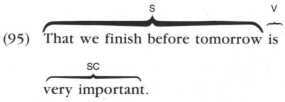

(95) That we finish before tomorrow is

very important.

Move the S after the SC.

269

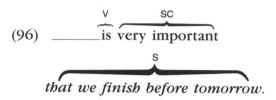

(96) _____is very important

that we finish before tomorrow.

Put *it* in the subject position.

(97) *It* is very important that we finish before tomorrow.

No other changes or adjustments are needed.

Note: This rearrangement can be done only when the subject has a verb form.

(98) To finish today is important.
(99) It is important to finish today.

It can not be done if the subject is a noun (example 100); example 101 is not correct English.

(100) The date is very important.
(101) X It is very important the date.

Exercise

Rearrange the sentences to focus on important subjects.

1. To practice with native speakers is helpful in learning a foreign language. *It is helpful in learning a foreign language to practice with native speakers.*
2. To listen to their ways of speaking is a big help.
3. Understanding them when they speak fast can be very difficult.
4. That they use contractions and slang has always been a problem for learners.
5. Later, not having had this practice may become a serious problem.

H2 Use of the Rearrangement with the Expletive *It*

This rearrangement of sentence patterns is used to give special emphasis to the information included in the subject. The rearrangement allows us to hear or read the verb and the subject complement first, so that we can turn all of our attention to the difficult subject at the end of the sentence.

This rearrangement also makes questions easier to ask and understand. Examples 103 and 105 are correct, but example 105 is much easier to form and much easier for a reader or listener to understand.

(102) statement

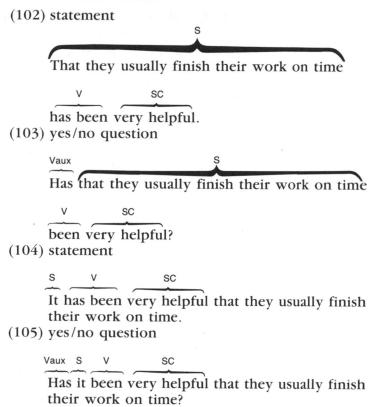

has been very helpful.

(103) yes/no question

Has that they usually finish their work on time

been very helpful?

(104) statement

It has been very helpful that they usually finish their work on time.

(105) yes/no question

Has it been very helpful that they usually finish their work on time?

Exercise

Rearrange each sentence to focus attention on the information in the subject or to make the sentence easier to understand.

1. Has that you speak Farsi fluently been helpful?
   Has it been helpful that you speak Farsi fluently?
2. That living in the United States hasn't improved her language at all is obvious.
3. Whether she can really use the language remains to be seen.

271

4. Was that you didn't get the job depressing?
5. That she had not been abroad came as a great surprise to us.

H3 Expletive *It* for Identification, Emphasis, Contrast

The end of a clause can be the position for new, important information. The speaker or writer can rearrange the parts of a sentence in order to focus the hearer's or reader's attention on this information.

Example 106 is a statement with the basic arrangement.

$$\quad\quad \overset{S}{\overbrace{\quad}} \quad \overset{V}{\overbrace{\quad}} \quad \overset{IO}{\overbrace{\quad\quad}}$$

(106) Phyllis bought her husband

$$\quad\quad \overset{DO}{\overbrace{\quad\quad\quad}} \quad \overset{Adv.}{\overbrace{\quad\quad\quad}}$$

an anniversary gift at a sports shop.

It is possible to rearrange the parts of this clause to focus attention on the adverbial or on any of the nouns—the subject (S), the indirect object (IO), or the direct object (DO). The following examples show these rearrangements.

(107) It was *at a sports shop* that Phyllis bought her husband an anniversary gift.
(108) It was *Phyllis* who bought her husband an anniversary gift at a sports shop.
(109) It was *for her husband* that Phyllis bought an anniversary gift at a sports shop.
(110) It was *an anniversary gift* that Phyllis bought for her husband at a sports shop.

Notice that in examples 109 and 110, the word *for* has been added to indicate the person who receives the benefits of the action.

The rearrangement in example 111 is used for identification. It puts the important information at the end of the independent clause. In that way the information gets the reader's or hearer's attention. It is used to answer questions.

(111) Who bought that new car?
(a) Benjamin.
(b) Benjamin bought it.
(c) *It was Benjamin who bought it.*

It is used for special emphasis or contrast.

> (112) I didn't know that. I thought *it was Dave who was shopping around for a new car.*
>
> *It may have been Dave who was shopping around, but it was Benjamin who bought one.*

Exercise

Using this rearrangement to focus on important nouns and adverbials, write the four sentences that come from:

Andreas bought five of his friends dinner yesterday for his birthday.

Refer to examples 107, 108, 109, and 110 if you need help.

1. *It was Andreas who bought five of his friends dinner for his birthday.*

2. _____

3. _____

4. _____

Exercise

Some statements have been made that you know are not true. Use the rearrangement with *it* to focus attention on the correct information.

1. Chicago is the largest city in the United States.
   It is New York City that is the largest city in the United States.

2. The metric system is used in the United States.

3. 2:00 p.m. is the same as 1300 hours.

4. We find Hawaii east of the North American mainland.

5. A thermometer measures weight.

Chapter 7
Contents

Chapter 7

7 *Punctuation*

A *INTRODUCTION*

Punctuation helps the reader understand the organization of the writer's ideas. Therefore, writers should keep the following principles in mind:

1. Use punctuation only when there is a reason for it, and only when there is a specific rule for its use in a particular situation.
2. Do not use the pronunciation of a word, phrase, or sentence in order to determine where to put punctuation; pronunciation and punctuation do not always relate to each other.
3. It is usually better (less confusing to the reader) to use too little punctuation than to use too much.

The following composition shows some of the forms and uses of punctuation:

(1)   George Washington

George Washington, the first President of the United States, is one of the most famous people in American history. In addition to serving as President (from 1789 to 1797), he had been a soldier in the French and Indian War, commander of the army in the American Revolution, and chairman of the Constitutional Convention. He was known for his hard work and fairness; he is considered one of the best American presidents.

This respected leader's name and face appear very often in the United States. One of the fifty states is named for him. Schools have been named for him: — Washington University in St. Louis, Mo., and Washington College in Chestertown, Md. The capital city of the country has his name. His birthday, which is in February, is observed as a major holiday. And his face is on the one-dollar bill and on the coin worth twenty-five cents. Is there someone like this in your country?

A *PUNCTUATION USES*

A1 **Separating Units**

Three of the units of a written message are paragraphs, sentences, and words. They are units of meaning. A writer puts them together to express his ideas. Punctuation helps the reader to see these separate units of meaning in a written message.

These units of meaning are signalled by indentation, capitalization, and end punctuation marks—periods, question marks, and exclamation points.

Paragraphs

A paragraph is usually indented. The composition about George Washington has two paragraphs. The indentation shows this clearly. The first sentence in the first paragraph is indented.

(2)   George Washington, the first President of the United States

There is also indentation before the first sentence in the second paragraph.

(3)   This respected leader's name and face appear

The indentation should be at least 5 letter spaces but not more than 10.

Sentences

Each sentence is signalled two ways. The first signal is a capital letter for the first word of the sentence (see Appendix A). The second signal is the mark at the end of each sentence. The end marks are the period, the question mark, and the exclamation point.

The exclamation point is not used often in compositions. It is used to show great excitement; this emotion does not usually occur in formal writing.

    (4) "Give me liberty, or give me death!"
      These are the famous words of Patrick Henry.

Note: A sentence cannot end with two periods. If the last word in a sentence already has a period, the sentence will not have two periods at the end. For example, *Md.* has a period because it is the abbreviation for *Maryland*; we would expect to add another period to signal the end of the sentence. However, we do not.

    (5) Washington College is in Chestertown, Md.

Note: If we use a question mark or an exclamation point, we add the end mark after the period in the abbreviation.

    (6) Have you ever been to Chestertown, Md.?
    (7) Yes, and I met John Wilkins, Jr.!

Exercise

Rewrite this paragraph correctly, using capital letters, end marks, and indentation.

there are natural time periods which we recognize in our calendars the problem with creating calendars is that the three natural time periods do not begin at the same time the result of this inconvenience is a calendar with months of different lengths and a leap year every fourth year

A2 **Joining Units**

One of the main jobs of punctuation is to show that two or more words, phrases, or clauses are connected. The punctuation signals to the reader that the writer has brought ideas together and is showing that the ideas are logically related.

Independent Clauses

Two independent clauses can be joined to form a compound sentence. One way to join them is with the conjunctions *and, but, or (nor), so, yet,* or *for* (when it means *because*). When one of these conjunctions is used to form a compound sentence, there is a comma after the first clause.

> (8) Clarice applied for admission to Washington University, but she was not accepted.

There is no comma after the conjunction.

> (9) X Clarice applied for admission to Washington University but, she was not accepted.

This rule applies only to independent clauses: it does not work with words, phrases, or dependent clauses.

> (10) X She filled out the application form, and sent it back to the admissions office.

If the independent clauses have commas in them, the reader may be confused to see another comma that signals the joining of independent clauses with a conjunction, because there are so many commas signalling different meanings. In this case, a semicolon is used in place of a comma.

> (11) X Robert had taken the TOEFL, the GRE, and another test, and he had done well on all of them.
> (12) Robert had taken the TOEFL, the GRE, and another test; and he had done well on all of them.

The second way to join independent clauses is with a semicolon, but without a conjunction.

> (13) He was known for his hard work and fairness; he is considered one of the best American presidents.

It is not correct to join two independent clauses with just a comma.

> (14) X He was known for his hard work and fairness, he is considered one of the best American presidents.

This mistake is called a **comma splice**.

Exercise

Add any needed punctuation to the following sentences.

1. He wanted to take two courses in chemical engineering, but he could not fit them into his schedule.
2. The lines at the bank were very long he did not have a lot of time to wait.
3. She wanted to open a checking account, cash some travelers checks, and change some money so she went to the bank very early.
4. However, she only had time to open the account and cash the checks.

Correct the punctuation mistakes in these sentences.

5. She could do her banking tomorrow after lunch or, she could do it this morning.
6. At first it was hard to think in terms of dollars and cents, she had to force herself not to convert every price into *yen*.
7. At registration he chose his courses then he paid his tuition and other fees.
8. He could take two mathematics courses, or take one mathematics course and a physics laboratory on Monday afternoons.

Sentence and Following Explanation, Example, List, or Quotation

A statement is sometimes followed by related information to make the statement clearer or to give the reader more information. If the statement is a grammatically complete sentence, the writer can put a period after it, and the sentence will be correct. However, when the writer has decided to provide more information to clarify the preceding statement, a colon can be used to show this relationship. This information can be an explanation.

(15) Washington was asked to be the President: he was respected for his leadership qualities.

The information can be an example.

(16) His name appears on the map: Washington state is in the northwest part of the country.

The information can be a list.

(17) Schools have been named for him: Washington University in St. Louis, Missouri, and Washington College in Chestertown, Maryland.

The information is often a quotation.

> (18) We should remember Patrick Henry's words today: "Give me liberty or give me death!"

The information after the colon can be in any form: a single letter, a word, a phrase, a sentence, a paragraph, several paragraphs, etc. However, it is important to remember that the statement before the colon must be a complete sentence. Example 19 is not correct, because the colon does not join a complete sentence with the list that comes after the colon: *We compared* is not a grammatically complete sentence.

> (19) X We compared: the portrait of Washington, his picture on the one-dollar bill, and his profile on the quarter.

The writer can use phrases like *the following* or *as follows* in addition to the colon in order to emphasize the connection between ideas.

> (20) Washington's picture appears on the following money: the one-dollar bill and the quarter.

Exercise

Complete the following sentences in any logical way. Decide whether example 15, 16, 17, or 18 shows how to punctuate the sentence, and write the number of the example. Then punctuate the sentence.

__18__ 1. The following quotation from (name of a book or person) tells us how to live properly (be sure the short quotation is in quotation marks) .

_____ 2. _____ is the most interesting place I have ever visited (give a reason) .

_____ 3. The food in my country is very different from food here. One big difference is the spices we use (list 2 or 3 that are not used very much here) .

_____ 4. Money here is different from money in my country (state one difference) .

_____ 5. One word can describe the weather here today (write the word) .

Sentence and Tag Question or Answer

One way of asking a question is by connecting a statement and a short question that asks if the statement is true. This short question is **tagged** onto the statement. Use a comma to join the statement and the tag question. (See Chapter 1, page 29.)

(21) Abraham Lincoln's profile appears on the penny, doesn't it?

Use a comma to connect *yes* or *no* with a short answer.

(22) Yes, it does.

Exercise

Complete the sentences and tag questions, and the short answers. Then add punctuation that is needed.

1. Roosevelt's profile is on the dime *, isn't it?*
   Yes, *it is.*
2. We made a lot of adjustments when we arrived in this country_____Yes _____
3. An informal style of English is not usually appropriate in compositions_____
   No_____
4. One kilo (kg. or kilogram) equals 2.2 pounds_____
   Yes_____
5. My classmates have found the American system of weights and measures difficult _____
   No_____

Items in a Series

A **series** is a list of 3 or more items. The items can be words, phrases, or clauses (but all the items in one series must be the same kind; see Chapter 5, page 196 on parallelism. Join items in a series with commas.

(23) George Washington was a soldier, a commander, and a president.

It is possible to eliminate the comma before the conjunction *and*. This is the writer's choice; there is no difference in meaning, although a writer may prefer one usage or the other. Just remember to be consistent: either always use the comma in this position or never use it. Both examples 23 and 24 are correct.

> (24) George Washington was a soldier, a commander and a President.

Note: This rule about items in a series works only when there are 3 or more items in the list; it does not apply if the list has only 2 items.

> (25) He was a soldier and a commander.
> (26) X He was a soldier, and a commander.

If the items in the series already have commas, use semicolons to make the relationships clear. In example 27, . how many places did my friends visit?

> (27) X My friends visited Washington, D.C., San Francisco, California, and New York City, New York.

Three of the places have commas in their names, so it is hard to know what the commas are signalling. Therefore, semicolons are used in order to make the sentences easier to understand. In example 28, it is clear that my friends visited three places.

> (28) My friends visited Washington, D.C.; San Francisco, California; and New York City, New York.

Note: Do not put a comma after the last item in a series.

> (29) X They visited Dallas, Houston, and San Antonio, on their vacation.

There are two other ways of joining the items in a series. One of these has commas but no conjunctions; the other has conjunctions but no commas. These two ways are correct, but they are very unusual. Therefore, they should not be used often.

> (30) Washington was a soldier, a commander, a president.
> (31) Washington was a soldier and a commander and a president.

Sometimes, for emphasis or clarity, a writer decides to number the items in a list of 2 or more items. If the list is written as part of a sentence, the numbers are put in parentheses.

> (32) George Washington served in three important periods of American history: (1) from 1752 to 1759,

as a soldier; (2) from 1775 to 1781, as Commander in Chief of the U.S. army; and (3) from 1789 to 1797, as President of the United States.

If the list is written like a list—vertically, not in a sentence—a period is put after each number.

(33) George Washington served in three important periods of American history:
1. From 1752 to 1759, as a soldier
2. From 1775 to 1781, as Commander in Chief of the U.S. Army
3. From 1789 to 1797, as President of the United States.

Note that there is no punctuation after each item in the list: the vertical arrangement makes it clear to the reader what the items of the list are.

Note: When we write items in a vertical list, we do not use a slash mark, closing parentheses, or a small circle after the number.

(34) X 1/ From 1752 to 1759, as a soldier
(35) X 1) From 1752 to 1759, as a soldier
(36) X 1° From 1752 to 1759, as a soldier

Exercise

Complete the following sentences. Fill in words and/or numbers to make logical statements. Decide which of the preceding examples shows how to punctuate the sentence, and write the number of the example. Then punctuate the sentence.

_23_ **1.** My three favorite classes in school have been _history, math_ and _geography_ .

_____ **2.** A visitor to my country should see (name 2 places) _____and_____.

_____ **3.** The largest cities in my country are_____ _____and _____.

_____ **4.** I think that the following three dates are the most
_____ important for world affairs in this century:
1_____ 2_____ and 3_____.

_____ **5.** Blank space is a way to give the reader information about the_____ _____
and_____in a written message.

A3 **Putting Extra Information Into Clauses**

Sometimes extra words, phrases, or clauses are put into a clause to provide more information. This information helps the readers because it clarifies an idea or because it shows how one idea is related to another. However, this material is not necessary: (1) the readers do not need it in order to understand the idea expressed in the clause, and (2) the material is not part of the grammatical structure of the clause.

Non-restrictive Information

Non-restrictive information can be added to a clause. The information can be an appositive, a noun clause, an adjective clause, or an adverb clause (see Chapter 5, page 224 and page 236 on restrictive and non-restrictive information). If this extra information is before or after the clause, use one comma to set it off from the clause.

> (37) They celebrate Washington's Birthday, which is in February.

If this extra material is put into the middle of the clause, use one comma before it and one comma after it.

> (38) His birthday, which is in February, is observed as a major holiday.

Exercise

Complete the sentences, and then add punctuation if necessary.

1. My native country _, *Malawi* ,_____is located in *Africa*_____.

2. The course which I find most interesting is _____.

3. In my country, the happiest holiday which is _____ _____occurs on_____.

4. _____is a famous person in my country who should be known all over the world.

285

5. More people should study_____
because it is a field in which the world needs more
knowledgeable people.

Explanations or Additions

Very short explanations or other added information can be
added to a clause. Parentheses or dashes are used to indicate
this added information.

Use a pair of parentheses to set off information that is
not very important to the discussion or ideas.

> (39) In addition to serving as President (from 1789 to
> 1797), he was a soldier in the French and Indian
> War, Commander of the Army in the American
> Revolution, and Chairman of the Constitutional
> Convention.

The discussion is about Washington's service to his country. Therefore, the dates of his Presidency are additional
information to help the reader who may not know when
Washington lived or when he was President.

Use one or two dashes to set off very short information
if the reader's attention should be drawn to it. While parentheses signal that the inserted information is not important,
dashes tell the reader to be sure to notice the information.
Example 40 has dates which are not signalled as important;
the parentheses indicate the lack of great importance.

> (40) He served as a soldier for a time in the French and
> Indian War (from 1756 to 1763).

Example 41 has dashes to indicate that the dates are important in the discussion.

> (41) That period—from 1756 to 1763—was critical in
> both American and European history.

Exercise

The underlined information has been inserted into the
sentences. Decide whether example 40 or 41 shows how
to set off each insertion. Write the number and then punctuate the insertion.

Newcomers to the United States are often confused by
American paper money because all the bills are the same

size. The one-dollar bill is as big as the five-dollar bill, the ten-dollar bill, the twenty-dollar bill, etc.

_40_ (There is a two-dollar bill, but it is not used very much.)

It is very important for the new arrival to learn to look at the numbers which appear frequently on each bill 15 times on the one-dollar bill, for example. Although a one-dollar bill may look like a ten-dollar bill they are the same size and although the number 1 may be mistaken for the number 10 , the words one and ten look quite different.

Phrases of Contrast

Sometimes a contrast between two ideas is expressed by a phrase added to an independent clause. The contrasting phrase is not part of the grammatical pattern of the clause where it appears. Often the phrase is introduced with *not* or *but (not)*. This contrasting phrase is set off from the clause by one or two commas.

(42) Some people have studied finance, *but* have little training in statistics.
(43) Many people in the United States want national, not local, gun control laws.

Exercise

Add any needed commas in the following sentences.

1. Some American money is the same size but not all.

2. The paper money not the coins can be confusing.
3. All American coins but not the penny are silver-colored.
4. This store will accept travelers checks but not personal checks.
5. Alice learned Spanish more slowly but more thoroughly than Edward.

One of the sentences has no commas in it. Which one? Why not?

Transitions and Sentence Modifiers

A **transition** is a word or a phrase that shows a logical connection between the idea in one independent clause and the idea in another independent clause. It is like a bridge between the two ideas. Use one or two commas to set off a transition in a clause. In example 44, the transition is *however*; it is inserted in the middle of a clause and is set off by two commas.

> (44) General Braddock's campaign against the French and Indians was disastrous. Washington, *however,* was not blamed for its failure.

Use one comma if the transition is at the beginning or end of a clause.

> (45) Washington was married in 1759. *For this reason,* he resigned from the army and became a farmer in Virginia.

A **sentence modifier** is also set off from the rest of the sentence with a comma.

> (46) *To tell the truth,* I do not know very much about history.

Exercise

Complete each sentence with one of the following transitions: **after a while**, **anyhow**, **however**, **in addition**, or **therefore**. Then punctuate the sentences.

1. It was snowing very hard yesterday afternoon, *therefore,* the airport was closed.
2. They studied very hard for the TOEFL. They bought special books for practice; _____ they took a special review class.
3. She let the dough rise. _____ she put the loaves in the oven for an hour.
4. I thought that we would not get home that night. We ran out of gasoline in the middle of nowhere. There was _____ an open gasoline station not too far away.
5. Pedro had not studied for the SAT; he got a very good score _____.

A4 *INDICATING SPECIAL STATUS OF WORDS*

In a sentence or a paragraph, some word or words may have unusual uses or may be used with unusual meanings. If the writer uses something in a special way, he should tell readers so that they can completely understand his ideas. The special status of words is indicated by quotation marks or underlining.

Unusual Words or Meanings

A writer can show that he is using words in an unusual way by putting quotation marks before and after them. The quotation marks signal that the use of the words is unusual.

> (47) Because of his service to the nation, George Washington has been called *"the father of our country."*

The five-word phrase in example 47 is unusual because the word *father* is not used in its usual way.

> (48) The sports announcer said that the score was 4 to "zip."

An announcement of this score might have the usual word *nothing* or *zero*.

Exercise

Complete the sentences, and add any needed punctuation.

1. The informal word for *gymnasium* is __"gym"_____.
2. The word *flunk* means _____.
3. American slang is hard to understand. For example, I did not know that *neat* also meant _____.

Direct Quotations

A **direct quotation** is a report of the exact words said or written by someone other than the writer. A writer must indicate when he uses someone else's words. He does this with quotation marks. In addition, he should indicate whose words they are.

> (49) At the end of his presidency, George Washington warned against *"permanent alliances"* with other countries.

The phrase *"permanent alliances"* is the exact phrase that Washington used.

The direct quotation may be of any length. It may be short, as in example 49, or it may be much longer.

> (50) In the Declaration of Independence, the states put forth the following principles: "We hold these truths to be self-evident, that all men are created equal, that they are endowed by their creator with certain unalienable Rights, that among these are Life, Liberty, and the pursuit of Happiness."

The 35 words in this direct quotation are exactly as they appear in the Declaration of Independence; the quotation marks tell the reader that this is an exact report of someone's words.

Exercise

Complete the sentences, and add any needed punctuation.

1. In English, we often use the following proverb: "People who live in glass houses should not throw stones."

2. A well-known proverb in (name of language) is _____.

3. In the United Nations Charter, the members state their intention to practice tolerance and live together in peace with one another as good neighbors. (The underlined words are the exact words in the Charter.)

4. _____, a famous person from my country, should be remembered for his/her idea that _____.

Foreign Words

If a writer uses foreign words, their special status is signalled by underlining. It is sometimes difficult to know when to underline. Many foreign words are borrowed and used in English; some of them are still considered foreign, while others are accepted as English. (If the writer is not sure whether a word is English, he should consult an English dictionary.)

> (51) In a book, a play often begins with a list of the dramatis personae.

290

In a printed book italics are used instead of underlining.

> (52) The *dramatis personae* are the characters in the play.

Exercise

Complete the following sentences, and add any needed punctuation.

1. In my language, the way to say "thank you" is *Khop Khon Khaa* ____. (Use English letters.)

2. A visitor to my country should know how to say ____(use English letters)____ ; this means _____.

3. Languages borrow words from other languages: ___(use English letters)___ is a foreign word we use in my language.

4. I have seen the word _____ in English, but I think that it is a foreign word borrowed and used in English.

Emphasized Words

A writer uses underlining (italics in a printed book) to show that certain words are especially important.

> (53) A direct quotation shows the _exact_ words used by someone besides the writer.

In example 53, the word *exact* is especially important: the writer has emphasized its importance with underlining. The underlining says to the reader, "Look at this word: it is very important."

Underlining should not be used very often in formal writing: a large number of emphasized words decreases its effect.

Exercise

Punctuate the sentences to show the word or words that should be emphasized to help the reader understand the message.

1. He was not careful in his writing. Although the rule said to put the hyphen _after_ a letter or number, he usually put it _under_ the letter or number.

2. The Washington Monument might be 168 meters high, but I do believe that it is 168,000 meters high.

Titles of Books, Stories, and Movies

Books and Other Separate Works

Underline the title of a book or any other printed material that appears separately and is not part of another, larger work.

(54) He had read <u>The Biography of George Washington, Gentleman Farmer</u> , but he did not find it very interesting.

(55) <u>The Washington Post</u> had quite a few advertisements for the Washington's Birthday sales.

<u>The Biography of George Washington, Gentleman Farmer</u> is the name of a book, and <u>The Washington Post</u> is the name of a newspaper.

Stories and Other Included Works

Use quotation marks to set off the titles of any work that does not appear separately, that is, included in another, larger work.

(56) George Washington's "First Inaugural Address in the City of New York, April 30, 1789" is included in the book <u>Inaugural Addresses of the Presidents of the United States</u> .

Washington's first inaugural address is one part of the book; it does not appear separately.

Movies, Television Shows

Use quotation marks to signal the name of a movie, a radio show, or a television program.

(57) "The Untouchables" was a popular television program in the United States in the 1950s.

Exercise

Complete the following sentences. Find the example (54, 55, 56, or 57) that shows how to punctuate each sentence, and write the number of the example. Then punctuate the sentences.

_55_ **1.** The biggest newspaper in my country is _An_ _Nakar_ .

_____ **2.** My two favorite books in English are_____ and _____ .

_____ **3.** _____ is a famous writer from my country. Two of his/her best-known works are_____ and_____ .

_____ **4.** For relaxation, I usually read __(specific name)__ or watch __(specific name)__ on television.

_____ **5.** The name of this book is_____ .

_____ **6.** If a person wants to understand my country better, he should read __(specific name)__ .

_____ **7.** The two movies I have enjoyed the most are _____ and _____ .

A5 Separating Parts of a Sentence or Phrase

Several ideas may be brought together in a phrase, a clause, or a sentence. However, it may be difficult for the reader to see the different parts of the writer's message. Therefore, punctuation can be useful in making the message clearer by visually separating parts of the message. The punctuation marks of separation are periods, commas, colons, semicolons, and slashes.

Dates

Dates can be written in formal and informal ways. The formal way is to use the name of the month, the number of the day, and the four digits of the year. Use a comma to separate the number of the day from the number of the year.

(58) George Washington was born on February 22, 1732.

When there is a full date—the month, the day, and the year—use a comma to separate the year from the word that follows it in the sentence.

(59) George Washington was born on February 22, 1732, in Virginia.

293

The informal way to write a date is fast and easy; it uses all numbers and slashes.

(60) She was born on *8/12/61*.

The first number is the month; the second number is the day; the third number is the last 2 digits of the year.

Note: Remember that in the U.S. the month comes before the day. August 12, 1961, is not 12/8/61; 12/8/61 is December 8, 1961. In compositions, it is better to use the formal way because (1) there is less chance for confusing the month and the day and (2) it is more appropriate.

Exercise

Complete the following sentences, and add any needed punctuation.

1. Convert to the formal way:
   a. United States Independence Day _July 4, 1776_
      7/4/76
   b. First manned orbital flight
      (U.S.S.R.) 4/12/61 _____
   c. End of World War I 11/11/18 _____
2. Convert to the informal way:
   a. Greatest aviation disaster:
      582 people died March 27, 1977 _____
   b. Beginning of the United Nations
      October 24, 1945 _____
   c. Official independence of
      Zimbabwe April 18, 1980 _____
3. The following sentence is not correct in English: X *He was born on 23/5/68.* What is the mistake? What did the writer probably mean to write?_____

Places

Use a comma to separate the parts of the name of a place. A city name should be separated from a state name.

(61) Washington, D.C., is larger than Washington, Pa.

Also, a city name and a state name should be separated from a country name.

(62) Paris, France, is larger than Paris, Texas, U.S.A.

In a sentence with a city name and a state name, the state name should have a comma after it.

(63) Paris, Texas, is not a large city.

Note: Do not put a comma between the number and the street name in an address.

    (64) X The President of the U.S. lives at 1600, Pennsylvania Avenue.

    (65) The President of the U.S. lives at 1600 Pennsylvania Avenue.

Note: Do not put a comma between the state abbreviation and the ZIP code in an address.

    (66) X The mailing address of the university is Arlington, TX, 76019.

    (67) The mailing address of the university is Arlington, TX 76019.

Exercise

Complete the following sentences. Decide which example or examples (61, 62, 63, 64, 65, 66 or 67) show how to punctuate each sentence, and write the number or numbers. Then punctuate the sentence.

  _61_ **1.** My school is in _Long Branch, New Jersey_ .

  _____ **2.** Life in ___(city and country of my birth)___ is
    different from life in ___(country where I am living now)___ .

  _____ **3.** The address where I live is _____
    _____ .

Numbers

Use a period—called a **decimal point** or a **point**—to separate the decimal digits from the whole numbers.

    (68) The Washington Monument is about 555 feet tall, that is, about 168.164 meters.

Note: Many writing systems use a comma in this case. Be careful not to do this in English.

    (69) X The monument is 168,164 meters tall.

Use a period to separate dollars from cents in a sum of money.

(70) That biography of Washington costs $25.95.

Do not use a comma in this case.

(71) ✗ That biography costs $25,95.

Use commas to separate and to group the digits in a number that is greater than 999. Start at the decimal point; count to the left; put a comma after each group of 3 digits.

(72) 999.95
  7,999.95
  51,043,972

Note: Some writing systems use a point in this case. Be careful not to do this in English.

(73) ✗ Washington, D.C., has about 700.000 people.

Note: Some writing systems use a space rather than a comma to group digits. Be careful not to do this in American English.

(74) ✗ Washington, D.C., has about 700 000 people.

Note: Do not use a comma to separate the digits in a year.

(75) ✗ Washington died in 1,799.
(76) Washington died in 1799.

Note: Do not use a comma to separate the digits in an address.

(77) ✗ They lived at 1,880 Columbia Road.
(78) They lived at 1880 Columbia Road.

Note: Do not use a comma to separate the digits in a ZIP code.

(79) ✗ Washington, D.C. 20,009
(80) Washington, D.C. 20009

Exercise

Complete the following sentences; use numerals, not words. Find the example or examples that show how to punctuate each sentence, and write the number or numbers. Then punctuate the sentences.

___72___ **1.** The distance by air from Washington, D.C., to Miami is 923 miles; that is ___1,485___ kilometers.

(Multiply by 1.6093.)

_____ 2. Absolute Zero is about – 273 degrees Celsius (Centigrade). It is _____ degrees Fahrenheit. (Multiply by 9/5, and add 32.)

_____ 3. The Sears Tower in Chicago has 110 stories and is 443 meters tall (443 meters = _____feet). (Multiply by 3.2808.)

_____ 4. This handbook cost $ _____. That is equal to _____ in my country; the exchange rate is _____ for $1.00 U.S.

_____ 5. My address in this country is the following:

_____   _____ (number and street) _____

_____ (city, state, and ZIP code) _____

Time

Use a colon to separate the hours from the minutes in time.

(81) Their plane arrived at 7:35 p.m.

Exercise

Complete the following chart and add needed punctuation. When it is noon in New York City, on May 31, tell the time and date in the following cities:

	Time	Date
1. Caracas (half hour later)	12:30	May 31
2. Jakarta (12½ hours later)	_____	_____
3. Kinshasa (6 hours later)	_____	_____
4. Adelaide (14½ hours later)	_____	_____
5. Dallas (one hour earlier)	_____	_____
6. Tokyo (14 hours later)	_____	_____

Direct Quotations and Reporting Verbs

When a person's exact words are written down, there is frequently an indication of the person who used the words. This indication usually includes a **reporting verb** such as *say, ask,* or *reply.* A comma separates the direct quotation from the **reporting verb**. (See also Chapter 7, pages 281 and 289.)

(82) Patrick Henry shouted, ''Give me liberty or give me death!''

(83) She answered, "I have never been to Chester-town."

If there is an exclamation point or a question mark to separate the direct quotation from the reporting verb, no comma is used.

(84) "Give me liberty or give me death!" shouted Patrick Henry.

Exercise

Add needed punctuation to the following sentences.

1. President Franklin Delano Roosevelt said , "The only thing we have to fear is fear itself."
2. "The only thing we have to fear is fear itself" is a famous quotation from President Roosevelt.
3. "The only thing we have to fear is fear itself" declared Franklin D. Roosevelt at the beginning of his presidency, in 1933.

Introductory Information Before an Independent Clause

Often a word, a phrase, or a dependent clause comes before an independent clause. Of course, this introductory material is related to the independent clause, but it is not part of the grammar of the clause. If the introductory material is not part of the grammar pattern of the independent clause following it, a comma is used for separation.

The introductory material may be an entire dependent clause.

(85) *After Washington left the Presidency,* he returned to his estate of Mt. Vernon.

It may be a phrase with a verb form, that is, a phrase showing an action or state.

(86) *After leaving the Presidency,* Washington returned to Virginia.

It may be a word or phrase that serves as an appositive (see Chapter 6, page 236).

(87) *Chairman of the Constitutional Convention,* Washington was a popular choice for the presidency.

It may be a word or phrase that serves as an adverb, that is, one telling *when, where, how, why,* etc.

> (88) *After the Revolutionary War,* Washington retired from public life.

When the introductory material is an adverb word or phrase, the writer has a choice: to use a comma for separation or not. If the adverb is short and simple, a comma is not especially helpful, because the reader does not need that extra help in reading the sentence.

> (89) *After the Revolutionary War* Washington retired from public life.

If the adverb is long or complicated, a comma is useful, because it helps the reader to see the two parts of the sentence—the introductory material and the main clause.

> (90) Because of insufficient support from the Congress and the large number of inexperienced and badly equipped soldiers, Washington had to avoid large battles with the British.

(There is a general principle that it is better to use too little punctuation than to use too much. However, a writer should remember that in the case of introductory adverbial information, a comma for separation is always correct.)

Note: Example 91 begins with a dependent clause, but there is no comma to separate it from the independent clause following it.

> (91) That the soldiers were suffering at Valley Forge was not a secret.

There is no comma of separation because the dependent clause is part of the grammar pattern of the independent clause: the clause *that the soldiers were suffering at Valley Forge* is the grammatical subject of the verb *was.* The comma of separation can be used only when the introductory information is not a part of the grammar pattern of the independent clause following it.

Exercise

Find the example (85, 86, 87, 88, 89, 90, or 91) that shows how to punctuate the sentence. Then add any needed punctuation.

_87_ **1.** A very important test the GRE sometimes makes people nervous.

_____ **2.** On Tuesday they are going to have their mid-term examination in computer science.

_____ **3.** When the plane landed the first thing we had to do was go through immigration.

_____ **4.** After the long flight of almost ten hours and the terribly hot and humid weather we were ready for a long sleep.

_____ **5.** I wrote a rough draft; before recopying it I checked the spelling very carefully.

_____ **6.** Satisfied with her grade on the report she began to work on her next physics project.

7. The following sentence has incorrect punctuation. What is the mistake?
That she arrived late, is generally known. _____

Information Following an Independent Clause

Often a word, phrase, or dependent clause comes after an independent clause. Sometimes this material has the following two characteristics:

1. It has no function in the grammar pattern of the independent clause.

2. It is not very closely related to the idea or ideas in the independent clause. The relationship is general, and often the material can be put in several places in the sentence.

In this case, use a comma to separate the independent clause from the information following it.

The information following it may be an entire dependent clause.

(92) He did not visit Mt. Vernon very often, because the war was not going well.

The information following it may be a phrase.

(93) he returned to Mt. Vernon, tired but satisfied with his job.

The information following it may be a word.

300

(94) Did Martha Washington spend some time in Valley
    Forge, too?

Note: Do not use a comma to separate an independent
clause from a dependent clause if they are very closely
related in meaning or if the dependent clause is part of the
grammar pattern of the independent clause.

(95) X Washington announced, that he wanted to retire
    after serving as President for two terms.

Example 95 is incorrect. There is a dependent clause: *that
he wanted to retire after serving as President for two terms.*
This dependent clause functions like a noun; it is the direct
object in the main clause. Therefore, there should not be
any comma of separation in the sentence.

(96) Washington announced that he wanted to retire
    after serving as President for two terms.

Exercise

Find the example (92, 93, 94, or 96) that shows how to punctuate the sentence. Then add any needed punctuation.

_93_ **1.** They returned to their dormitory having com-
        pleted the long registration process.

_____ **2.** I did not finish registering yesterday, and I did not
        get all the courses I wanted either.

_____ **3.** She was generally satisfied with her schedule al-
        though she had not gotten all the courses she
        wanted.

4. The following sentence is incorrect. Explain the mistake.
    Which example shows the mistake?
    *Many people think, that the United Nations is an im-
    portant organization which performs important duties.*

Preventing Misreading

Use a comma of separation to prevent misreading. A comma can help the reader to separate two ideas that could be
confused.

(97) X With Martha Custis Washington settled at Mt.
    Vernon.

The reader could be confused. Is this sentence about one
person—Martha Custis Washington—or about two people

301

—Martha Custis and George Washington? To help the reader avoid this confusion, the writer should use a comma.

> (98) With Martha Custis, Washington settled at Mt. Vernon.

Note: The comma to prevent misreading should not be used often; it is a better idea to rewrite the sentence to avoid the possibility of confusion. Moreover, this comma should be used only when the possibility of confusion is obvious: when two interpretations exist. It should not be used in general to make a sentence clear.

Exercise

Add commas of separation to the following sentences, so that the readers will be able to understand the ideas more easily.

1. Because he injured his eye glasses would be helpful.
2. Just before the plane came down the runway lights went on.
3. In baseball bats are not all the same size.
4. Inside the book was more interesting than the dull cover had led me to expect.
5. As a complement to psychology statistics is a good choice for a course to take.

Names of People, Last Name First

In English, the usual order for a person's full name is first name (given name), middle name, and last name (surname, family name). However there are times when a person's name is written in another order: last name, first name, and middle name. This order is often found on application forms, class rolls, and bibliographies. When this second arrangement is used, a comma separates the last name from the first and second names.

> (99) Washington, Martha Custis
> Roosevelt, Franklin Delano
>> Martha Custis Washington
>> Franklin Delano Roosevelt

Note: There is no comma between the first name and the middle name.

Note: It is very important for students to use the comma correctly when they write their names, especially if their names are very different from English names.

A6 Showing A Choice

A quick and easy way to show a choice is with a slash. The writer uses the slash to separate the possibilities. For example, in example 100, the choice is between the word *and* and the word *or.*

> (100) The students had to read Washington's first inaugural address and/or his farewell address.

The *and/or* means that there are three possibilities. Each student had to do one of the following reading assignments:

1. Washington's first inaugural address
2. Washington's farewell address
3. both of Washington's addresses

A7 Showing Something Has Been Removed

Punctuation can tell the reader that a particular word, sentence, or paragraph is a shortened version.

Contractions indicate shortened words. They are formed by joining words and removing letters. An apostrophe shows the location of the omitted letter(s).

> (101) He's not studying English this year.
> (102) He isn't studying English this year.

Note: A few contractions have irregular spellings.

cannot/can not	can't
will not	won't

Abbreviations are shortened names. Use a period after initials in a name and after other abbreviations.

> (103) Dwight D. Eisenhower's home in Gettysburg, Pa., was not very far from Washington, D.C.

In a direct quotation, 3 periods are used to show that a word or words have been omitted in the middle of a sentence or paragraph. This is called **ellipsis**.

> (104) The previous sample composition has the claim that "George Washington . . . is one of the most famous people in American history."

Exercise

Add apostrophes and periods where they are necessary.

1. Professor Jameson made an unusual statement: "Although studying cant guarantee a good grade, Im sure that it wont hurt your grade."

2. In Chapter 7, the fifth principle says, "Use punctuation only when there is a specific rule for its use."

3. John F. Kennedys family comes from Boston, Massachusetts.

4. In his book, *Follow the Lemmings*, Peter Cross says that lemmings, "are the most interesting creatures on earth."

Appendix

Appendix

A. **Spelling**
B. **Some Common Transitive Two-Word Verbs**
C. **Verb + Verb Combinations**
D. **Irregular Verbs**
E. **Indirect Objects in Sentence Patterns**
F. **Comparative and Superlative Irregular Forms**
G. **Some Adjectives and their Prepositions**

A **SPELLING**

These six spelling rules should be used when the grammar in a sentence requires a special form of a word, for example, the past tense of a regular verb, the plural of a noun, or the comparative form of an adverb.

Some of the rules are complex: they require several steps. However, these rules are not difficult, if the questions are answered in a step-by-step procedure. Answer each question with a *yes* or a *no*. If there is a *no* answer, the rule does not apply; otherwise, the rule does apply. Also, there are charts which show how to use the step-by-step procedure.

After the rules there are some exercises. These exercises have some common words and some unusual ones. The rules can be used even if a particular word is not known. Then, if the student wants to, he or she can find the word in a dictionary.

Some of the spelling rules refer to vowel and consonant letters. The vowel letters are: *a, e, i, o,* and *u.* The other 21 letters are consonant letters. However, for these six spelling rules, *w, x,* and *y* should not be considered as consonant letters.

A1 **Spelling Rule #1: Doubling the Final Consonant**

Use this rule to form:

1. The past tense of a verb: V + *ed*

    (1) pla*n* + ed = pla*nn*ed

2. The past participle of a verb: V + *ed*

    (2) prefe*r* + ed = prefe*rr*ed

307

3. The present participle of a verb: V + *ing*

    (3) si*t* + ing = si*tt*ing

4. The comparative form of an adjective: Adj. + *er*

    (4) bi*g* + er = bi*gg*er

5. The superlative form of an adjective: Adj. + *est*

    (5) re*d* + est = re*dd*est

Double the final consonant when all three questions have *yes* answers:

1. Does the simple form of the verb or the positive form of the adjective or adverb end with only one consonant letter?

2. Is there only one vowel letter before the one final consonant?

3. Is the stress (or accent) on that one vowel?

(Following are some words in which the accent does not fall on the last syllable, and the final consonant is not doubled: alter — altered, altering; listen — listened, listening; solicit — solicited, soliciting.)

Note: Consider *qu* as one consonant, not as a consonant and a vowel.

    (6) equi*p* + ed = equi*pp*ed

Note: Instead of double *c,* write *ck.*

    (7) picni*c* + ed = picni*ck*ed

The following chart shows how the three questions and their answers lead to correct spelling.

Question	want + ed	wait + ing	narrow + er	prefer + ed	big + est
1	NO: 2 consonant letters	YES:	YES:	YES:	YES:
	wa*nt* + ed	wai*t* + ing	narro*w* + er	prefe*r* + ed	bi*g* + est
2		NO: 2 vowel letters	YES:	YES:	YES:
		wa*it* + ing	narro*w* + er	prefe*r* + ed	bi*g* + est
3			NO: stress on another vowel	YES:	YES:
			ná*rr*ow + er	prefé*r* + ed	bí*g* + est

Question	want + ed	wait + ing	narrow + er	prefer + ed	big + est
	NO doubled letter	NO doubled letter	NO doubled letter	DOUBLED LETTER	DOUBLED LETTER
	wanted	waiting	narrower	preferred	biggest

Exercise

Write the past tense or past participle forms.

1. answer + ed = _answered_
2. tow + ed = _____
3. sin + ed = _____
4. extend + ed = _____
5. unseat + ed = _____
6. defer + ed = _____
7. acquit + ed = _____
8. open + ed = _____
9. skid + ed = _____
10. tax + ed = _____

Write the simple forms.

11. occurred = _occur_ + ed
12. trekked = _____ + ed
13. called = _____ + ed
14. abutted = _____ + ed
15. mimicked = _____ + ed

Exercise

Write the present participle forms.

1. play + ing = _playing_
2. conceal + ing = _____
3. nag + ing = _____
4. enter + ing = _____
5. stab + ing = _____
6. prefer + ing = _____
7. sign + ing = _____
8. span + ing = _____
9. stow + ing = _____
10. bud + ing = _____

Write the simple forms.

11. missing = _miss_ + ing
12. whetting = _____ + ing

309

13. dimming = _____ + ing
14. rigging = _____ + ing
15. canning = _____ + ing

Exercise

Write the comparative and superlative forms.

1. new + er = *newer*
2. trim + er = _____
3. glad + er = _____
4. fast + er = _____
5. flat + er = _____
6. narrow + est = _____
7. broad + est = _____
8. thin + est = _____
9. quiet + est = _____
10. wicked + est = _____

Write the positive forms.

11. thicker = *thick* + er
12. tallest = _____ + er
13. sadder = _____ + er
14. fullest = _____ + est
15. hotter = _____ + est

A2 ## Spelling Rule #2: Cancelling the Final *e*

Use this rule to form:

1. The past tense of a verb: V + *ed*
   (8) use + ed = used
2. The past participle of a verb: V + *ed*
   (9) exclude + ed = excluded
3. The present participle of a verb: V + *ing*
   (10) arrange + ing = arranging
4. The comparative form of an adjective: Adj. + *er*
   (11) pale + er = paler
5. The superlative form of an adjective: Adj. + *est*
   (12) sure + est = surest

Cancel the final *e* on the simple form of a verb or on the positive form of an adjective or adverb.

(13) use + ed = us~~e~~ed = used

Note: Do not cancel the second *e* of a double *e* when adding *ing*.

(14) agre~~e~~ + ing = agreeing

Note: Do not cancel the *e* in *be*.

(15) be + ing = being

Note: An *ie* in the simple form becomes *y* before *ing*.

(16) l~~ie~~ + ing = lying

Exercise

Write the past tense or past participle forms.

1. name + ed = _named_
2. eliminate + ed = _____
3. clothe + ed = _____
4. defame + ed = _____
5. lie + ed = _____
6. universalize + ed = _____
7. precede + ed = _____
8. stare + ed = _____
9. place + ed = _____
10. eye + ed = _____

Write the simple forms.

11. abused = _abuse_ + ed
12. loped = _____ + ed
13. imbibed = _____ + ed
14. freed = _____ + ed
15. axed = _____ + ed

Exercise

Write the present participle forms.

1. seize + ing = _seizing_
2. innoculate + ing = _____
3. sense + ing = _____
4. tune + ing = _____

    5. see + ing = _____

    6. die + ing = _____

    7. dye + ing = _____

    8. obscure + ing = _____

    9. raze + ing = _____

10. be + ing = _____

Write the simple forms.

11. exuding = _exude_ + ing

12. vying = _____ + ing

13. coping = _____ + ing

14. lapsing = _____ + ing

15. proving = _____ + ing

Exercise

Write the comparative or superlative form.

    1. large + er = _larger, largest_

    2. brave + er = _____

    3. wide + est = _____

    4. simple + est = _____

    5. polite + est = _____

Write the positive forms.

    1. freer = _free_ + er

    2. rarest = _____ + er

    3. truer = _____ + er

    4. gravest = _____ + er

    5. bluest = _____ + er

A3 Spelling Rule #3: Changing Final *y* to *i*

Use this rule to form:

    1. The past tense of a verb: V + *ed*

      (17) tr*y* + ed = tr*i*ed

    2. The past participle of a verb: V + *ed*

      (18) den*y* + ed = den*i*ed

    3. The comparative form of an adjective: Adj. + *er*

      (19) happ*y* + er = happ*i*er

4. The superlative form of an adjective:
   Adj. + *est*

   (20) sorr*y* + est = sorr*i*est

5. The plural of a noun: N + *s*

   (21) countr*y* + s = countr*i*es

6. The third person singular of a present tense verb:
   V + *s*

   (22) den*y* + s = den*i*es

Change the final *y* to *i* when the answer to this question
is *yes:* Is the letter in front of the final *y* a consonant letter?

Note: When *s* is added to make a noun plural or a verb
form, (1) the final *y* changes to *i,* and (2) *e* is added before
the *s.*

   (23) countr*y* + s = countr*i* + *e* + s

The following chart shows how the question and its answer
lead to correct spelling.

	delay + ed	friendly + est	try + ed	try + s
Question	NO: a is a vowel letter	YES:	YES:	YES:
	delay + ed	friendly + est	try + ed	try + s
	NO CHANGE	CHANGE y to i	CHANGE y to i	CHANGE y to i ADD e before s
	delayed	friendliest	tried	tries

Exercise

Write the past tense or past participle forms.

1. relay + ed = *relayed*
2. rely + ed = _____
3. ready + ed = _____
4. deploy + ed = _____
5. supply + ed = _____
6. buoy + ed = _____
7. scurry + ed = _____
8. toy + ed = _____

9. defray + ed = _____

10. hurry + ed = _____

Write the simple forms.

11. pried = _pry_____ + ed

12. married = _____ + ed

13. decried = _____ + ed

14. scurried = _____ + ed

15. defied = _____ + ed

Exercise

Write the comparative and superlative forms.

1. lazy + er = _lazier, laziest_____

2. silly + er = _____

3. dopey + er = _____

4. costly + er = _____

5. shy + er = _____

6. happy + est = _____

7. grey + est = _____

8. funny + est = _____

9. nosy + est = _____

10. noisy + est = _____

Write the simple forms.

11. sorrier = _sorry_____ + er

12. snappiest = _____ + est

13. steelier = _____ + er

14. angriest = _____ + est

15. friendlier = _____ + er

Exercise

Write the plural forms of the nouns.

1. mystery + s = _mysteries_____

2. day + s = _____

3. galaxy + s = _____

4. spy + s = _____

5. baby + s = _____

6. toy + s = _____

7. body + s = _____

8. flurry + s = _____

9. key + s = _____

10. county + s = _____

Write the singular forms.

11. guppies = *guppy* + s

12. buoys = _____ + s

13. slurries = _____ + s

14. treys = _____ + s

15. calories = _____ + s

Exercise

Write the third person singular present tense forms.

1. play + s = *plays*

2. parry + s = _____

3. deny + s = _____

4. obey + s = _____

5. defy + s = _____

6. rely + s = _____

7. rally + s = _____

8. deploy + s = _____

9. buy + s = _____

10. say + s = _____

Write the simple forms.

11. buoys = *buoy* + s

12. assays = _____ + s

13. tallies = _____ + s

14. annoys = _____ + s

15. spies = _____ + s

A4 **Spelling Rule #4: Adding *es* after *h, s, x,* or *z***

Use this rule to form:

1. The third person singular of a present tense verb:
V + *s*

(24) watc*h* + s = watch*es*

2. The plural of a noun: N + *s*

(25) pas*s* + s = pass*es*

315

Appendix A

Add *es* if the answer to the question is *yes:*
Is the last SOUND of the simple or singular form

[s] as in *miss?*
[z] as in *maze?*
[š] as in *rush?*
[ž] as in *garage?*
[č] as in *watch?*
[ǰ] as in *judge?*

The following chart shows how the question and its answer
lead to correct spelling.

	pass + s	match + s	epoch + s
Question	YES: [s] as in *miss*	YES: [č] as in *match*	NO: [k] as in *back*
	ADD *es* passes	ADD *es* matches	DO NOT ADD *es* epochs

Exercise

Write the third person singular.

1. mash + s = _mashes_
2. curse + s = _____
3. match + s = _____
4. stomach + s = _____
5. nudge + s = _____
6. ax + s = _____
7. axe + s = _____
8. miss + s = _____
9. amaze + s = _____
10. box + s = _____

Write the simple forms.

11. aches = _ache_ + s
12. fazes = _____ + s
13. hedges = _____ + s
14. fixes = _____ + s
15. buzzes = _____ + s

Exercise

Write the plural noun forms.

1. match + s = *matches*
2. dish + s = _____
3. gauge + s = _____
4. outrage + s = _____
5. boss + s = _____
6. monarch + s = _____
7. hose + s = _____
8. ketch + s = _____
9. tax + s = _____
10. mirage + s = _____

Write the singular nouns.

11. choices = *choice* + s
12. addages = _____ + s
13. guesses = _____ + s
14. crazes = _____ + s
15. witches = _____ + s

A5 **Spelling Rule #5: Adding *es* after *o***

Use this rule to form:

1. The third person singular of a present tense verb: V + *s*

   (26) go + s = go*es*

Note: There is an exception to this rule.

   (27) solo + s = solo*s*

2. The plural of a noun: N + *s*

   (28) potato + s = potato*es*

Add *es* if the simple form of the verb ends in *o*.

Some nouns ending in *o* form the plural by adding *s*, some by adding *es*, and some have two possibilities. If you are not sure of the correct spelling of the plural, check a dictionary.

Singular	Plural in *s*	Plural in *es*
buffalo	buffalos	buffaloes
cargo	cargos	cargoes

317

Singular	**Plural in s**	**Plural in es**
echo		echoes
hero		heroes
piano	pianos	
potato		potatoes
solo	solos	
tomato		tomatoes
tobacco	tobaccos	
veto		vetoes

Add *s* if the word is an abbreviation:

kilo(gram)	kilos
photo(graph)	photos

Add *s* if the word has a vowel letter before the *o*:

zoo	zoos
studio	studios

Add *s* if the word is a proper noun:

Eskimo	Eskimos
Filipino	Filipinos

Exercise

Write the third person singular.

1. go + s = _goes_
2. buffalo + s = _____
3. do + s = _____
4. solo + s = _____
5. echo + s = _____

Exercise

Write the correct plural forms.

1. potato + s = _potatoes_
2. piano + s = _____
3. kangaroo + s = _____
4. kilo + s = _____
5. hero + s = _____

Write the correct singular forms.

6. cargos = _cargo_ + s
7. tomatoes = _____ + s

8. Eskimos = _____ + s

9. cargoes = _____ + s

10. zoos = _____ + s

A6 **Spelling Rule #6: Changing *f* to *v* and adding *es***

Use this rule to form:

1. The plural of a noun: N + *s*

(29) wi*fe* + s = wi*ves*

Some English nouns end in *f* or *fe* in the singular. The plural is formed in the regular way (by adding *s*) or with the ending *ves*. A few words allow both possibilities. If you are not sure of the correct spelling of the plural, check a dictionary.

Singular	**Plural in *s***	**Plural in *ves***
belief	beliefs	
chief	chiefs	
handkerchief	handkerchiefs	
hoof	hoofs	hooves
knife		knives
leaf		leaves
life		lives
loaf		loaves
proof	proofs	
roof	roofs	
safe	safes	
scarf	scarfs	scarves
self		selves
shelf		shelves
thief		thieves
wife		wives

Exercise

Write the correct plural forms.

1. roof + s = _____

2. loaf + s = _____

3. wife + s = _____

4. handkerchief + s = _____

5. knife + s = _____

319

Write the correct singular forms.

6. scarfs = _____ + s

7. scarves = _____ + s

8. lives = _____ + s

9. chiefs = _____ + s

10. selves = _____ + s

A7 **Capitalization**

Use a capital letter in the following situations:

1. Capitalize the first letter of every sentence.

(30) *C*apitalization can help a reader.

2. Capitalize the first letter of every word in a proper noun. (the name of a person or a place, for example)

(31) *G*eorge *W*ashington was the first president of the *U*nited *S*tates.

3. In the title of a book or a film, capitalize the first word and all other important words (not articles, short conjunctions, short prepositions, for example).

(32) *War and Peace*
(33) *For Whom the Bell Tolls*
(34) *A Bell for Adano*

4. Capitalize the first letter of a direct quotation.

(35) Patrick Henry said, ''*G*ive me liberty or give me death!''

5. Capitalize the first letter of each item in a list when the list is (1) numbered and (2) arranged vertically (like the five items in this list).

(36) **1.** Publication schedule
    2. Sales overview
    3. Upcoming conferences
    4. Staff additions
    5. Job descriptions

Exercise

Capitalize where necessary.

1. the tallest building in the world is the sears tower; it has 110 stories and is 1,454 feet (443 meters) tall. it is in chicago, where there are several other skyscrapers.
2. the united nations moved to its current location in new york in 1951.
3. one of the most famous speeches in literature is in a play by shakespeare. hamlet begins his speech with the phrase "to be or not to be."
4. Have you ever read ernest hemingway's *the old man and the sea?*

A8 **Hyphenation**

Use hyphenation in the following cases:

1. A compound number

    (37)   47   forty-seven
    (38) 147   one hundred forty-seven

2. Fractions

    (39) 2/5   two-fifths

3. A word divided at the end of a line or writing

    (40)   im-
          possible
    (41)   impos-
          sible

Note: Be sure to put a hyphen next to the letter in front of it.

Note: Check a dictionary to determine where a word can be divided.

    (42) X   imposs-
          ible

Exercise

Add hyphens where necessary.

1. The Secretariat Building of the United Nations has thirty nine stories.
2. The United Nations has more than one hundred twenty member nations.
3. Have you ever seen the Citicorp Building in New York?

B SOME COMMON TRANSITIVE TWO-WORD VERBS

The blank space indicates the position of a pronoun direct object (DO):

Separable	call____up	He called *her* up.
Inseparable	take after____	She takes after *him*.

add____up
admit to____
agree on____
air____out
allow for____
apply for____
ask for____
ask____out
attend to____

back____out
back____up
bawl____out
beat____out
become of____
black____out
block____up
blow____down
blow____in
blow____out
blow____up
blurt____out
break____down
break____in
break in(to)____
break____off
break____out
break____up
bring____about
bring____off
bring____on
bring____out
bring____up
brush____off
brush____out
build____up
bump into____
burn____down
burn____up
buy____out
buy____up

call____back
call for____
call____in
call____off
call on____
call____out
call____up

care about____
care for____
carry____off
carry____on
carry____out
carry____over
cash____in
catch on to____
check in(to)____
check____out
check____over
cheer____on
cheer____up
chew____up
chop____down
chop____up
clean____off
clean____out
clean____up
clear____off
clear____out
clear____up
clog____up
close____down
close____out
close____up
cloud____up
come across____
come by____
come into____
come over____
come through____
cool____off
count____in
count on____
count____out
count____up
cross____off
cross____out
cut across____
cut____down
cut____off
cut____up

deal with____
depend (up)on____
dip into____
disagree with____

dispose of____
do____over
do without____
draw____out
draw____up
dream about____
dream of____
dress____down
dress____up
drink____up
drive____back
drive____out
drop____off
dry____off
dust____off
dwell on____

eat____up

fall for____
feel like____
fight____off
figure on____
figure____out
fill____in
fill____out
fill____up
find____out
fix____up
follow____through
follow____up

get____across
get after____
get around____
get____back
get____in
get in(to)____
get____off
get on____
get____out
get____over
get over____
get through____
get____together
give____away
give____back
give____off
give____out

give_____up
go about_____
go after_____
go for_____
go into_____
go over_____
go through_____
go without_____
grow on_____

hand_____down
hand_____in
hand_____out
hand_____over
hang around_____
hang onto_____
hang_____up
have_____on
head for_____
head into_____
hear about_____
hear from_____
hear of_____
help_____out
hold_____back
hold_____in
hold_____off
hold_____out
hold_____up
hunt_____up

insist (up)on_____

jack_____up

keep at_____
keep_____down
keep to_____
keep_____up
knock_____out

laugh_____off
lay_____aside
lay_____down
lay_____off
lay off (of)_____
lead_____on
leave_____off
leave_____on
leave_____out
let_____down
let_____in
let_____off
let_____out
light_____up
line_____up
live_____down
live off (of)_____
live on_____
live through_____

look after_____
look at_____
look for_____
look into_____
look_____over
look_____up

major in_____
make_____out
make_____over
make_____up
mark_____down
mark_____up
meet with_____
mix_____up
mop_____up
move_____up

open_____up

part with_____
pass_____out
pass_____up
pay_____back
pay_____off
pay_____out
pick on_____
pick_____out
pick_____up
plan on_____
play_____down
play_____up
plow into_____
plug_____in
plug_____up
point_____out
pull_____down
pull_____in
pull_____out
pull_____over
pull_____through
pull through_____
pull_____together
pull_____up
push_____down
push_____up
put_____across
put_____aside
put_____away
put_____down
put_____in
put_____off
put_____on
put_____out
put_____over
put_____together
put_____up

quiet_____down

read_____through
read through_____
rinse_____off
rinse_____out
rip_____off
root for_____
run_____in
rub_____off
rub_____out
rule_____out
run across_____
run against_____
run for_____
run into_____
run_____off
run over_____

save_____up
see about_____
see_____off
see to_____
sell_____off
send for_____
send_____off
set_____off
set_____up
settle on_____
sew_____up
show_____off
shut_____down
shut_____off
shut_____out
shut_____up
side with_____
single_____out
sleep on_____
slow_____down
slow_____up
speak about_____
speak for_____
speed_____up
spell_____out
stand for_____
stand_____up
stick to_____
stir_____up
straighten_____out
straighten_____up
stumble across_____
stumble into_____
stumble on(to)_____
stumble over_____
subscribe to_____
sum_____up

take after_____
take_____away
take_____back

Appendix B

take____down
take____in
take____off
take____out
take____over
take____up
talk about____
talk____over
tear____down
tear____up
tell____apart
tell____off
tell on____
think of____
think____over
think____through
think____up
throw____away
throw____over
throw____up

thumb through____
tie____up
tire____out
total____up
touch on____
touch____up
try____on
try____out
tune____up
turn against____
turn____around
turn____down
turn____in
turn into____
turn____off
turn____on
turn____out
turn____over
turn____up

use____up

wait for____
wait on____
warm____up
wash____off
wash____out
wash____up
wear____out
wind____up
wipe____off
wipe____out
work on____
work____out
write____down
write____in
write____off
write____out
write____up

C VERB + VERB COMBINATIONS

I. Verb + *to* V: We can *afford to buy* it.
II. Verb + V-*ing*: I *admit feeling* angry.
III. Verb + O + *to* V: The doctor *advised him to stop* smoking.
IV. Verb + O + V: I *felt the boat rock*.

Note: Verb + *to* V has a different meaning from Verb + V-*ing*.

A dot indicates the possibility of a combination.

Verb	I *to* V	II V-*ing*	III O + *to* V	IV O + V
admit		•		
advise		•	•	
afford	•	•		
agree	•			
allow			•	
anticipate		•		
appear	•			
appoint			•	
appreciate		•		
arrange	•			
ask	•		•	
attempt	•	•		
avoid		•		
bear	•	•		
beg	•	•		
begin	•	•		
bother	•	•		
call on			•	
care	•			
cause			•	
challenge			•	
choose	•		•	
come	•			
command			•	
compel			•	
consent	•			
consider		•		
continue	•	•		
convince			•	
dare	•		•	

Verb	I to V	II V-ing	III O + to V	IV O + V
decide	•			
delay		•		
demand	•			
deny		•		
deserve	•	•		
desire	•			
determine	•			
detest		•		
dislike	•	•		
dread	•	•		
drive			•	
enable			•	
encourage			•	
endeavor	•			
enjoy		•		
escape		•		
expect	•		•	
fail	•			
fear	•	•		
feel				•
finish		•		
forbid		•	•	
force			•	
forget	•	•		
get	•	•	•	
give up		•		
go		•		
happen	•			
have				•
hate	•	•	•	
hear				•
help			•	•
hesitate	•	•		
hope	•			
imagine		•		
instruct			•	
intend	•	•	•	
invite			•	
keep (on)		•		
lead			•	

Verb	I *to* V	II V-*ing*	III O + *to* V	IV O + V
learn	•			
let				•
like	•	•	•	
listen to				•
love	•	•		
make				•
manage	•			
mean	•		•	
mind		•		
miss		•		
need	•		•	
neglect	•	•		
notice				•
notify			•	
observe				•
offer	•			
order			•	
permit		•	•	
persuade			•	
plan	•	•		
pledge	•			
postpone		•		
practice		•		
prefer	•	•	•	
prepare	•			
pretend	•	•		
proceed	•			
promise	•			
propose	•	•		
put off		•		
quit		•		
recall		•		
recommend		•		
refuse	•			
regret	•	•		
remember	•	•		
remind			•	
request	•		•	
require			•	
resent		•		

Verb	I *to* V	II V-*ing*	III O + *to* V	IV O + V
resist		•		
risk		•		
resume		•		
see				•
seem	•			
select			•	
smell				•
stand	•	•		
start	•	•		
stop	•	•		
suggest		•		
swear	•			
teach			•	
tell			•	
tempt			•	
tend	•			
threaten	•			
trust			•	
try	•	•		
urge			•	
volunteer	•			
want	•		•	
warn			•	
watch				•
wish	•		•	

D **IRREGULAR VERBS**

Present	Past	Past Participle
arise	arose	arisen
awake	awoke	awoken/awakened
be	was/were	been
bear	bore	borne/born*
beat	beat	beaten
become	became	become
befall	befell	befallen
begin	began	begun
behold	beheld	beheld
bend	bent	bent
bereave	bereaved	bereaved/bereft*
bet	bet	bet
bid	bade/bid*	bidden/bid*
bind	bound	bound
bite	bit	bitten/bit
bleed	bled	bled
blow	blew	blown
break	broke	broken
breed	bred	bred
bring	brought	brought
broadcast	broadcast	broadcast
build	built	built
burn	burned/burnt B	burned/burnt B
burst	burst	burst
buy	bought	bought
cast	cast	cast
catch	catch	catch
chide	chided	chided
choose	chose	chosen
cling	clung	clung
clothe	clothed/clad	clothed/clad
come	came	come
cost	cost	cost
creep	crept	crept
cut	cut	cut
deal	dealt	dealt
dig	dug	dug
dive	dove/dived	dived
do	did	done
draw	drew	drawn
dream	dreamed/dreamt B	dreamed/dreamt B
drink	drank	drunk
drive	drove	driven
dwell	dwelled/dwelt	dwelled/dwelt

Present	Past	Past Participle
eat	ate	eaten
fall	fell	fallen
feed	fed	fed
feel	felt	felt
fight	fought	fought
find	found	found
flee	fled	fled
fling	flung	flung
fly	flew	flown
forbid	forbad(e)/forbid	forbidden/forbid
forecast	forecast	forecast
forget	forgot	forgotten/forgot B
forgive	forgave	forgiven
forsake	forsook	forsaken
freeze	froze	frozen
get	got	gotten/got B
gild	gilded/gilt	gilded/gilt
give	gave	given
go	went	gone
grind	ground	ground
grow	grew	grown
hang	hung	hung
have	had	had
hear	heard	heard
hide	hid	hidden
hit	hit	hit
hold	held	held
hurt	hurt	hurt
keep	kept	kept
kneel	kneeled/knelt	kneeled/knelt
knit	knit/knitted	knit/knitted
know	knew	known
lay	laid	laid
lead	led	led
lean	leaned/leant B	leaned/leant B
leap	leaped/leapt B	leaped/leapt B
learn	learned/learnt B	learned/learnt B
leave	left	left
lend	lent	lent
let	let	let
lie	lay	lain
light	lit/lighted	lit/lighted
lose	lost	lost
make	made	made
mean	meant	meant
meet	met	met

Present	Past	Past Participle
mislay	mislaid	mislaid
mislead	misled	misled
mistake	mistook	mistaken
misunderstand	misunderstood	misunderstood
mow	mowed	mowed/mown
outdo	outdid	outdone
overcome	overcame	overcome
overdo	overdid	overdone
overdraw	overdrew	overdrawn
overtake	overtook	overtaken
partake	partook	partaken
pay	paid	paid
prove	proved	proved/proven
put	put	put
read	read	read
rewind	rewound	rewound
rid	rid	rid
ride	rode	ridden
ring	rang	rung
rise	rose	risen
run	ran	run
say	said	said
see	saw	seen
seek	sought	sought
sell	sold	sold
send	sent	sent
set	set	set
sew	sewed	sewed/sewn
shake	shook	shaken
shave	shaved	shaved/shaven
shear	sheared/shore	sheared/shorn
shed	shed	shed
shine	shone	shone
shoot	shot	shot
show	showed	showed/shown
shred	shredded/shred	shredded/shred
shrink	shrank/shrunk	shrunk
shut	shut	shut
sing	sang	sung
sink	sank/sunk	sunk
sit	sat	sat
slay	slew	slain
sleep	slept	slept
slide	slid	slid/slidden
sling	slung	slung
slit	slit	slit

Present	Past	Past Participle
smell	smelled/smelt B	smelled/smelt B
sow	sowed	sowed/sown
speak	spoke	spoken
speed	speeded/sped	speeded/sped
spell	spelled/spelt B	spelled/spelt B
spend	spent	spent
spill	spilled/spilt B	spilled/spilt B
spin	spun	spun
spit	spit/spat B	spit/spat B
split	split	split
spoil	spoiled/spoilt B	spoiled/spoilt B
spread	spread	spread
spring	sprang	sprung
stand	stood	stood
steal	stole	stolen
stick	stuck	stuck
sting	stung	stung
stink	stank/stunk	stunk
stride	strode	stridden
strike	struck	struck
strive	strived/strove	strived/striven
swear	swore	sworn
sweat	sweated/sweat	sweated/sweat
sweep	swept	swept
swell	swelled	swelled/swollen
swim	swam	swum
swing	swung	swung
take	took	taken
teach	taught	taught
tear	tore	torn
tell	told	told
think	thought	thought
thrive	thrived/throve	thrived/thriven
throw	threw	thrown
thrust	thrust	thrust
tread	trod	trod/trodden
unbend	unbent	unbent
unbind	unbound	unbound
undergo	underwent	undergone
understand	understood	understood
undertake	undertook	undertaken
undo	undid	undone
unwind	unwound	unwound
uphold	upheld	upheld
upset	upset	upset

Present	Past	Past Participle
wake	waked/woke	waked/woke/woken
wear	wore	worn
weave	wove	woven
wed	wedded/wed	wedded/wed
weep	wept	wept
wet	wetted/wet	wetted/wet
win	won	won
wind	wound	wound
withdraw	withdrew	withdrawn
withhold	withheld	withheld
withstand	withstood	withstood
wring	wrung	wrung
write	wrote	written

*different forms for different meanings
B = British form

E   *INDIRECT OBJECTS IN SENTENCE PATTERNS*

     S   V   IO   DO

I. I asked *him a question.*

     S   V   DO   to + IO

II. He admitted his mistake *to the teacher.*

     S   V   DO   IO

III. He answered the question *for everyone.*

Verb	I IO DO	II to	III for
admit		•	
announce		•	
answer			•
ask	•		
bet	•		•
bring	•	•	•
build	•		•
buy	•		•
call	•		•
cash			•
change			•
charge		•	•
choose	•		•
cost	•		
demonstrate		•	•
deny	•	•	
design	•		•
describe		•	•
distribute		•	
do	•	•	•
draw	•		•
explain		•	•
find	•		•
fix	•		•
get	•		•
give	•	•	
guarantee	•	•	•
hand	•	•	
introduce		•	

Verb	I IO DO	II to	III for
leave	•	•	•
lend	•	•	•
mail	•	•	
make	•		•
mention		•	
offer	•	•	
owe	•	•	
pay	•	•	
play	•		
prepare			•
prescribe	•		•
promise	•	•	
pronounce			•
prove		•	
read	•	•	
recommend		•	•
refund	•	•	
refuse	•	•	
repeat		•	•
report		•	
save	•		•
say		•	
sell	•	•	
send	•	•	
show	•	•	
speak		•	
state		•	•
suggest		•	•
talk		•	
take	•	•	
teach	•	•	•
telephone		•	
tell	•	•	
throw	•	•	
wish	•	•	•
write	•	•	

F COMPARATIVE AND SUPERLATIVE IRREGULAR FORMS

Positive	Comparative	Superlative
bad	worse	worst
far	farther further	farthest furthest
good	better	best
little	less	least
many much	more	most
well	better	best

Note: Example 1 below is incorrect because it has two indications of the comparative: the word *more* and the irregular form *better*.

(1) X more better

Note: *Further* and *furthest* are used for distance and degree.

(2) They walked two miles further than we did. (distance)
(3) At our next meeting, let's discuss this problem further. (degree)

Farther and *farthest* are used only for distance.

(4) They walked two miles farther than we did.

Examples 2 and 4 have the same meaning.

Note: *Well* can be used as an adjective or an adverb. As an adjective, it describes people's health; it is the opposite of *ill* or *sick* (American English).

(5) Mary has not been well since last Tuesday.

The adjective *good* is not used to describe health (except in very informal conversation).

As an adverb, *well* is the opposite of *badly* or *poorly*.

(6) His car has been running very well since you gave it a tune-up.

G SOME ADJECTIVES AND THEIR PREPOSITIONS

acceptable to
accustomed to
afraid of, about
amazed at
angry about, at, with
annoyed at, with
anxious about
ashamed of
aware of
bored by, with
busy with
capable of
careful about, of, with
careless about, of, with
certain about, of
comparable to
composed of
concerned about
confident about, of
confused about
(un)conscious of
(in)considerate about, of
(dis)courteous to
critical of
dedicated to
dependent on
different from, than, to
disappointed about, at, in, with
doubtful about, of
eager for
easy on, with
eligible for
enthusiastic about
envious of
equal to
essential to, for
excited about
experienced in
expert at, in, with
familiar with
famous for
fond of
full of

glad about, of
good at, to, for
grateful for, to
(un)happy about, with
harmful for, to
homesick for
(dis)honest about, in, with
hungry for
identical to, with
ignorant about, of
independent of
interested in
jealous of
kind to
known for
mad at
made from, of, with
necessary for, to
parallel to
particular about
(im)patient with
perpendicular to
pleased about, at
polite to
popular with
positive about, of
preferable to
prepared for
proud of
qualified for
ready for
rich in
right about
rude to
sad about
safe from
(dis)satisfied about, with, by
sensitive about, to
scared of
serious about
separate from
sick with

shocked at
sorry about, for
(dis)similar to
suitable for
(un)successful in
sure about, of

suited to
tired from, of
surprised about, at
wrong about
typical of

Index

Index

a, 133, 134–135, 139, 140
abbreviations, 206, 303
ability, modals of, 119, 120
a bit, 165
abstract nouns, 48
action, activity, 4, 5–7
   continuing, 91, 92, 101, 108–109
   habitual, 91, 95–96
   repeated, 91, 94, 101, 108, 109
   status expressed by verb, 89, 91–92,
     101–104
   time expressed by verb, 89, 91–92,
     94–98, 108
   see also doer of action; receiver of
     action
active voice, 259, 262, 263
actual, 183
actually, 166, 183
addition:
   conjunctions of, 190
   sentence connectors of, 205
   short, punctuation of, 286–287
   see also explanation
addresses, punctuation and form of, 295,
   296
adjective(s), 136, 153–158, 162
   of age, 159, 160
   of color, 159, 160
   comparative form, 138, 154, 170–172,
     App. A
   comparative meanings, 173–177
   compound, with number, 183
   (de)emphasizers of, 165
   ending in -ly, 162
   form, 154
   general, 159, 160
   irregular comparative and superlative
     forms, App. F
   meaning, 153, 154
   in noun phrase, 53, 153–155, 159, 160
   noun used as, 54, 157, 159, 160
   as object complement, 9
   participial, 157–158
   placement of, 76, 153–154, 159
   positive form, 170–172
   possessive, 75–76, 142
   and prepositions, 155, App. G
   quantifiers as, 148
   of shape, 159, 160
   of size, 159
   as subject complement, 11
   superlative form, 138, 154, 170–172,
     App. F

superlative meaning, 177–178
   without noun, 153
adjective clauses, 153, 155, 156, 239,
   240, 285
   as dependent clauses, 211–212,
     217–226
   non-restrictive, 224–225, 285
   restrictive, 219, 224–226
   who/whom problem, 220–221
adjective-equivalents, 155–157, 216
   as dependent clause, 211–212
   infinitives as, 156, 241–242, 244–245
   past participles as, 158, 240–241
   present participles as, 156, 157–158,
     237, 238–239
adjective phrases, 153, 155, 159
adverb(s), 83, 161–170
   as adjective-equivalents, 157, 161
   comparative form, 161, 170–172
   comparative meanings, 173, 176
   (de)emphasizers of, 165
   form, 161
   formation with -ly, 162
   of frequency, 168, 252–254, 255
   of manner, 164, 167, 168–169
   meaning, 161, 162, 163
   negative, 252–254, 255–256
   of place, 167, 168–169
   placement of, 161, 163, 165, 166, 167,
     168–169
   placement in noun phrase, 159
   pronoun use of (there, then), 71
   of reason, 164
   relative pronouns for, 220
   superlative form, 161, 170–172
   superlative meaning, 177–178
   of time, 102, 167–169, 183
adverb clauses, 161, 162–163, 238, 285
   as dependent clauses, 211, 213, 217,
     298
   punctuation of, 211, 238, 298–299
adverb-equivalents, 162–164
   as dependent clauses, 211, 216
   infinitives as, 163–164, 241–244
   past participles as, 240–241
   present participles as, 163–164,
     237–238
adverbial, 13, 255–256
   emphasized by expletive it, 272
   of frequency, negative, 252–254
   see also adverb(s)
adverb phrases, 161, 162–163, 238
   as adjective-equivalents, 157

341

Index

Index

Index

short, punctuation of, 286–287
expletive:
  defined, 269
  it, 258, 269–273
  there, 199–200, 258, 266–269

–f or *–fe,* plural in *–fs, –fes, –ves,* App. A
falling intonation, 14, 21, 30, 33
far, 143, App. F
farther, farthest, App. F
feel, 11, 103
feminine, 63–64
few, 145, 146
fewer, 145, 159
fewest, 145
films, titles of, 292, App. A
final letter of word, change in, doubling,
  or drop of, *see* consonant, final; *–e,*
  final; *–y,* final
first:
  adverb of indefinite time, 168
  ordinal number, 151–152
first person, 60–61, 68
  shall vs. *will,* 97
  see also I; me; us; we
focus, subject–verb inversion for,
  257–258, 266, 268, 269, 270,
  272–273
  see also emphasis
for:
  as coordinate conjunction, 191, 279
  with objects, 7, 261, 272, App. E
foreign words, 290
forget, 103, 113
formal speech:
  conditional without *if,* 126
  emphasizers and de-emphasizers, 165
  prepositions, 179
  restatement questions in, 31
formal writing, 165, 252, 278, 291
  see also written English
fortunately, 166
forty, 149
fractions, App. A
  plus *of,* 147
fragment, sentence, 3, 234–236
frequency, adverbs of, 168
  negative, 252–254, 255
frequently, 168
from, 7
full forms vs. contractions, 90, 99,
  105–106, 117, 251
further, furthest, App. F
fused sentence, 207
future, continuous, 115
future perfect, 105
future time, 89, 96–98
  contrary–to–fact statements, 127
  expressed by past tense, 118
  expressed by simple present tense,
    91–92, 98, 118

modals, 115, 118, 119, 121, 122, 123,
  124
past combined with, 96
progressive form, 98, 115
sequence of tense in reported speech,
  229–230
use of present progressive, 98, 101–102
future time clause, 97

games, 49
general reference:
  pronouns, 67–68
  use of determiners for, 53, 140
geographical features, 42
geographical names, 42, 141–142
gerund, 57, 112
  negative, 114
  as noun-equivalent, 57–58, 239–240
  possessive form and, 113
  verb agreement, 86
  verb +, 112–113, App. C
  verbs of sense plus objective case and,
    113–114
gerund phrase, as object of preposition,
  181
get, 11, 240
  in passive voice, 263
  past participle, 107
got, gotten, 107, 263
grammatical parallelism, 196, 282
Greek forms of nouns, 45
grow, 11

habitual activity, 91, 95–96
had, 16, 29
  contraction, 105–106, 117
  in past perfect, 105–106
  in short answer and tag statement, 25,
    200
had best, had better, 119, 123
had to, 119
half (of), 147
hardly ever, 14, 168
has, 90
  contractions, 99, 105
  in questions, 16, 18, 29
  in short answer and tag statement, 25,
    200
has got, 107
have, 90, 103, 240
  contraction, 99, 105, 117
  meaning *possess,* 107, 260
  negation, 250, 251
  in question, 16, 17–18, 29
  in short answer and tag statement, 25,
    200
  in simple perfect, 104–105
have got, 107
have got to, 119, 124
have to, 119, 124
he, 17, 24, 61, 62, 63–64, 65, 200

346

Index

Index

Index

Index

reflexive pronoun, 68–69
    uses of, 69–70
reinforcement, sentence connectors of,
    206
relationship, expressed by possessive, 78
relative clauses, 156, 222–223
relatively, 165
relative pronoun, 217–220, 222
    omission possible, 219, 225–226
relevance, expressed by verb, 89,
    108–112, 115
    current, 94
remain, 11
remember, 103, 113
repeated action, 91, 94, 101, 108, 109
repeated information, and ellipsis, 192,
    198
    errors, 222–223
reported exclamations, 233–234
reported imperative, 231–233
reported speech, 111, 228
    and sequence of tenses, 228–230
reporting verbs, 228, 297
requests:
    imperative, 34
    for permission, modals, 118–119
restatement, 16
    sentence connectors of, 206
restatement questions, 16, 31–32
restrictive adjective clauses, 219,
    224–226
restrictive appositive, 236
restrictive information, 285
result, *see* cause and effect/result
rising intonation, 21, 22, 26, 30, 31–32,
    33, 214
run-on sentence, 207

–s:
    in noun plural, 44, 46
    in noun singular, 45
    in third person singular present tense,
        90, 116
    in uncountable nouns, 48, 49
    vs. *–es,* spelling rules, App. A
seasons, 42, 133
second, 151
second person, 60–61, 68
    see also you
see, 103, 113
seem, 11, 103
seldom, 14, 168, 252
self, 68
selves, 68
semicolon, 277, 293
    in compound sentences, 189,
        204–206, 207, 210, 279
    series punctuation by, 283
sense, verbs of, 113–114
sentence(s), 277, 278
    affirmative, 14

basic parts of, 3–4, 83
complex, 111, 189, 209–227, 235
compound, 188–209, 210, 235
compound/complex, 235
conditional, 125–127
contrary-to-fact, 115, 127
declarative, 13–15; *see also* statements
exclamatory, 37–39
imperative, 32–37
interrogative, 16–32; *see also* questions
negative, 14
object parts of, 5, 6–10
simple, 3, 188, 193, 196, 235
types of, 13, 235
sentence connectors, 204–206
sentence fragments, 3, 234–236
sentence modifiers, 161, 166–167
    comma used with, 166, 288
sentence pattern, 3–13
    with indirect object, 6–8, App. E
    with intransitive verb, 4–5
    with linking verb, 11–13
    with object complement, 9–10
    with transitive verb, 5–6
sentence pattern rearrangement, 38,
    249–273
    with expletive *it,* 269–273
    with expletive *there,* 266–269
    negation, 14, 191, 249–257
    passive voice, 259–266
    subject–verb inversion, 202, 254, 255,
        257–259, 266–267
    see also question word order
separable transitives, 84, App. B
separation of units:
    marks of, 293
    punctuation for, 277–278, 293–303
sequence:
    sentence connectors of, 206
    subordinate conjunctions of, 213
sequence of tenses, in complex
        sentences, 111, 210, 228
    in reported exclamations, 233–234
    in reported speech, 228–230
    unchanging situation exception, 230
series, 194, 282–284
several (of), 146
shall, 16, 29
    conditional, 126
    contraction, 117
    future expressed by, 97
    modal meanings, 119, 121, 122
    negatives, 117
    past tenses, 230
    in short answer and tag statement, 25,
        200
she, 17, 24, 61, 62, 63–64, 65, 200
    third person singular present tense
        form, 89–90
she's (she is, she has), 99
ships, 64

354

Index

reported imperative in, 232–233
reported speech in, 228–230
as sentence fragment, 234–235
sequence of tenses in, 210, 228–230, 233–234
as subject of independent clause, 301
unchanging situation statement in, 230–231
uses of, 211–212
in various types of sentences, 235
wh–subordinate, 216–226
who/whom problem, 220–221
subordinate conjunctions, 212–213
such, 226–227
such...that, 227
suggestion (imperative), 35–36
summary, sentence connectors of, 206
superlative, 138, 161, 170–172
  form, 170–172
  irregular forms, App. F
  meaning, 177–178
  spelling rules, App. A
  the with, 138, 171

tag, 282
tag question, 16, 28–31, 282
  end punctuation, 30
  intonation of, 30
  response to, 30
  word order, 29
tag statement, 23, 199–200, 282
  defined, 199
  negative, 23, 199, 200
  pronoun as subject in, 24, 71, 199
  use of *there,* 71, 199–200, 267
  verb form and order in, 199–200
taste, 11, 103
television programs, titles of, 292
temporary verb form, 101
tenses, *see* past tense; present tense;
    sequence of tenses
–th, 152
than, 173, 174–175, 176
that:
  as demonstrative, 143
  as relative pronoun, 219, 223
  as subordinate conjunction, 211, 213
  unexpressed, 213, 225
  wrong use of, 173
the, 134, 135, 136–138, 139, 140, 141–142
the following, 281
their, 66, 76
  wrong use, 56
theirs, 66, 77
  wrong use, 56
them, 61, 62, 64, 65, 66, 181
themselves, 69
then:
  as adverb substitute, 170
  pronoun use of, 71

there, 167
  as adverb substitute, 170
  expletive, 199–200, 258, 266–269
  pronoun use of, 71
  in subject position, 24, 30, 71, 199–200, 267
  in tag statement, 71, 199–200, 267
  in yes/no question, 267
therefore, 204, 210
these, 143
they, 61, 62, 64, 65, 66
  as general reference pronoun, 67–68
  wrong use, 56
things, 60, 62
  comparison of, 173, 177
  identification by empty *it,* 11–12
  relative pronouns for, 219, 220
  use of articles, 136, 138, 140
third person, 60–61, 69
  see also he; her; him; it; she; them; they
third person singular, 86, 90
  modals, 116
  spelling rules, App. A
this, 143
those, 143
though, 213
three–word verbs, 83–84, 85
thus, 170
time, 11, 71
  adverb of, 102, 167–169, 183
  adverbial of, 13
  expressed by possessive, 75, 78
  expressed by verb, 89, 91–92, 94–98, 115
  future, 89, 91–92, 96–98
  past, 89, 92, 94–96, 109–110
  present, 89, 91–92, 108–109
  punctuation of, 297
  questions, 20, 163
  sentence connectors of, 206
  subordinate conjunctions of, 213
times of day, 134
titles:
  of books, stories, films, etc., 292–293, App. A
  of people, 42
to, with objects, 7, 261, App. E
to + verb, 57, 112, 156, 163
  see also infinitive
too, 165, 166, 243
  as coordinate conjunction, 190
  in ellipsis, 198, 202
  as emphasizer, 198, 202, 243
to what extent, 161, 182, 211
transitions, 204–206
  defined, 288
  enclosed by commas, 204–205, 288
  use of, 204
transitive verbs, 5–6, 7–8, 259
  inseparable, 84, App. B
  separable, 84, App. B

356

Index